Java
Programming
Basics

JAVA PROGRAMMING BASICS

**Edith Au
Dave Makower
and the
Pencom Web Works**

MIS:
PRESS

A Subsidiary of
Henry Holt and Co., Inc.

MIS:Press

A Subsidiary of Henry Holt and Company, Inc.

115 West 18th Street

New York, NY 10011

http://www.mispress.com

Limits of Liability and Disclaimer of Warranty

The Author and Publisher of this book have used their best efforts in preparing this book and disck and the programs contained in them. These efforts include the development, research, and testing of the theories and programs to determine their effectiveness. However, the Author and Publisher make no warranty of any kind, expressed or implied, with regard to these programs or the documentation contained in this book. The Author and Publisher shall not be liable in any event for incidental or consequential damages in connection with, or arising out of, the furnishing, performance, or use of this book and these programs.

Trademarks

Java ™ and HotJava ™ are trademarks of Sun Microsystems. Roaster ™ is a trademark of Natural Intelligence, Inc. Additional trademarks and product names in this book and the accompanying diskc appear in initial capital letters or all capital letters. Readers, however, should contact the appropriate companies for more complete information regarding trademarks and registration.

ISBN 1-55828-469-9

99 98 97 96   6 5 4 3 2 1

Associate Publisher: Paul Farrell
Managing Editor: Cary Sullivan
Development Editor: Andrew Neusner
Production Editor: Anthony Washington
Associate Production Editor: Carmen Walker

Dedication

Edith Au:

    To my family.

Dave Makower:

    To my parents, Jordan and Esther Makower, who have always supported me in my odyssey through life.

Acknowledgments

This book is not the work of one, or even two people. In particular, we'd like to thank our editor Andy Neusner, and our publisher Paul Farrell, as well as Anthony Washington and everyone else at Henry Holt who made this book possible. Our technical editor, Chuck McManis, was of immeasurable help throughout, providing insight beyond any available published matter.

Large portions of the book were written by individuals at Pencom Web Works. Mark Mangan contributed most of Chapter 2, and was deeply involved in every aspect of the project from beginning to end. A good deal of Chapter 1 and all of Chapter 13 are the work of Jonathan Wallace.

Linda DiSanto contributed heavily to Chapter 3. Laurie Caro contributed quite a few of the illustrations. Thanks also to Ellick Quach and to the Systems Administration staff at Pencom for not locking us out of the file server, and particularly Donald "I love you, man!" Chow for staying up late to make sure the CD-ROM went out on time.

Bill Bates, working at Netscape, graciously wrote the JavaScript appendix.

Patrick Naughton gave valuable insight into the story of how Java came to be.

Thanks to the many individuals and groups who contributed applets and other material, including (in no particular order) Sun Microsystems, Natural Intelligence, Paul Burchard, Paul Coddington, Pete Keleher, Mark Masse, Russ Ethington, Dario Laverde, Alan Phillips, Osamu Satoh, Ted Phelps and Dale Gass. Professor Peter B. Henderson from SUNY at Stony Brook, Diana Cioffi at Pencom, and Nelson Yu at the University of Alberta provided helpful comments. In addition, there are individuals who deserve our personal thanks.

Edith Au

I whole heartedly thank Johnathan Wallace and Ellick Quach for giving me the opportunity and support. This book would not have happened without them. I also would like to thank Professor Tzi-cker Chiueh from SUNY at Stony Brook, who initiated my interest in the Internet.

During the course of putting together this book, the following people have taken times to answer my questions: Sanford Barr, Brett Henriksen, Marc Rovner, Rick Tait, and Tony Zhang. Thanks to Tony Zhang for giving me rides to Java SIG meetings.

Thanks also go to everyone on comp.lang.java and NYC Java SIG. I learned a lot from your questions and answers. Last of all, I want to thank my family and friends for their enormous support. Special thanks to Rao for taking care of me when I was sick.

Dave Makower

I owe a great debt of gratitude to Professor Ken Perlin at NYU, who made it possible for me to take the time to master Java— by making it mandatory. In addition, I thank Professor Edmond Schonberg at NYU for his suggestions on the conceptual examples in Chapter 1. I'd also like to thank my family and my girlfriend Valerie, without whom I probably would never have eaten during the past few months.

Contents

Part One
The Overview

Part Two
The Java Language

Part Three
Programming with Java

Part Four
Other Issues

Pencom Systems Incorporated is a 23 year old, $63 million software services company specializing in staffing, contract programming, and systems administration. This year its newest business unit, Pencom Web Works (PWW), was created to meet the growing demand for corporate IS solutions using Web-based technologies.

Intranet Development

Using the same powerful, easy-to-use technologies that have become ubiquitous on global networks, Pencom is helping companies develop their own corporate Intranets.

PWW specializes in building applications which allow users to interact with Java "smart" forms and securely distribute sensitive corporate data across private networks, or the Internet. PWW can build platform independent workflow applications and intermediate programs for databases that tie all these resources into a Web browser. Using HTML, CGI, and Java, PWW can help companies rethink the way they work and communicate internally.

Web Site Development

In addition to sophisticated object-oriented analysis and design for internal networks, Pencom Web Works is an accomplished developer of external Web sites. PWW can customize your corporate image into a dynamic, interactive site in cyberspace—intuitively structured and loaded with whatever functionality and multimedia you require. Moving beyond simple HTML, PWW is versed in the latest tags, the latest browsers, sophisticated CGI scripting, Java applet development, Javascript, and a host of popular Netscape extensions, such as Shockwave Director and Real Audio Player.

In conjunction with Pencom Systems Incorporated, PWW also offers training, contract programming, and system administration services. Pencom has the resources, technical expertise, and industry knowledge to provide you with a total Web solution.

Write **pww-info@pencom.com** for more information.

Part One

The Overview

CHAPTER 1

The Object-Oriented Worldview

Object-Orientation: A Shift in Paradigm

Java combines two great benefits in one computer language: its customization for the World Wide Web, a major theme of the rest of this book, and its object-orientation, which we will discuss in this chapter.

The introduction of object-orientation (OO) was one of the great revolutions in computer software. Like most paradigm shifts, the innovations introduced by OO now seem self-evident, but only in retrospect.

Sidebar: Acronym Alert

People often use the acronym **OO** to stand for anything object-oriented, yielding acronyms such as the following:

- **OOP** - Object-oriented programming
- **OOA** - Object-oriented analysis
- **OOD** - Object-oriented design
- **OOM** - Object-oriented methodology

This book does not deal in depth with concepts of object-oriented analysis, design or methodologies. You will, however, frequently find us referring to OOP and OO concepts in general, so it's good to be familiar with these acronyms.

The Old-Fashioned Way

Before OO, there was a major disjunct between the way software worked and the way we see the world. This created a significant problem, because a major function of software—particularly in the business world, but also in science, engineering and other domains—is to model the world and support real-life *activities*. Software, however, is a discipline that was created from the processor up, by technologists whose main concern was not, at first, to *intuitively* model the world. Instead, software began with machine language, intended to direct the processor to perform tasks. Each succeeding generation of computer languages bundled a number of the commands of the predecessor generation into single commands that were, at the same time, successively more English-like—but without greatly increasing consideration for the fundamental problem of modeling the world.

The unique genesis of computer languages created a problem unknown in any other domain of engineering—the builder's tools and the architect's job were uniquely unsuited to each other. In fact, the architect and the builder almost entirely lacked a common language. Imagine if the architect's blueprints had to be translated into an unrecognizable format before the builder could do his job. Even worse, imagine that, in order to get the job done, the architect is forced to think in a "design language" suitable to communicate with the builder but completely unsuited to analyzing the structure of a house.

Computer languages developed from the processor up, and analysis developed from the real world down. The two inconsistent disciplines meet, and often do battle, on the disputed field of software design. This conflict is in large part responsible for the fact that so many software projects still fail spectacularly, so many decades after the invention of software, which ought to be a maturing tool.

OO is not a panacea, but it does go a long way toward addressing the schism between analysis and code.

Procedural Programming vs. Object-Oriented Programming

The difference between *procedural programming* and *object-oriented programming*—as indicated by the term "object-oriented" itself—is indeed a question of orientation, or point-of-view.

The procedural programmer looks at a problem, and analyzes the solution in terms of *algorithms* which embody the *steps* necessary to solve that problem. First, broad procedures are described (e.g. "retrieve the records," "sort the list," "save the file," etc.). Gradually, each broad, high-level[1] process is broken down into smaller, more and more detailed subproce-dures ("compare record *a* with record *b*," "swap record *a* and record *b*," etc.), and finally each of these subprocedures is described in terms of individual low-level operations that make it up ("add these two numbers," "assign this value to that memory location," etc.). This process is called *algorithmic decomposition*. Naturally, these procedures are described in terms of the data they act upon, but the solution is viewed from the point of view of the procedures. The data is viewed as *separate* from the procedures, and the procedures act upon the data.

The object-oriented programmer looks at a problem as a system of interacting objects, where an object consists of both data *and* all of the relevant procedures which make sense on that data. *Object-oriented decomposition* involves identifying the objects in the system, and assigning to each object the operations which are appropriate to that object.

The Procedural Approach

Using a traditional, *procedural* approach, imagine that it is your job to create a software program that approximates the functionality observed in a patch of forest. You walk through the woods, jotting down all the behaviors you observe:

- Running

- Jumping from tree to tree

- Storing nuts for the winter

---

[1] In the world of computers, the term *low-level* is used to refer to the extremely detailed, close-up view of something, while the term *high-level* is used to refer to more abstract, general view. Imagine an aerial view of a mountain. The *higher* you fly, the more the details blend together and mesh, allowing you to focus on an overall picture of the mountain as a whole. The *lower* you fly, the more details you see—trees, houses, birds, rocks, people—and the less you see of the mountain itself.

- Photosynthesis
- Singing
- Eating grass
- Eating mice
- Hooting
- Howling

And so forth. Having made a complete list of these behaviors, you start organizing charts illustrating the relationship between these behaviors, for example, nut-finding precedes nut-storing, and a hooting phase both precedes and follows mouse-eating.

Because things (data) and the processes that act on them (behavior) are treated separately, it is likely that data structures and the operations which refer to and alter them may find themselves spread out in different parts of a large program, which soon comes to resemble a potfull of spaghetti. If you decide to change something in your system—specifying that all plants are green or all animals have fur—there is no single place to make the change; you can't just change the data structures for animals or plants, because procedures throughout the program may depend on those data structures. Instead, you have to perform a search and replace mission throughout the spaghetti, attempting to find all of the code which refers to animals or plants and updating it to accommodate the new features of the data structure. Even then, you run the risk that a seemingly benign change in one place will have some completely unforeseen effect somewhere else in the program. Ironically, the blueprint produced by the architect, which was intended to serve as a guide to the end result of the program, is completely useless as a guide to the innards of the program itself. Unlike the blueprint of a house, which serves both as an image of what is wanted and later (with appropriate modifications) as a guide to what has been built, an old-fashioned software design document tells you little or nothing about what is actually inside the black box. It is only a representation of how the software was intended to appear from the outside.

The Object-Oriented Approach

OO presents a much more comfortable and intuitive way to view the world. An OO architect, strolling through the forest, would begin by writing down:

- Tree
- Plant
- Mouse
- Deer
- Owl
- Thrush
- Wolf

And so on. Having identified the different entities at hand, the architect then looks to simplify the picture even further by classifying some of the above in terms of their relationship to one another: for example, trees and plants are members of the plant family, wolves, mice and deer are mammals; the owl and thrush are birds. The process of classification followed by an OO analyst is, for obvious reasons, extremely similar to that followed by taxonomists since Cuvier, classifying animals into phyla, families, and species. Having identified a number of entities, the architect then thinks about assigning behaviors to them: howling and predation to the wolf, photosynthesis to trees and plants, flying to the owl and thrush, mouse-eating to the owl, etc. The behavior can be assigned at the most abstract level available: flying is a function performed by class bird, while mouse-eating is a function performed only by subclass owl. (Thrushes do not eat mice.) However, if a behavior is later added or modified—for example, gliding is added, a version of flying which does not require wingbeats—the change must be made only at the level of the parent class, bird, and is automatically propagated everywhere else it is required in the system. Compare this to the job of searching through hundreds of thousands or even millions of lines of code, looking for bird-related routines that now must be modified to accommo-date gliding.

To the relieved architect, and her client, what OO accomplishes is rather miraculous. If we are modeling a house in the real world, we create a house in the software. If we are modeling a forest, we create software trees and animals, behaving like the real ones. This is not fanciful or an exaggeration. A software squirrel, like a real one, is a collection of attributes and functions—fur and nut-hunting—that which collaborate to produce a result. In the philosophy of OO, an object is a bundle of data and related functions. Thinking of an object as a little software machine whose job is to collaborate in a greater work allows us to avoid problems that would never become clear in old-fashioned programming.

Introduction to Object-Oriented Concepts

Anyone wishing to program in an object-oriented language like Java—or anyone wishing to communicate with those who do such programming—needs to have a basic understanding of the concepts underlying object-oriented programming in general.

What is an Object?

The most basic way in which object-oriented programming differs from procedural programming is in the way it looks at the relationship between data and procedures. In procedural programming, data and procedures are viewed as two separate things. One defines data structures, and then one defines procedures to act on these data structures. In object-oriented programming, on the other hand, data structures are grouped together with the procedures that operate on them. The resulting entity—a set of data, combined with the relevant operations on that data—is called an *object*.

Objects Have State

The data members of an object are often referred to as the object's *state*, or its *attributes*. For example, if you have created an object to represent a circle, the attributes of that circle would probably include the locations of its four corners, and perhaps the colors of its outline and interior. In Java, the attributes of an object are stored in its *variables*.

Objects Have Behavior

An object's operations, or *methods* as they are referred to in Java, define the *behavior* of the object. The methods of a `Rectangle` would very likely include drawing, moving, resizing, erasing, changing color, etc.

You may often hear people refer to *messages* in object-oriented parlance. When you call one of an object's methods, you are essentially sending it a *message* to perform that operation—it's essentially like saying to the `Rectangle`, "draw yourself." Note that with the grouping of data and operations comes the notion that an object *behaves*, rather than being acted upon from the outside.

Encapsulation and Data-Hiding

We have seen that an object has state and behavior. The grouping of state and behavior into a single unit is called *encapsulation*. Ideally, all operations that might affect an object's data are defined as methods of the object, and thus encapsulated as part of the object. If this is the case, then no outside entity needs to have direct access to the object's data. Outside entities call the object's methods, and only the object's own methods can act directly upon its data. Thus, encapsulation provides a way of shielding an object's data from any direct manipulation from the outside. This concept is known as *data-hiding*.

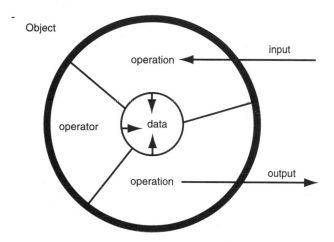

If, somewhere in your program, you want to move a Rectangle, you don't directly access the data members in which the four corners are stored. Those variables belong to the Rectangle object itself, and they are part of its *private* representation. Instead, you send a message to the Rectangle, by calling one of its methods, asking it to move itself a certain distance in *x* and in *y*.

Theoretically, all of an object's data members are to be treated as *private*, and the only way to access on any data contained in an object is by calling one of the object's methods to either alter that data or to report on its value. In practice, it is often more convenient or practical to keep most of the data private, while allowing certain data to be *public*, directly accessible from outside. Object-oriented languages typically have facilities to control the visibility of an object's data and methods. We will examine how Java handles this in Chapter 8.

One of the key advantages of encapsulation and data-hiding is that you can change an object's internal representation without changing the way it looks to the outside. For instance, after writing a significant portion of your program, you may discover that you don't need to store all four corners of a `Rectangle`; all you need is the upper left and lower right corner, and the other two can be inferred from there. This is not a problem in an object-oriented program. Since outside objects don't know or care about the internal representation of your `Rectangle`, all of your changes can be localized within the `Rectangle` object itself. No other part of the program needs to change, because no other part of the program contains references to the object's internal data.

Classes

A *class* is a set of objects that share attributes and behavior. Every object belongs to a class. In fact, one cannot create objects without first specifying the attributes and behavior of a class, thereby defining the "blueprints" by which objects of that class may be created. Like a blueprint, the definition of a class does not itself create any individual objects, but rather it defines the specifications for their creation.

Thus, before we can create any `Rectangles`, we must first define `Rectangle` to be a class; in the class definition, we provide a specification of the variables and methods which embody a `Rectangle`. Below is what that class definition might look like in Java. If it looks like a foreign language, that's because it is—for now, anyway. Don't worry about understanding all of the details just yet. Just get what you can from it, and let the comments (any text starting with `//`) be your guide:

```
class Rectangle {
// variables define the Rectangle's state

    // the four corners
    Point upLeft;
    Point upRight;
    Point lowLeft;
    Point lowRight;

    // outline and fill colors
    Color outlineColor;
    Color fillColor;

// methods define the Rectangle's behavior

    void draw() {
       // method to draw a Rectangle
       }

    void erase() {
       // method to erase a Rectangle
    }

    void move(int x_dist, int y_dist) {
       // method to move a Rectangle
    }

    Point[] getCorners() {
       // method to return array of corner Points
    }

    Color getOutlineColor() {
       return outlineColor;
    }
```

```
Color getFillColor() {
   return fillColor;
}


Point getPosition() {
   // method to calculate and return the center point
}


// ... etc.
}
```

The important thing to gain from this example is to see that all of the relevant code for a Rectangle is provided inside the class definition. The class *encapsulates* the data and methods that embody a Rectangle. By defining this class, we have not actually created any individual Rectangles; we have merely defined what a Rectangle *is*. Having completed this class definition, we can then create one or more individual objects of class Rectangle:

```
// code to create four individual rectangles
Rectangle thisRect = new Rectangle();
Rectangle thatRect = new Rectangle();
Rectangle myRect = new Rectangle();
Rectangle yourRect = new Rectangle();
```

We refer to the individual objects (thisRect, thatRect, myRect, yourRect) as *instances* of the class. In a drawing program, there may be many Rectangles on the screen at one time. They are each distinct objects, but they are all instances of the same class. The act of creating such an instance from the blueprint provided by the class definition is called *instantiating* the object.

Having instantiated these objects, the code outside of the class can use statements like the following to send messages to the individual objects, asking them to perform actions and report information.

```
thisRect.draw();
thatRect.erase();
myRect.move(distance_x, distance_y);
whichColor = yourRect.getFillColor();
```

Inheritance

Not only can we use classes to describe and create objects, but we can also describe relationships among classes themselves. We can group similar classes together into more general *superclasses*, and divide classes into more specific *subclasses*. Thus, `Polygon` and `Oval` can be seen as subclasses of the same superclass, `Shape`; we can further specify that `Circle` is a subclass of `Ellipse`, and both `Triangle` and `Rectangle` are subclasses of `Polygon`. `Square`, in turn, is a subclass of `Rectangle`.

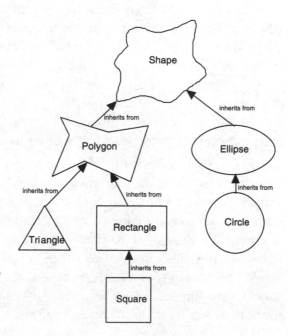

This hierarchical grouping yields families of classes, organized on the basis of their similarities. It turns out to be very useful to define classes this way. Since a subclass is seen as "belonging to" its superclass, there are certain operations and attributes which they will share. This is the essence of the concept of *inheritance*. We say that a subclass *inherits* characteristics from its superclass. In Java, we say that the subclass `extends` the superclass.

Thus, if a `Rectangle` has four corners, an outline color, and a fill color, and `Square` is a subclass of class `Rectangle`, then a `Square` has four corners, an outline color, and a fill color. In our definition of class `Square`, we don't need to specify that it has these attributes—they come "for free;" they are implicitly inherited from class `Rectangle`.

A subclass inherits both variables and methods from its superclass. Thus, `Square` also inherits methods to get and set its outline color and its fill color.

In Java, a superclass may have many subclasses, but a subclass can only inherit from one superclass. This model of inheritance is called *single inheritance*. Some languages, such as later implementations of C++, allow for *multiple inheritance*, where a class may inherit from one or more superclasses. Java does not support multiple inheritance. In Chapter 8, we shall discuss the advantages and disadvantages of this feature, and what mechanisms Java provides in order to get by without it.

The power of inheritance is that it allows code to be reused. Programmers often need to program very similar objects over and over again. Rather than having to "reinvent the wheel" with each new project, inheritance allows programmers to build up libraries of classes—or to use prefabricated class libraries— whose quality has already been thoroughly tested, and whose general functionality can be reapplied again and again. Through subclassing, these general classes can easily be made more specific, to suit many individual situations.

Polymorphism

Very often, it is beneficial for related objects, whose internal implementations may differ, to present themselves as essentially similar on the outside. This is especially useful when you want to have a collection of objects, such as an array.

Imagine a drawing program, which stores a list of Shapes that appear on a drawing surface. When the screen is updated, the program needs to step through its list of Shapes, and call each one's draw() method.[2] Clearly, all Shapes need to have a draw() method. But, although Square, Circle, Ellipse, and Rectangle are all descended from class Shape, we are going to need very different instructions to draw a Rectangle than to draw an Oval.

Object-oriented languages facilitate this through a mechanism known as *polymorphism*. Originating from the Greek words *poly* (many) and *morphos* (form, shape), polymorphism is a facility by which objects may present a similar interface, but differ in implementation—in other words, they look the same on the outside, but they may be different on the inside.

Thus, the class Shape declares a method called draw(). The subclasses of class Shape may each declare their own draw() methods as necessary, *overriding* the draw() method declared in their superclass. To the program, each object in the list is simply a Shape. It steps through the list, and calls draw() on each one. Each object, however, knows how to respond to a call to draw(), and will do so according to its own definition.

---

[2] Note the parentheses in our reference to the draw() method. In many programming languages, and particularly in Java, one often places parameters for a method between the parentheses. For example cos(theta) might be a call to a method in which we pass theta in as a parameter and calculate its cosine. When there are no parameters, we use the empty parentheses to distinguish methods, such as draw() and getCurrentItem() from variables such as myInt and currentItem. In addition, it is common when writing about programming to refer to a method by its name followed by the empty parentheses, even if that method does take parameters. The use of the empty parentheses in prose is a shorthand, and does not necessarily imply that the method has no parameters.

Abstraction

All of the features of object-oriented programming, combined together, produce a powerful mechanism for *abstraction*. Abstraction can be defined as the stripping away of irrelevant details in order to concentrate on relevant information. It is a means for coping with complexity, and it is a natural part of problem solving. Informally, abstraction can be described as "looking at the big picture."

When you turn on your computer in order to balance your checkbook, you don't care about the details underlying the checkbook program. You simply think of it as a checkbook, and you concentrate on the task at hand. You don't care about the software, or the data bus, or the microprocessor, or the VLSI circuits, or the electrons scurrying back and forth along channels of silicon. These details—as critical as they are to the functioning of the system—are hidden from you by layers and layers of abstraction; and well they should be, or how would you ever get anything done?

Similarly, a class is an abstraction for a bundle of data and operations. Once the attributes and behavior of a class have been defined, that level of detail has been dealt with, and it can be "abstracted away." Encapsulation and data-hiding allow the details to reside entirely within the object. Having completely described a class of objects, inheritance allows the programmer to define subclasses, abstracting away the details that have already been dealt with, and concentrating on the relevant information that makes the subclass special. Polymorphism allows us to abstract away irrelevant differences between objects, treating them as functionally the same.

Appropriately, we can view the very concept of object-oriented programming itself as an abstraction for all of these features.

Real-World Modeling With OOP: An Example

One of the most often stated advantages of object-oriented programming is that it facilitates the modeling of real-world systems. In light of the above discussion of abstraction, this premise rings true: real-world systems are inherently complex, and abstraction helps us to deal with complexity.

To bring our discussion of OOP a little more into the real world, let's look at a somewhat scaled-down version of a real-world system. We will look at an object-oriented approach to modeling the problem, and how it differs from a procedural approach. We will see how the object-oriented approach makes use of all of the concepts described above—objects, classes, encapsulation, data-hiding, inheritance and polymorphism—in order to handle the complexity of the problem and deal with changes in the system.

Imagine we are programming the central control unit for a system of phones. We can model a phone as an object. Thus, we need a class to represent a phone.

class Phone

Variables: (state)	Methods:(behavior)
offHook	ring()
connected	pick-up()
otherParty	hang-up()
location	dial (number)
	connectTo(party)
	isBusy()
	getLocation()

The variables of class `Phone` might include a Boolean (true/false) variable to represent whether the phone is on or off the hook; another Boolean to represent whether or not the phone is connected to another party; a number to represent who the phone is connected to; and some indication of the location of the phone.

We need to define methods to ring the phone; to respond to the phone being picked up or hung up; to dial a specific number; to connect the phone to another party; to tell us whether the phone is busy or not; and to tell us where the phone is located.

In the real world, however, there are many different types of phones. There are rotary phones, touch-tone phones, pay phones, etc. In terms of their details, these different types of phones may differ greatly. The specifics of the `dial()` method for a rotary phone, a touch-tone phone, and a pay phone may differ substantially.

In a procedural language like C, there is no inheritance, so if we want to have a collection of `Phones`, we need to embed all of the possible information for every different type of phone in a single data type, including a field indicating which type of phone we are dealing with in each particular instance. All code that deals with phones will need to first ascertain what type of phone we are dealing with, and then use that information to decide how to proceed, typically via a `case` statement.[3] Thus, in C, the code for `dial()` might look vaguely like this:

---

[3] A case statement is simply a switch based on a single value. It essentially says, "If the value is *a* do this; if the value is *b* do that; if the value is *c* do something else," and so on.

```
void dial(Phone *P, Number n) {
  switch(P -> phoneType) {
    case rotary:
      /* specific operations for rotary phones*/
      break;
    case touch_tone:
      /* specific operations for touch-tone phones*/
      break;
    case pay_phone:
      /* specific operations for pay phones*/
      break;
  }
}
```

The problem with this is that the code for `ring()` contains a similar `case` statement, and so does the code for countless other procedures. What if we now decide to add cellular phones into the system? We have to search through the code to find all of the scattered places where these `case` statements occur, and add to each one a `case` for cellular phones. Clearly, searching for these statements will be extremely tedious and error-prone. We also have to alter the existing `Phone` data structure, including in it any information which is relevant to cellular phones, and accounting for any way in which this change will affect code that depends on the implementation of this data structure. All `Phones` will then have space allocated for this information, whether they use it or not. Furthermore, all of this requires altering existing code, possibly introducing bugs into a working system.

In an object-oriented language like Java, however, the code for `dial()` and `ring()`—and any other relevant methods—is encapsulated in the `Phone` class itself. Each different type of phone is simply a subclass of `Phone`, and may provide it's own definition for `dial()` or `ring()`, overriding any default definition provided in `Phone`.

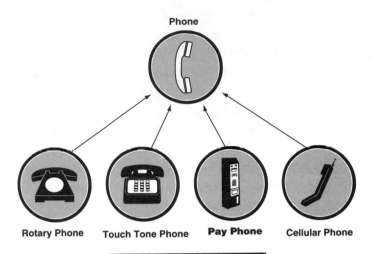

Phone

Rotary Phone   Touch Tone Phone   Pay Phone   Cellular Phone

A class hierarchy for phones.

If we want to include cellular phones in our model, we simply create a new subclass of Phone called CellularPhone, and in this class we define whatever variables and methods distinguish a CellularPhone from other types of Phones. To whatever extent all phones are alike, this information is simply inherited from Phone and reused as is.

When we add CellularPhone to our object-oriented model, the existing code for the classes RotaryPhone, TouchTonePhone, and PayPhone is completely unaffected by the change. More importantly, any code which relies upon these classes can continue to function unaltered. There is no need to change anything that is already working.

In the object-oriented model, dealing with collections of Phones is simple and efficient. Because of polymorphism, we can have, say, a list of Phone objects, each of which will respond according to its own definition when presented with a call to the ring() method. As far as the part of the program dealing with the list is concerned, they are all Phones. The details of how to handle each different type of Phone are abstracted away; such details are irrelevant to the task of managing a list of Phones.

Summary

Object-oriented programming (OOP) strives to deal with the complexity of real-world systems through a number of mechanisms for *abstraction*. Such mechanisms aim to hide irrelevant details while focusing only on information which is relevant to the task at hand.

Rather than view data and operations as separate entities, the object-oriented approach combines data and related operations into entities called *objects*. Each individual object is created as an *instance* of a *class*. The class definition specifies the *attributes* and *behavior* of all objects which are instances of that class. In Java, attributes and behavior are embodied by *variables* and *methods*, respectively.

The idea that an object's variables and methods are somehow wrapped up together in a single unit is known as *encapsulation*. Encapsulation facilitates *data-hiding*, wherein an object's variables are hidden from the outside world, and, theoretically, may only be accessed by calling the object's methods. The methods may act upon the data, or report to the outside as to what is stored there, but they act as a shield, controlling access to the data and ensuring that outside entities—unaware of the details of the object's implementation—may not alter the data in inappropriate ways.

Classes of objects are grouped together into more general superclasses, according to their similarities. Additionally, via *inheritance*, a programmer may define subclasses of existing classes in order to extend their functionality. To the extent that a subclass is the same as its superclass, it does not need to redefine variables and methods defined in the superclass—these variables and methods are *inherited* implicitly. Defining a subclass involves merely adding in any new functionality that is needed, and *overriding* those methods in the superclass which are no longer applicable and need to be revised for the new class. Inheritance thus allows for software to be reused, and obviates the need for a great deal of repeated effort.

Through inheritance, object-oriented languages also support *polymorphism*, by which objects may differ in their internal implementation, while providing a consistent outside appearance. Polymorphism is particularly useful in facilitating collections of heterogeneous objects. Because the differences are handled by the objects themselves, these differences can be abstracted away by the part of the program managing the collection.

All of these features together make object-oriented programming a powerful tool for modeling complex systems, and facilitate the creation of software that can be easily reused and adapted without damaging the functionality of existing code.

JAVA
PROGRAMMING
BASICS

CHAPTER 2

Java in Context

The History of Java

In 1991 Sun Microsystems' "Green" team set out to develop an operating system for household appliances. What they eventually created was Java—a revolutionary yet intuitive next step in the phenomenal evolution of the World Wide Web. When Sun gave this small team its charter, the Web did not yet exist. Its vague, free-spirited objectives were built around a concept of securely distributing code on heterogeneous networks. It was not until the network of networks would take hold and spawn a powerful, ubiquitous platform that Java would find its logical home. When Java finally met the Web browser, it simply made sense.

The seeds of Green were planted in the spring of 1990, when 25-year-old Sun programmer Patrick Naughton mentioned to CEO Scott McNealy that he was leaving the company to join the ranks of a rival corporation, where he felt they were doing things right. McNealy responded by asking Naughton to draw a plan reflecting what he would do if he were the chief. The next morning Naughton sat at his terminal and wrote a brutally honest assessment of Sun's problems; going beyond mere criticism, he included an outline for a new division to develop a new kind of product.

McNealy received Naughton's twelve screens of email and was impressed. He forwarded it to his managers, who in turn sent it around. Soon, Naughton was convinced to stay and offered the resources to make some real changes. Together with senior programmer James Gosling, he established a team committed to the idea of producing simple, easy-to-use computers for real-world applications that they could sell to everyday consumers. This represented a fundamental departure from the Sun business plan, which had historically been geared toward high-tech programmers. Naughton's basic idea was to move away from the heavy high-powered machines and operating systems that make up the Sun product line and toward something that hid the sophisticated and arcane workings of computer science from the user.

Although the Green development team was not quite certain what they had come together to make, they were sure it should be simple, easy to use, and appealing to the mass market. At the time, Gosling remarked that the chips in consumer appliances were being used badly. Rather than a variety of incompatible remote controls to operate some of the increasing number of chip-based household appliances, why not network them together and tie them into a single, handheld interface? The idea was that one could centrally control the toaster, refrigerator, and home security system. Although this represented a completely new arena for the largest manufacturer of Internet servers, it fit firmly within Sun's guiding ethos—"the network is the computer."

At first, Gosling's team wanted to use C++, but they quickly realized they needed something more robust and reliable.

Unlike computer users, consumers would not put up with their toaster crashing when the microwave sent it some funny code. The most apparent stumbling block was that C++ is compiled for particular chips, while consumer electronic manufacturers incorporate a variety of chips into their appliances. In addition, they regularly include the cheapest bits of silicon they can find, switching chips with new models to reduce costs. Gosling decided that they needed a new language, one that was simple, secure, robust, and—most importantly—made to run along heterogeneous networks on a variety of hardware and software architectures.

So Gosling set to work on a new language. Originally he named it Oak, after the tree that sat outside his office. The team started with C++ as the basic model, then set out to reduce and simplify the language. By making it leaner and meaner—stripping away many of the more complicated, error-causing features in C or C++—they made it more robust and crash-proof.

Along with this new computing environment, the Green team developed a Personal Digital Assistant–like handheld computer named *7, which had a graphical interface that included animations of the various appliances in the house. There was no keyboard or menus; users were meant to drag and drop functional icons into different appliances. With this handheld device, homeowners could program the VCR and set the coffee machine boiling all with a few finger strokes.

Sun soon realized that the qualities of this new programming environment offered possibilities that extended beyond the original concept of a household network. With Oak, designed inherently to be secure and platform independent, bits of code could be passed around between the home, office, cars, computers, televisions, anything with a chip. By the fall of 1992, Sun had formed FirstPerson Inc., a wholly owned subsidiary focusing on business and consumer applications for Oak.

By spring of the following year, FirstPerson felt it had finally found the right fit for its new technology—the information superhighway. At the time, Time Warner had been receiving proposals for its new plan to build an interactive TV system. The highly hyped idea of an interactive, networked television was widely hailed as the next great medium. Although Sun seemed to have superior technology and had been all but offered the project, Silicon Graphics stepped in and captured the deal.

It seemed, however, that neither the nation's network infrastructure nor public demand warranted or could handle such a system. The telephone wires did not have the bandwidth for real-time video, while the cable networks would have to be re-engineered to support two-way data communication. More importantly, studies of television viewers demonstrated that they did not want to pay for it. The set-top box phenomenon of the early 1990s would eventually fizzle out; but at the time, Sun needed a use for its new language, which until then represented an increasingly expensive experiment.

Still on the lookout for a home for the new technology, Sun entered negotiations with 3DO, which made television-based game machines. Again the deal fell through, as 3DO was only interested if they could buy the technology outright. Early in 1994 FirstPerson drew up a new business plan centered around CD-ROM development and looked forward to entering the world of online services. Interest and possible uses seemed to be waning and by the spring, FirstPerson was dissolved.

Although Marc Andreessen and the National Center for Supercomputing Applications (NCSA) had put the World Wide Web on the map in the spring of 1993 with the introduction of Mosaic, neither Sun nor anyone else saw the natural fit with Java. Not until mid-1994, that is, when Sun co-founder Bill Joy pumped new life into the project. Realizing that Green had developed a secure, robust, platform-independent language environment, he set Gosling and Naughton to work to make it fit into the now emerging information superhighway, which had found its interface in the Web browser.

In the fall of 1994, Naughton and fellow programmer Jonathan Payne developed their own browser. Initially named Webrunner, it had the ability to download and execute mini-applications, dubbed *applets*. At the same time, Joy realized that a firm plan of selling or licensing this technology was not the answer. Rather, in the same way that Netscape captured 80% of the browser market share, Sun would unleash Java onto the Net by simply giving it away. In the real world of business, it is naturally counterintuitive to develop a product and then give it away. Sun, however, is in the business of selling hardware, which accounts for nearly all of its $6 billion a year in revenue. Even its other software development projects, such as Solaris and SunOS, are aimed at selling more Sun workstations. In this bold move to gain market share, Sun reasoned that this new Internet software would ultimately increase its bottom line by helping to sell Internet servers.

Around this time, Sun set to work on finding a new name for its hot product. Oak was an unexciting name; it was also already taken. Naughton describes long days of hacking, continually re-energizing with frequent stops at a local coffee shop. They often bought chocolate-covered Java beans, which inspired the name. The marketing department loved it; Java was simple, interesting, and reflected the caffeinated, dynamic nature of what it brings to the Web.

Two years after the introduction of Mosaic, in the spring of 1995, Sun formally introduced Java and HotJava (formerly the Webrunner browser). Andreessen, who had moved on to head up technology at Netscape saw what Sun had created and said, "What these guys are doing is undeniably, absolutely new. It's great stuff." His company signed a deal to incorporate the technology, and by the end of 1995 there were free beta versions of Java-capable Netscape Navigator browsers being downloaded all over the world.

In its long and winding development trail, based on various business plans, Java had a single axis on which it revolved—the network. To run effectively on a heterogeneous network, code had to be platform-independent and secure. Java has evolved into something more than just a quick solution to these problems. It is indeed a serious, heavyweight programming language with many useful features built in from the ground up. There are a host of buzzwords used to describe Java: simple, familiar, object-oriented, secure, robust, portable, architecture-neutral, high-performance, multithreaded, extensible, and dynamic. It is all this and more.

Advantages of Java

Compiled *and* Interpreted

A popular comic sketch from the early days of the TV show *Saturday Night Live* featured a mock commercial for a product whose claim to fame was that it was "a floor wax *and* a dessert topping!" Like the wonder-product advertised in this sketch, Java bridges the gap between interpreted languages and compiled languages: it's compiled *and* interpreted.

Compiled languages, such as C or C++, are designed as a way for humans to describe the actions they want a computer to perform, typically via text that looks like a shorthand for English (or some other human language). Once the programmer has finished typing in this description, a program called a *compiler* translates this description into a sequence of instructions—actual machine instructions for a specific chip on which the program is meant to run. The instructions are not executed as they are generated; they are stored in a file called an *executable file*, or simply an *executable*. Compilation is thus a necessary intermediate step between writing a program in one of these languages and running it. After compilation, the executable can be invoked whenever the user wishes, and the machine instructions contained therein will be executed.

Interpreted languages, such as BASIC, Tcl, and UNIX shell languages, are also typically written in a text form resembling a human language. Unlike compiled languages, however, which must be translated into machine instructions and stored in this form for later use, interpreted languages are not stored in the native language of the machine. Most interpreted languages actually store programs in the same form in which they are written. When such a program is invoked, it is read in the way it was written and translated to machine instructions "on the fly," by a program called an *interpreter*. Thus, in a purely interpreted language, there is no intermediate compilation step.

Java combines these two approaches. After a programmer types in source code in the Java language, he feeds that source code to the Java compiler, a program that, like all compilers, translates source code into instructions. The instructions are stored in a file, as a sequence of bytes. These bytes, in order, represent the instructions that comprise the program. The instructions, stored in this form, are called *bytecodes*.

Bytecodes, however, are *not* machine instructions for a specific chip, as is the case with purely compiled languages. Rather, the bytecodes are instructions for a *virtual* machine—an "imaginary" chip, if you will. It is the job of another program, the Java interpreter, to read the bytecodes and generate instructions for the actual physical machine and operating system on which it is running. The Java interpreter acts as a stand-in, emulating the behavior expected of the virtual machine. The Java virtual machine, therefore, is just a specification for how a machine should behave in response to a given set of instructions. This behavior is implemented not in hardware, but in software, and is embodied by the Java interpreter and run-time system.

Thus, Java is compiled *and* interpreted, in that order. As we shall see, this hybrid scheme is a significant advantage for Java.

Architecture-Neutral and Portable

Because different computers use different chip architectures, the instruction sets are not interchangeable. Thus, if you have developed a program you want to run on a different machine from the one for which you have compiled it, you have to go back to your source code and recompile it for the new machine. Additionally, if the new machine runs under a different operating system than the machine for which you originally wrote the code, the services provided by the operating system may differ, as may the ways in which your program calls on those services. You will then have to alter your source code itself, often quite significantly, in order to produce a version that will even compile for the new operating system. This process of altering and recompiling a program for a different platform is known as *porting*; software developers often go through a great deal of effort and write many lines of additional code in order to make their software more portable.

Software consumers typically buy programs written in compiled languages. What the consumer buys in these cases is typically the executable form of the program, not the source code, which is usually proprietary to the individual or company that developed the software. Thus, if the consumer decides to buy a new computer or switch to a new operating system, it is likely that none of the old software will work on the new machine. If he is fortunate and all the software manufacturers have gone to the trouble of porting their software, he can buy new versions of all of his old software, often at great expense. If he is unfortunate, some or all of the software manufacturers may have decided that it was too much trouble to port the software to the new platform, and the consumer will have to find alternate solutions.

Recall that Java is compiled not to native machine instructions, but to bytecodes. The bytecodes themselves are *architecture-neutral*. A sequence of bytes is a sequence of bytes (as long as the hardware accepts the notion of eight-bit bytes, as all modern hardware does). It is the Java interpreter that interprets these bytecodes as instructions for the Java virtual machine. Thus, if you have a Java interpreter for your machine, any code written in Java and compiled to bytecodes will run on your machine. If you want to run the same compiled code on a different machine, you can, as long as that machine has a Java interpreter.

The Java interpreter is written in ANSI C, and the designers put a great deal of effort into making the code portable. Availability of the Java interpreter for various platforms is discussed in Chapter 4. The Java compiler is written in Java, and is therefore architecture-neutral.

Familiar and Simple

Java is familiar because it is syntactically based on C and C++. To programmers familiar with these popular languages, Java code should be easily intelligible, and the transition to writing in Java should be very straightforward.

Java is simple because the designers deliberately removed features found in its predecessors, on the grounds that these features made the language unnecessarily complex or introduced too much room for programmer error. One example is *multiple inheritance*, a feature whose value is often debated among object-oriented language designers and one that the designers of Java decided to remove from the language. We discuss the problems caused by multiple inheritance in Chapter 8, as well as the solution that Java provides, which solves most problems for which multiple inheritance was devised.

Many other features of C++ were by-products of the attempt to keep C++ as backward-compatible with C as possible.

Although C++ is an object-oriented language, it allows many ways to "break" the abstractions on which object-oriented programming is based. Although Java keeps much of C's syntax and functionality, it is a language in its own right, not merely a new and improved version of an existing language. As a result, the designers were free to do away with anything they felt compromised the goals of the language as a whole. The result is a simpler, more purely object-oriented language.

Object-Oriented

Java provides all the benefits of an object-oriented language. Code written in Java can be reused through inheritance without sacrificing the functionality of already-implemented systems. Because programmers are freed from having to reinvent the wheel with each new project, development time can be decreased.

NOTE

The central concepts of object-oriented programming (OOP) and the advantages that they provide are discussed in detail in Chapter 1. For programmers, Chapter 8 discusses the specific manner in which Java implements these concepts.

Multithreaded

The concept of objects interacting with one another in a dynamic system brings with it, to some extent, an implicit notion of *concurrency*. It is natural to think of several objects doing whatever it is that they do, all at the same time, communicating with one another as necessary, or simply performing their own tasks, completely oblivious to each other. A *multithreaded* language provides support for several independent sequences of instructions within the same program to be executed simultaneously. Each independent sequence of instructions, combined with the data necessary for the execution of those instructions, is called a *thread*. Because today's computers typically use one processor, implementing multithreaded operation generally involves some mechanism by which concurrency can be simulated; each thread is given a tiny slice of time (typically measured in microseconds) in which to perform a few operations, and then the processor is turned over to the next thread, and the next, finally cycling back around, and so on. This all happens so fast that the net effect is the appearance of simultaneous execution of all the active threads.

There is quite a bit of programming involved in pulling this type of thing off. It's generally acknowledged that the best way to do this is to provide support for it directly in the language, so that most of the burden of maintaining the threads is taken off the shoulders of the programmer. There have been several attempts to extend C and C++ to provide them with mechanisms for concurrency—the languages themselves predate much of the modern work on multithreaded systems—but none of these efforts has proven superior enough to rise to the top as a standard.

Java was designed from the start as a multithreaded language. The designers of the language provide a simple and flexible mechanism by which most of the complexities of maintaining the threads are handled by the Java run-time system. This has the advantage that the programmer need not be concerned with the mechanics of thread maintenance; it also provides another advantage as multiprocessor machines become a reality. Because the language looks at threads from a high level of abstraction, there is no need for a Java program to be modified to run on a multiprocessor machine. The details of handling threads will be quite different on these machines, and the Java run-time system itself, when implemented on these machines, will have to be adjusted in order to deal with these details; but Java programs themselves, which do not concern themselves with the details, will not need to be rewritten or recompiled to function as intended.

Dynamic Loading and Late Binding

As a Java program runs, it loads code for the each object class it needs as necessary. Because the data and operations that pertain to a given object are encapsulated within that object, code is loaded in small bundles that make sense and that are likely to be needed together. Contrast this with programs written in traditional languages, which load themselves into memory in large chunks, much of which may not even be accessed during the entire run of the program. Java programs take up only as much memory as they need at any given time. This is one of the key advantages of *dynamic loading*.

When one Java object calls a method of another Java object—for example, when a crossword applet calls the `Puzzle` object's `displayPuzzle()` method, it is not until that call is actually made that the runtime system figures out where in memory the instructions for the `displayPuzzle()` method are called and *binds* the call to that sequence of instructions. This approach, called *late binding*, is partially a by-product of dynamic loading; after all, if you haven't loaded the `Puzzle` object into memory until it is needed, there is no way to know in advance exactly where in memory the instructions for its `displayPuzzle()` method will be. As a result, there is no choice but to use late binding.

From an object-oriented point of view, this has two immediately obvious advantages. First, imagine there are three different classes of puzzles, each of which has its own version of the `displayPuzzle()` method. The method is not bound until it is called, so you are assured that the correct method for this particular `Puzzle` object will be called. Also, what happens if you change the implementation of the `displayPuzzle()` method for one of the `Puzzle` classes? You don't have to recompile your whole applet, just the code for the class you changed. The applet as a whole is unaffected.

Heavy Compile-Time Checking

The Java language follows a certain *specification*, or set of rules. One function of these rules is to keep the language from being able to produce instruction sequences that would be senseless, impossible, or dangerous for the virtual machine to follow. Another function is to help enforce the object-oriented nature of the language by treating each class of objects as a distinct data type.

The Java compiler does extensive checking to make sure that the rules of the language are obeyed. The result of this is a *robust* language; that is, any errors in the code are discovered early by the compiler. When the compiler discovers an error, it does not produce executable code. Thus, any code that has made it past the compiler is guaranteed to have followed these rules. Unlike C or C++, Java makes it difficult or impossible for programmers to circumvent the rules, either intentionally or by mistake.

Heavy Run-Time Checking

Some errors are impossible to catch when a program is compiled. They may depend on the state of the environment as the program is being run. Because Java is interpreted, Java bytecodes are processed by the Java run-time system before any machine code is actually executed on the processor. This gives the run-time system an opportunity to do run-time checking of the code, to make sure that it does not do anything that could corrupt memory or do other damage.

In addition, Java code that is loaded over the network (such as an applet running in a World Wide Web page) is treated as "untrusted." That is, there is no guarantee that this code was created by a legitimate Java compiler that correctly implemented all the run-time checks. There is also no guarantee that the person who wrote this code did not include instructions that might compromise the security of the system running the applet. As a result, network-loaded (*outside*) code is tagged so that the run-time system can keep track of it. Outside code is fed through a bytecode verifier to make sure that it follows all the language rules, and outside code is restricted from performing suspicious actions, such as reading or writing to disk, asking for unrestricted access to the network, and so on. These security protections are discussed in detail in Chapter 12.

The Java API

Most programming languages come with a certain set of standard libraries that provide basic functionality, such as console input and output, string and file manipulation, and mathematical functions and constants. Java includes these features and more as part of the Java API (application programmer's interface). The API provides packages of classes that the programmer can use to construct full-featured working applications. It includes all the things you would expect to be included with a language, as well as support for multithreading, exception handling, graphics, audio, and network support.

Additionally, the API includes a package of classes known as the *Abstract Window Toolkit* (AWT), which consists of prefabricated graphic user interface (GUI) widgets, such as scrollbars, menus, buttons, check boxes, radio buttons, and so on. The Java run-time system collaborates with the local windowing system on whatever platform it is running on in order to create and manage these widgets. To the Java program itself, however, these windowing systems all look alike, because the AWT provides the programmer with a consistent interface for directing the creation and management of the widgets.

Publicly Accepted

It has been less than a year since Java was announced, but the industry is lining up behind it in force. Nearly every day, messages circulate on the Internet that yet another software developer has announced support for Java in one form or another. Vendors such as Borland, Symantec, Metroworks, and Natural Intelligence have announced Integrated Development Environments for Java, and these are starting to hit the market.

The promise of Java as a tool for the development of cross-platform client-server applications has the industry buzzing with excitement. With this wave of support from the industry, Java has the push it needs to achieve a wide client base and gain public acceptance.

Disadvantages of Java

Requires Object-Oriented Approach to Programming

Java is deeply rooted in the object-oriented approach. As a result, for those programmers unacquainted with object-oriented programming, there is a bit of a learning curve associated with it. It's sometimes difficult to keep track of the members and methods of an object if some of those members and methods were inherited from its parent class, and some from its parent's parent class, and so on. The class that represents a Java applet, for example, has four levels of superclasses, each of which contributes some of the attributes and behavior that define an applet. For the beginner, this can be difficult to keep track of.

Fortunately for those unacquainted with object-oriented programming, there are books like this one, to help sort it all out.

Slower than Machine Code

Because of the additional processing involved in translating each instruction (perhaps after verification) from bytecode to machine code, not to mention the run-time checking, Java runs significantly slower than programs compiled directly to machine code. This is, however, a temporary disadvantage, because of two coming advances.

One is the so-called *just-in-time compiler*, a special variant of the Java interpreter. It not only interprets Java code and translates it to machine code, but it saves the machine code in native form, so that as that section of the program is executed again, it does not have to be translated into machine code a second, or third, or hundredth time.

The second solution to this problem lies in a new line of microprocessors—picoJAVA, microJAVA, and UltraJAVA—announced by Sun Microelectronics in February 1996 and scheduled to be released from mid-1996 to late 1997. These new chips implement the Java virtual machine in hardware, rather than software, speeding up the performance of Java immensely.

However, until the just-in-time compiler and the Java microprocessor become a reality, Java remains an impractical choice for applications that require optimum performance.

Security Target

Because Java is designed to accommodate network-loaded executable code, it is a natural target for hackers. In fact, no open system is perfectly safe. Any system attached in any way to the Internet faces some form of risk. Although the designers of the language took security issues into account when they designed the language, they were aware that there may be something they overlooked.

Their solution was to make the source code for the Java runtime system open and public. Anyone who is curious can obtain the source code from Sun and inspect the code carefully for any sign of a security hole. Although there is a risk that a malicious hacker will find the security hole first, the people at Sun put their faith in the academic and industrial community as a whole, which will gain from increasing the security of the Internet and lose from the degradation of that security. In fact, some have already found problems with Java's security implementation. See Chapter 12 for more details on security issues.

Summary

Java represents a solution for a need that now exists. The World Wide Web is quickly becoming a ubiquitous tool for business, study, and entertainment—a common interface to access stores of information housed and published on the Internet. To take the functionality of the Internet to the next level—beyond simply calling and displaying data—the Web calls for greater multimedia and interactivity capabilities.

In order for executable content to be distributed practically on the Web, it must be simple, secure, and platform-independent. Although Java was originally developed with entirely different applications in mind, the fact that it has these features has rendered it an ideal fit for the Web.

JAVA
PROGRAMMING
BASICS

Viewing and Using Java Applets

What is a Java-Enabled Browser?

A *Java-enabled browser* is a Web browser that can run applets embedded in HTML pages. This opens up a new dimension for Web pages. No longer are Web pages limited to so-called *static* content: fixed text and still images on a page that cannot itself respond to user input without sending a message back to the server for a brand-new page. With a Java-enabled browser, Web pages "come to life" with animation, in-line audio, and real-time interactivity.

What are HTML Tags?

HTML pages contain only text. The secret of HTML is in *tags*, special keywords surrounded by angle-brackets; for example, <H1> (meaning "Heading 1") and <B> (meaning "Bold"). These tags are essentially cues for the Web browser to do something special at this point when displaying the page.

Some HTML tags come in begin-end pairs that enclose the text to which they pertain. For example, <B> and </B> signify, respectively, the start and end of a section of text to be formatted in bold type. <H1> and </H1> signify, respectively, the start and end of a level-1 heading. In general, a slash (/) in a tag signifies the end of a begin-end pair.

Many HTML tags contain additional text items between the angle brackets that give the Web browser more information so that it can respond appropriately to the tag. These additional items are called *attributes*. Some tags have required attributes, without which the tag cannot be interpreted; some attributes are optional.

NOTE

In this book, to refer to a tag without explicitly including its attributes, we use an ellipsis (...) inside the angle brackets. This is just a notation we use for convenience; the tag does not appear this way in the actual HTML file.

There is a tag, <IMG ...>, that informs the Web browser that the page needs to contain an image. One required attribute of this tag is the SRC attribute, which the HTML designer sets equal to the text of a Uniform Resource Locator (URL) for that image, as in:

```
<IMG SRC="http://the_machine.acme.com/some_dir/my_image.gif">
```

The Web browser uses this URL to request the image from the server so that it can display it for you at this location in the page.

There is also a tag that informs the Web browser that a certain image or bit of text is a *hyperlink*; this tag uses an attribute that names the URL of the location to which the link points. Hyperlink text is typically displayed in a different color from normal text, and if you click on that text your Web browser knows to request the document at the location pointed to by the URL for that link.

There are many more tags that comprise the standard HTML vocabulary. This is not a book on HTML, so we do not go into them here.

How are Applets Embedded into Web Pages?

N O T E

According to all versions of the HTML specification, HTML tags are to be processed in a case-insensitive manner. That is, the Web browser should respond identically to tags such as <APPLET>, <Applet>, and <applet>. At the time of this writing, however, there is a bug in the Macintosh version of the appletviewer that comes with Sun's Java Developer's Kit, such that the tag will *only* be recognized if it is in all lowercase letters, i.e., <applet>. The bug may be fixed by the time you read this.

A Java-enabled browser, in addition to recognizing the standard HTML tags, will recognize the tag <APPLET ...>, which signifies that a Java applet should run in this space on the page. Within the <APPLET ...> tag, the HTML page designer includes attributes indicating the URL at which the Java bytecode instructions that comprise the applet can be found. Whenever the browser encounters an <APPLET ...> tag, it will call up its Java module to load and run those instructions, displaying the applet right in the Web page.

If a traditional (i.e., non-Java-enabled) browser comes across a page with an <APPLET ...> tag, it will simply ignore the tag; it is part of the HTML specification that browsers should ignore any tags they do not understand. As we shall see, this feature allows considerate HTML designers to include alternate material, such as static images, for the benefit of those who do not have Java-enabled browsers; this way, such users aren't kept completely in the dark when they navigate to a page with an applet.

We will discuss the <APPLET ...> tag, its proper syntax, and its attributes in greater detail later in this chapter.

Security Risks of Java-Enabled Browsers

Although the idea of interactive Web pages is a very attractive one and the arguments in favor of such pages are compelling and exciting, it would not be appropriate to launch into a wholehearted endorsement of Java applets without stopping to ask some questions about security.

An *applet* is basically a program. It is a set of instructions for your computer to execute. Ordinarily, you run a program on your computer by consciously installing and invoking it. Any well-informed user is aware that some programs—viruses, for example—may contain damaging instructions or cause sensitive information to be transmitted to someone who shouldn't see it. As a result, a wise user does not run programs whose origin or intentions are suspect. It is always a question of the user's judgment.

Unlike other programs, an applet runs when you use a Java-enabled browser to navigate to a Web page. The browser sees the <APPLET> tag, loads the applet—typically from the network—and then runs it on your machine. The step where you consciously decide to install and run the program is no longer part of the scenario. This may represent a serious security risk if applets were not in some way constrained from doing anything that might damage your system (such as deleting files).

Fortunately, there are significant constraints on Java applets and the activities that they may and may not engage in. The exact nature of these constraints is highly dependent on the specific Java-enabled browser you are using to view the applets. An entire chapter of this book is devoted to discussions of security concerns as they relate to Java. If you are concerned about security—and we think you *should* be concerned, although not necessarily worried—you should at least skim Chapter 12 before installing and running any Java-enabled browser.

What Java-Enabled Browsers are Available?

The HotJava Web Browser

In all of the hype about Java and HotJava, many people have gotten the misconception that they are one and the same. In fact, they are not. *Java* is a programming language, which is the focus of this book. *HotJava* is a specific Web browser written by the people at Sun Microsystems to showcase the features of the Java language.

The HotJava browser was the first Web browser developed to display embedded applets on Web pages. It was included with alpha versions of the Java Development Kit. The most recently released version of the HotJava browser was version 1.0 Alpha3, made available in September 1995. Although the Java language itself has since been through its beta stage and was released in a final 1.0 version in January 1996, Sun has not yet released an updated version of the HotJava browser (at the time of this writing).

The alpha version of the HotJava browser was not intended to be a full-fledged Web browser. The main purpose of this release was to let people see the power of Java and test-drive the language. The most important drawback of the alpha version of the HotJava browser is that *it can only run Java applets written in the alpha version of the Java language.* The growing pains that the language itself went through in transition through its beta stage rendered the alpha code obsolete. Although there are still a few alpha applets floating around the Web from the old days, most of it has been updated to be compatible with the beta and final versions of the Java language. As a result, until Sun comes out with an update, HotJava is not really a viable choice as a Java-enabled browser.

NOTE

This book is based on the final version 1.0 of the Java language. There are significant differences between the alpha versions and later version of the language, rendering them incompatible with one another; even the HTML tags are different. This book contains *no* alpha code. Version 1.0 Alpha3 of the HotJava browser *cannot* display any of the applets included in this book or its accompanying CD-ROM.

Netscape Navigator 2.0

Netscape Navigator 2.0, from Netscape Communications Corporation, is the first general-purpose browser to run Java applets written using the beta and final versions of the Java language. Unlike version 1.0 Alpha3 of the HotJava browser, Netscape Navigator 2.0 (often referred to simply as *Netscape*, or the Netscape browser) is a full-fledged, fully supported Web browser, which supports version 1.0 of the Java language. Netscape will run applets written according to either the beta or final specifications of the Java language; it will not run alpha code.

At the time of this writing, Netscape is the *only* browser that supports Java 1.0 applets. As a result, this is the browser we will focus on in this chapter. By no means, however, is Netscape the only browser manufacturer that has pledged to support Java. By the time you read this, there may well be a handful of others available. Although the features of these individual browsers may differ (especially with respect to security; see Chapter 12), there should be no significant difference in the way an applet looks under one browser or another.

Downloading Java-Enabled Netscape Navigator 2.0

Do I Need to Download Netscape at All?

You might already have access to a Java-enabled browser, without even knowing it. If you are working in a networked environment, your system administrator may have already installed the latest version of Netscape. Before you go to the trouble of downloading or installing the browser, consult with your system administrator.

If you already have the Java-enabled version of Netscape, you can skip this section, and go on to the next section, which outlines the Java-specific features of Netscape 2.0 (page 58).

If you're running Netscape and you're not certain whether your version supports Java, you can select **About Netscape...** from Nctscape's Help menu. If your browser supports Java, there will be a special Java-compatible logo on the About Netscape page.

Platform Requirements

Netscape 2.0 supports Java on Windows 95, Windows NT, and UNIX (Sun Solaris 2.3 and 2.4, SunOS 4.1, IRIX, OSF1, HP-UX). Netscape 2.0 for the Macintosh does not include support for Java. However, a beta version with the awkwardly long name Netscape Navigator 2.0 Java B1, was made available for PowerPC-equipped Macs in February 1996. By the time you read this, it will probably have been updated, and there may well be a final version available for the Macintosh.

NOTE The version of the Java run-time system included in Netscape Navigator 2.0 Java B1 for the Macintosh is version beta1. There are known bugs with this version of the Java run-time system, and there are a few subtle incompatibilities with the final version of the language. As with any beta software, you should expect that the behavior of this program may be quirky at times and may cause your machine to crash. Use it at your own risk.

Doing the Download

The easiest way to download Netscape Navigator 2.0 is to use a Web browser. Simply point your Web browser to Netscape's home page at

```
http://home.netscape.com
```

and follow the obvious links from there.

Alternatively, if for some reason you cannot use a Web browser to download the software, you can use a text-based FTP session. We have included an example here. The actual commands you need to enter will differ, depending on the platform for which you are downloading the software. Following is the relevant information for each platform.

Windows 95/Windows NT

1. Open an FTP session to: `ftp.netscape.com`
2. Change to the directory: **/2.0/windows**
3. Get the file: **n32e20.exe**

NOTE Although this directory also contains an executable for Windows 3.1, that version of Netscape Navigator 2.0 is not Java-enabled, at the time of this writing.

UNIX

1. Open an FTP session to: `ftp.netscape.com`

2. Change to the directory: **/2.0/unix**

3. Get one of the appropriate files:

> **netscape-v20-export.alpha-dec-osf2.0.tar.Z**
>
> **netscape-v20-export.alpha-dec-osf2.0.tar.gz**
>
> **netscape-v20-export.hppa1.1-hp-hpux.tar.Z**
>
> **netscape-v20-export.hppa1.1-hp-hpux.tar.gz**
>
> **netscape-v20-export.i386-unknown-bsd.tar.Z**
>
> **netscape-v20-export.i386-unknown-bsd.tar.gz**
>
> **netscape-v20-export.i486-unknown-linux.tar.Z**
>
> **netscape-v20-export.i486-unknown-linux.tar.gz**
>
> **netscape-v20-export.mips-sgi-irix5.2.tar.Z**
>
> **netscape-v20-export.mips-sgi-irix5.2.tar.gz**
>
> **netscape-v20-export.rs6000-ibm-aix3.2.tar.Z**
>
> **netscape-v20-export.rs6000-ibm-aix3.2.tar.gz**
>
> **netscape-v20-export.sparc-sun-solaris2.3.tar.Z**
>
> **netscape-v20-export.sparc-sun-solaris2.3.tar.gz**
>
> **netscape-v20-export.sparc-sun-solaris2.4.tar.Z**
>
> **netscape-v20-export.sparc-sun-solaris2.4.tar.gz**
>
> **netscape-v20-export.sparc-sun-sunos4.1.3_U1.tar.Z**
>
> **netscape-v20-export.sparc-sun-sunos4.1.3_U1.tar.gz**

NOTE

For each UNIX platform, there are two format options available: **.gz** and **.Z**. The **.gz** files are smaller than the **.Z** files, which means they take less time to download. However, in order to unzip a **.gz** file, you must have **gzip** running on your UNIX system. If your system doesn't have **gzip**, then you should download the **.Z** file.

Macintosh

1. Open an FTP session to: `ftp.netscape.com`
2. Change to the directory: **/pub/MacJava**
3. Get the appropriate file: **Mac2.0JavaB1.hqx**

Sample FTP Session

The following is a sample FTP session to download the Windows 95/Windows NT version of Netscape Navigator 2.0. The process is similar for each of the supported platforms, although Mac users are more likely to be using an FTP program with a graphical user interface such as Fetch or Anarchie. Just substitute the appropriate directory and file names. You should use anonymous as your user name (ftp will also work as a shortcut). When prompted for a password, *do not use your password from your local system*! Instead, substitute your own complete email address for the generic one we've included in the following.

It's a good idea to change to a temporary directory before beginning the FTP session.

NOTE

```
$ ftp ftp.netscape.com
Connected to ftp20.netscape.com.
220 ftp20 FTP server (Version wu-2.4(17) Tue Feb 20 09:08:35
PST 1996) ready.
Name (ftp.netscape.com:edith): anonymous
331 Guest login ok, send your complete e-mail address as
password.
Password: username@machine.org
230-Welcome to the Netscape Communications Corporation FTP
server.
```

```
<< informational messages >>
230 Guest login ok, access restrictions apply.
Remote system type is UNIX.
Using binary mode to transfer files.
ftp> cd 2.0/windows
250 CWD command successful.
ftp> bin
200 Type set to I.
ftp> get n32e20.exe
local: n32e20.exe remote: n32e20.exe
200 PORT command successful.
150 Opening BINARY mode data connection for n32e20.exe
(3269120 bytes).

226 Transfer complete.
3269120 bytes received in 7.2e+02 seconds (4.5 Kbytes/s)
ftp> bye
221 Goodbye.
$
```

Unpack the Archive

Windows 95/Windows NT

After the FTP session, you should have a file named **n32e20.exe** in your current directory (the temporary directory). All you need to do is run this executable and follow the on-screen setup instructions that the program provides.

After the installation, you can delete **n32e20.exe** and the temporary directory.

NOTE

There is no need to set the CLASSPATH variable to run Netscape on Windows 95/Windows NT.

UNIX

N O T E

The instructions included here are specifically for the Solaris version of Netscape. They should be essentially similar for all versions, but to be sure of any particular differences, you should carefully read the **README** file included with the release.

You should have the downloaded file in your current directory (the temporary directory). To unzip a **.Z** file, type:

```
% zcat filename.tar.Z | tar -vxf -
```

To unzip a **.gz** file, type:

```
% gzip -dc filename.tar.gz | tar -vxf -
```

After unpacking the archive, you can move the unpacked directory to the desired location and then delete the **.Z** or **.gz** file. You should then make sure that, wherever the Netscape executable is located, you have included that location in your **$PATH** variable.

Netscape needs a file called **moz2_0.zip** in order to run applets. After unzipping the **.Z** or **.gz** file, you should see **moz2_0.zip** under the **netscape** directory. Copy the file to one of the following directories:

```
/usr/local/netscape/java/classes/
/usr/local/lib/netscape/
$HOME/.netscape/
```

If you are not a system administrator, you probably don't have write access to **/usr/local/**. In this case, you should copy **moz2_0.zip** to the **.netscape** directory under your home directory. If you are a system administrator, then you may want to copy the file to one of the first two directories so that your users do not need to make redundant copies of the file in their home directories and to ease the upgrade process, should a new version of this file be released.

NOTE

There is no need to set your CLASSPATH to point to **moz2_0.zip** if you have the file in any of the previously mentioned locations. If the file is located anywhere else, however, you will need to include the complete path of the file in your class path, for example:

```
% setenv CLASSPATH <unusual_path>/moz2_0.zip
```

Macintosh

Netscape 2.0 Java B1 for the Macintosh is distributed as a BinHex-encoded (**.hqx**) file. To decode this file, you need the freeware StuffIt Expander from Aladdin Systems, available from many places online, including (but not limited to) AOL, CompuServe, and the following URL:

```
ftp://mirrors.aol.com/pub/info-mac/cmp/stuffit-expander-
352.hqx
```

Another way to get StuffIt Expander, if you use Eudora for email, is to send an email message from your Eudora return address to get-stuffit@ultranet.com. UltraNet will send you a copy of StuffIt Expander.

If you already have StuffIt Expander and you used a program like Netscape Navigator 2.0, Fetch, or Anarchie to download the Java-enabled Netscape, then it's very likely that these programs automatically invoked the Expander when you finished your FTP session, and you don't need to manually decode anything. Otherwise, you can decode the **.hqx** file by simply dragging it onto StuffIt Expander.

After the **.hqx** file is decoded, you should be able to see the installer application, **MacJava 2.0b1 Install**, on your hard drive. Simply double-click this application, and it will guide you through the installation process. When you're done, you can throw away the installer and the **.hqx** file if you wish. However, because this is a beta version, you might want to keep the installer around, just in case you need to re-install.

After Unpacking the Archive

Regardless of which platform you are using, you should carefully read the **README** file distributed with the release for any last-minute changes, important notes, or known incompatibilities/bugs. This is especially true for UNIX, as different UNIX systems may require different settings.

Java-Specific Features of Netscape Navigator 2.0

Java Applets

The most obvious Java-specific feature of Netscape Navigator 2.0 is its ability to display Java applets. That's why we're here.

The Java Console

The Java-enabled version of Netscape provides a console to display messages from embedded applets. Under normal circumstances, you will not need to see these messages; however, should some sort of error occur, this is most likely where the error message will appear. If an applet seems to be working improperly, freezes up, or has difficulty loading, you might want to check the Java console to see if it is displaying any error messages.

The Java console window is not displayed by default. To display the console window, simply select **Show Java Console** from the Options menu.

Disabling Java

You may decide that you do not want applets to be run at all. Perhaps you are concerned about security risks or tired of waiting for them to load when you navigate to pages that contain them. You can choose to disable Java by selecting **Security Preferences** from the Options menu and selecting the **Disable Java** option in the dialog box that appears.

As we mentioned briefly earlier in this chapter, there are certain items on HTML pages that are intended as alternate material for users of non-Java-enabled browsers. If you disable Java using the method we have just described, you will see neither the applets nor the alternate material. This is because your browser is a Java enabled browser, and as such, it still recognizes the <APPLET ...> tag, even if it is currently set not to load or display applets.

JavaScript

Another new feature of Netscape 2.0 is JavaScript. It is stretching things a bit to say that JavaScript is a Java-related feature of Netscape 2.0. In fact, JavaScript is not Java, and the two are only slightly related. We mention JavaScript here mostly to resolve any confusion caused by the name. In fact, JavaScript is supported by even those incarnations of Netscape 2.0 that do not support Java applets (such as the Windows 3.1 and Macintosh 68K versions).

JavaScript, known originally and briefly as LiveScript, is a Netscape-specific scripting language that borrows some of Java's syntax but is much simpler and less powerful. JavaScript is intended to allow nonprogrammers to provide some simple and limited interactivity to Web pages. There are certain simple things for which it may be more convenient to use JavaScript than Java. For example, you can write a Java applet that displays a few buttons on a page and updates a text box based on the buttons clicked. JavaScript, however, can accomplish a simple task like this with less code and fewer steps than Java.

Links to Some Interesting Applets

You now have your Java-enabled browser set up and ready to go. Now what do you do? In this section, we'll provide you with the URLs of some interesting applets that can give you a general idea of what Java can do. Now, fire up your browser and get ready to play!

PC Scoreboard

http://www.cnet.com/Content/Reviews/Compare/Pc100/

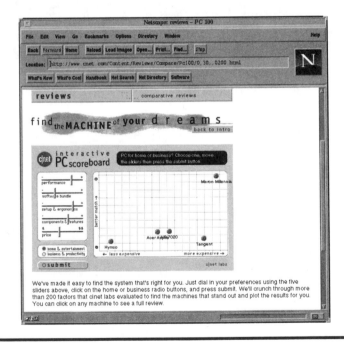

Figure 3.1 PC Scoreboard. Reprinted with permission from C|NET: The Computer Network © 1996.

Looking to buy a PC? This applet can help you sort out the peaches from the lemons. You simply dial in your priorities and preferences with regard to performance, bundled software, ease of setup, components/features, and price range. The interactive buyer's guide processes your input and plots the five closest matches on a grid.

One neat feature of this applet is the pop-up help box, which responds to the position of the mouse and provides information about anything you point to. This is the kind of thing you could never accomplish with standard static HTML pages.

This applet demonstrates an interactive way of delivering useful information. Savvy Web site developers are aware that this type of feature not only provides a useful service but attracts many users. A Web site that attracts many eyes is also very attractive to advertisers, who are often willing to pay to place their ads in front of those eyes.

Masse Doodle

http://www-ugrad.cs.colorado.edu/~masse/Java/MasseDoodle/MasseDoodle.html

Figure 3.2 Masse Doodle. Courtesy of Mark Masse.

This one is purely for fun. Remember when you were little, if you were lucky enough to get invited to the right birthday party, you could get one of those doodle pads with the translucent gray cellophane sheet on the front and the sticky back? Well it's back. There's not much to explain here. Just draw on the screen, and when you want to erase it, use the handle to wipe it away and start fresh.

If you've convinced your boss to let you have access to the Internet for business purposes, don't let her catch you playing with this.

Financial Portfolio Demo

http://java.sun.com/applets/applets/StockDemo/index.html

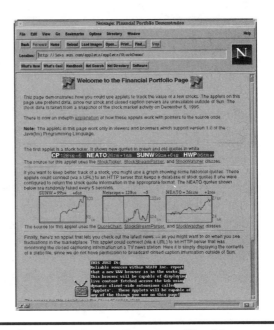

Figure 3.3 StockDemo. Courtesy of Sun Microsystems.

On the opposite end of the spectrum from Mark Masse's doodle pad is this demonstration from Sun Microsystems. Lest you get the impression that Java is only good for fun and games, this page demonstrates that Java is not just a toy, but can be used to develop serious business tools. Using the built-in network support of the Java language, the applets on this page take real-time feeds of changing data and display them in a useful form.

Most of the data shown here is actually static or fake, because Sun does not have permission to broadcast the type of data these applets are intended to display. The applets themselves, however, can be easily downloaded to your site and configured to display real data—if your site has access to the appropriate servers.

Notice that there are three applets running on the same page. The multithreaded nature of Java allows these three running applets to share your microprocessor without letting things get too slow. As a matter of fact, as I type these words on a 66MHz 486DX machine, the applets are running in a Netscape window in the background. Because the applets know how to be friendly not only to each other, but to other processes as well, I can type in my word processor with no discernible decrease in speed.

CyberAgent

http://www.mks.com/tools/java/dale/agent/CyberAgent.html

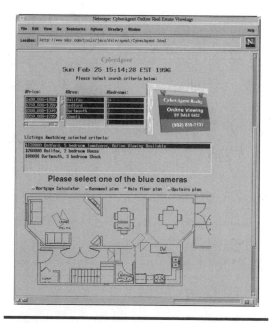

Figure 3.4 CyberAgent. Courtesy of Dale Gass.

CyberAgent is a virtual real-estate agent. You select the price range, geographical area, and number of bedrooms, and it suggests homes from its database. You can then see a floor plan and photos of these homes. The applet includes a configurable mortgage planner so you can figure out the monthly damage to your bank account.

Notice how the author of this applet took what could have been dry, uninteresting material and spiced it up with some animation, audio, and interactivity.

Chat Touring

http://www.cs.princeton.edu/~burchard/www/interactive/chat/

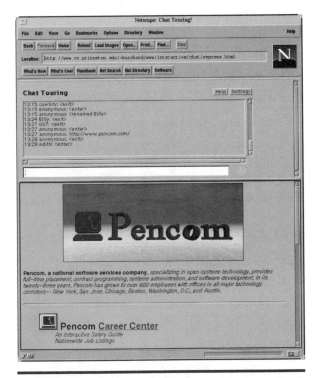

Figure 3.5 Chat Touring. Courtesy of Paul Burchard.

This is a fascinating little applet by Paul Burchard of Princeton University. It is actually connected to an application running on the server, which facilitates communication between all browsers currently running the applet from that site. It serves as a chat room. Navigate to this page and you can have a text-based chat with anyone in the world who happens to be there at the time—or anyone with whom you have arranged to meet.

What makes this particular chat room unique has to do with the bottom frame. While chatting with someone on the other end, if you want to show them a certain Web page, you simply enter the URL in the text-entry box. When you do this, everyone currently in the chat room is "teleported" to that URL—just in the bottom frame of their Web browser. The top frame is still connected to the chat room.

Another feature of this applet is that you can (on entry to the chat room) select someone to be your "tour guide." If you do this, then you will only be teleported to URLs entered by that person; URLs entered by others will have no effect on your browser.

This applet is a good demonstration of how client-server applications can be built in Java. The server application runs on the host, allowing communication between the various applets (clients) running on people's Web browsers. The clients don't interact directly with each other. All interaction is passed through the server application, which then broadcasts it to the clients.

If you'd like to host your own Chat Touring rooms from your Web site, we've included the entire Chat Touring package—server application, client applet, source code, and all—on the CD-ROM accompanying this book. It is distributed free of charge under the GNU Library General-Purpose License. Instructions for installation can be found at:

```
http://www.cs.princeton.edu/~burchard/www/interactive/chat/ins
tall.html
```

The NPAC Visible Human Viewer

http://www.npac.syr.edu/projects/vishuman/VisibleHuman.html

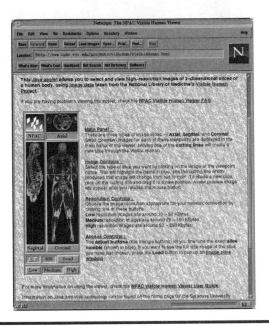

Figure 3.6 NPAC Visible Human Viewer. Courtesy of Paul Coddington and the Northeast Parallel Architectures Center at Syracuse University.

This is one of my personal favorites, although Edith finds it a little nauseating. This applet provides a glimpse of the educational potential of Java and of the Web as a whole. The NPAC Visible Human Viewer gives you a neat graphical interface to select cross-section images of the human anatomy and then downloads those images in either low, medium, or high resolution. It uses image data taken from the National Library of Medicine's Visible Human Project.

Teachers can use an applet like this as an aid in presenting lessons on human anatomy and to inspire the imaginations of their students. Whether you're into biology or just like to see cool images, this is a pretty fascinating applet.

Adding Applets to Your Own HTML Pages

NOTE

This discussion will assume a basic familiarity with HTML. If you don't know HTML and you're interested in learning, you can start by looking online, at http://www.stars.com/Vlib/Misc/Tutorials.html. If you'd rather learn from a book, then you might try John December and Mark Ginsburg's *HTML and CGI Unleashed* (Sams.net, 1995).

Adding an applet to your own HTML pages is actually fairly simple. You do not necessarily need to have written the applet yourself. If someone has already compiled the applet, you don't even need the **.java** source files. All you need are the relevant **.class** files containing compiled Java virtual machine instructions (bytecode).

Briefly, all you need to do is have the compiled **.class** file(s) for the applet accessible—not necessarily in the same directory as the HTML file, although this is certainly convenient—and then include in the HTML file the appropriate tags containing the relevant information needed to load the applet. Very shortly, we'll explain what we mean by *accessible*, *appropriate tags*, and *relevant information*.

A Simple Example: Bouncing Heads

Included with the Java Development Kit on the CD-ROM accompanying this book, you will find a directory filled with sample applets. You can run these applets directly from the CD-ROM by using the **Open File** command in your Java-enabled browser to open the HTML pages included in each applet's directory.

In order to show how easy it is to include applets in your Web pages, we're going to grab some of the executable files from the CD, put them on your hard drive, and write some simple, home-grown HTML pages that reference them.

A nice simple one to start with is "Bouncing Heads." This is probably not one you'd really like to have on your home page, but as a first applet to embed in a page, its simplicity makes it attractive.

In any convenient directory, create a subdirectory called **bouncing**. From the directory containing the "Bouncing Heads" demo, copy the following files to your new **bouncing** directory:

- **bouceitem.class**
- **bounceimage.class**
- the **images** directory, with its contents
- the **audio** directory, with its contents

Now change to your new **bouncing** directory, and using any text editor you like that supports long file names (such as the Windows NotePad accessory, vi or emacs under UNIX, or SimpleText on MacOS), create a text file called **mybounce.html**. Enter the following text into your file, and save it in your **bouncing** directory:

```
<html>
<head>
<title>Bouncing Heads Applet</title>
</head>
<body>
<h1>Bouncing Heads</h1>
Ladies and gentlemen, we proudly present the Bouncing
Heads!!!!
<hr>
<applet code=BounceItem.class width=500 height=300>
Uh-oh.  If you can read this, you're not using a <i>Java-
enabled browser</i>.
</applet>
```

```
<hr>
</body>
</html>
```

NOTE If your editor automatically appends a **.txt** extension to saved files, (such as with the Windows 95 Notepad), disable this feature. If you can't, you can use another editor.

Viewing the Applet

Once you've saved the HTML file, you can start up your Java-enabled Netscape browser and choose **Open File** from the File menu. Navigate to the **bouncing** directory, and choose the HTML file you just created. You should see the applet running, embedded in your own HTML page.

About the `<APPLET ...>` Tag

It is important to realize that when we say a page "contains" an applet, or an applet is "embedded" in a page, we do *not* mean to imply that either the applet source code or the executable code is contained within the HTML file itself. Rather, what the HTML page contains is an `<APPLET ...>` tag in which you provide the URL and some other information that the Java-enabled browser uses to obtain and run the already-compiled **.class** file for your applet. There is also an `</APPLET>` end tag, signifying a return to normal HTML. Between these two tags, you may place zero or more `<PARAM ...>` tags in which, as we shall see, you can pass information (*parameters*) to an applet as it begins execution.

In fact, `<PARAM ...>` tags are the only thing between the `<APPLET ...>` and `</APPLET>` tags that a Java-enabled browser cares about. That is, you can place anything you want between these two tags, and a Java-enabled browser will simply ignore it and will not display it, concentrating only on the <APPLET ...> tag itself, and any supplied <PARAM ...> tags, until it sees an </APPLET> tag, which tells it to go on reading HTML as normal. This turns out to be a useful feature.

When a non-Java-enabled browser comes across the <APPLET ...> tag, it does what it always does when it sees a tag it cannot recognize: it ignores the tag and goes on reading the file. It ignores any <PARAM ...> tags for the same reason. What's left is anything else you placed between the <APPLET ...> and </APPLET> tags. This additional material (which, you recall, is ignored by the Java-enabled browser) is simply formatted and displayed as normal HTML by a nonenabled browser.

Thus, anything (not only straight text but tags for graphics, links, formatting, and so on) that you place between the <APPLET ...> and </APPLET> tags, other than applet parameters, can be viewed as alternate material for those who do not have Java-enabled browsers. It is very common for designers of applet-powered HTML pages to place between these tags a static image of the applet and/or an explanatory message letting users of non-Java-enabled applets know what is going on in this space. Notice that in our examples, we have stuck to explanatory messages, just to keep things simple.

Attributes of the <APPLET ...> Tag

The text within the <APPLET ...> tag (other than the word APPLET) defines the *attributes* of the <APPLET ...> tag (not to be confused with the object-oriented notion of the attributes of a class). The following are the attributes defined for the <APPLET ...> tag:

Attribute	Meaning
CODE="*AppletFileName*.class"	This attribute specifies the name of the applet class to be loaded, that is, the name of the already-compiled **.class** file in which the executable Java bytecode for the applet is stored. This attribute *must* be specified. (*Note:* the double-quotes shown are optional.)

Attribute	Meaning
CODEBASE="*URLofAppletDirectory*	This attribute specifies the URL of the directory in which the applet resides. This may be specified as an absolute URL, or it may be specified relative to the directory in which the HTML file resides. If the applet resides in the same directory as the HTML file, then the CODEBASE attribute may be omitted entirely. (*Note:* the applet does not need to be on the same server as the page that references it. This has implications with regard to security; see Chapter 12 for details.)
WIDTH=*x_pixels* HEIGHT=*y_pixels*	These attributes specify the width and height of the space on the HTML page that will be reserved for the applet. This attribute *must* be specified. In Netscape, you can optionally specify a percentage of the page width/height, rather than an absolute number of pixels.
NAME="*NameOfApplet*	A name for the applet may optionally be specified so that other applets on the page may refer to this applet, or perhaps more accurately, this *instance* of this applet. This facilitates inter-applet communication. The name need not match the name of the **.class** file. In fact, you may have more than one copy of the same applet running independently on the same page, with different NAME attributes specified.
ALIGN=*AlignmentSpecifier*	This optional attribute specifies where on the page the applet will appear. Possible values for *AlignmentSpecifier* are: TOP, BOTTOM, LEFT, RIGHT, MIDDLE, ABSMIDDLE, ABSBOTTOM, TEXTTOP, and BASELINE.
HSPACE=*number*	Used only when ALIGN is set to LEFT or RIGHT, this attribute specifies the amount of horizontal blank space the browser should leave surrounding the applet.
VSPACE=*number*	Used only when some vertical alignment is specified with the ALIGN attribute (TOP, BOTTOM, etc.), VSPACE specifies the amount of vertical blank space the browser should leave surrounding the applet.
ALT="*SomeDescriptiveText*	Text-only browsers will display this text where the applet would normally go. This attribute is optional.

Another Example: Tumbling Duke

The following example is slightly more involved, as it uses the <PARAM ...> tag to pass information into the applet.

Gather the Files Needed to Run the Applet

First, create a directory anywhere you like and call it **MyTumbler**. We'll use this directory to launch the applet from.

In the directory where the demo applets are stored, you should find a subdirectory called **TumblingDuke**. Change to this directory, and copy the following items to your new **MyTumbler** directory:

- the file **TumbleItem.class**
- the directory **images**, including its contents

Create a Web Page to Contain It

Create an HTML file with the following text, and save it in your **MyTumbler** directory with the title **mytumble.html**:

```
<html>
<head>
<title>Tumbling Duke</title>
</head>
<body>
<h1>Tumbling Duke Applet</h1>
<hr>
<applet code="TumbleItem.class" width=600 height=95>
<param name=maxwidth value="120">
<param name=nimgs value="16">
<param name=offset value="-57">
<param name=img value="images/tumble">
If you had a Java-enabled browser, you could see the following
image move right on this Web page: <br>
<img source="images/tumble/T1.gif">
```

```
</applet>
<hr>
<a href="TumbleItem.java">The source.</a>
</body>
</html>
```

Run the Applet

By this time, you should know how to run an applet. Just invoke the appletviewer with the URL of the referencing HTML page as an argument, or open the HTML page from your Java-enabled browser. (On the Mac, you can simply drag the page to either the Netscape 2.0 Java B1 icon, or the AppletViewer icon.)

About the `<PARAM ...>` Tag

A smart programmer knows that the most useful programs are those that can be customized to the users' needs without having to be redesigned, rewritten, or recompiled. As a result, programmers will typically write programs so that they accept *parameters*, outside information that you pass in so that the program knows how you'd like it to behave in the particular circumstances in which you've invoked it. Applets take their parameters from `<PARAM ...>` tags.

Each `<PARAM ...>` tag has a name attribute, such as maxwidth, and a value attribute, such as 120. These represent what programmers call *tuples*, which are simply name/value pairs; for the purposes of the `<PARAM ...>` tag, one value corresponds to each named parameter. Inside the program, the applet can refer to that parameter by name to find its value. In the preceding example, the applet uses the parameters to figure out where the image files comprising the animation are located and various information about how to format the applet within the HTML page.

You can make the TumbleItem applet play any animation you want and have it move across the applet's area of the screen, just by changing the parameters in the HTML page. (Of course, you'd have to supply your own animation images.) The beauty of this is that it allows you to change the functionality of the applet without having to recompile it.

To see this for yourself, you can use an animation we've supplied for you on the CD-ROM. In the directory containing the examples for this book (see Appendix D for a listing of the CD-ROM contents), you will find a subdirectory called **images**. The **images** directory contains a subdirectory called **globe**. Copy the **globe** directory, with its contents, to the **images** directory within the **tumbling** directory. The path to the globe directory should now be **.../MyTumbler/images/globe/**.

Now, create a new HTML file in the **MyTumbler** directory, and call it **myglobe.html**:

```
<html>
<head>
<title>My Globe Animation</title>
</head>
<body>
<h1>Parameterized Animation Applet</h1>
<hr>
<applet code="TumbleItem.class" width=600 height=95>
<param name=maxwidth value="150">
<param name=nimgs value="8">
<param name=offset value="50">
<param name=img value="images/globe">
If you had a Java-enabled browser, you could see the following
image move right on this Web page: <br>
<img source="images/globe/T1.gif">
</applet>
<hr>
<a href="TumbleItem.java">The source.</a>
</body>
</html>
```

When you view this HTML page, you should see the globe spinning and moving across the screen. Not only have we changed the animation, but we have also changed the direction in which it moves. So you see, a single applet can be used for many different pages if it has been thoughtfully designed to accept parameters.

NOTE If you want to include animation on your Web pages, the best way is to use the Animator demo applet that comes with the JDK. We didn't use it here because it has lots of parameters and we wanted to keep things simple. However, as the previous example shows, parameters generally make applets much more practical.

Useful Tips for Placing Your Applets on a Web Server

At first, you may be using applets only for experimentation on pages that only you have access to. If you have Web pages that are available to the Internet as a whole, however, you will likely want to put applets on these pages so that others can access them. Be the first on your block to have an animated home page!

Here are a few tips for doing this correctly:

- Make sure that the Web server (HTTP server) knows about the directory in which you keep your HTML pages and/or applets. You may need to talk to your system administrator to find out how to make this directory known to the server and what the URL of this directory is or should be.

- Make sure you have set the directory in which your HTML pages and/or applets are stored so that the directory is executable. The simplest way to do this is to navigate to the directory and execute the following command (don't forget the dot):

```
% chmod +x .
```

- Make sure that any HTML files you want to be accessible have been made world-readable, and any applets are world-readable and world-executable. The simplest way to do this is to navigate to the directory containing these files and execute the following commands:

```
% chmod +r *.html *.class
% chmod +x *.class
```

- It is not necessary to store an applet in the same directory as the HTML page that references it. In fact, it doesn't even need to be on the same machine as the HTML page. You may have pages scattered about your directory tree that reference the same applet. A common example is an animator applet that can be parameterized to display any group of images. It would be inefficient to have multiple copies of that applet all over your disk. Use the CODEBASE attribute of the <APPLET...> tag to specify the location of the directory actually containing the **.class** file(s) for the applet. This location may be a relative URL (that is, relative to the HTML file containing the tag), or it may be a complete URL to a directory anywhere on the Web that contains the executable applet.

- If you're a programmer and you want your source code to be publicly visible, include a link to the source (**.java**) file(s) on the page containing the applet and make sure all of these **.java** files are world-readable. This helps others learn from your code and lets you demonstrate your programming genius. If, on the other hand, you want to protect your proprietary source code from prying eyes while allowing people to use your applets, either keep the source code off the public server or just make sure that the source code files are not world-readable:

```
% chmod o-r *.java
```

Summary

The Java-enabled browser has become the first vehicle for the distribution of interactive, executable content on the Web. Using a Java-enabled browser is no more difficult than using a traditional Web browser.

The notion of applets extends the functionality of HTML pages, while leaving the HTML standard itself basically intact, allowing Java-enabled browsers to view both applet-powered pages and static HTML pages. Furthermore, the syntax of the <APPLET ...> tag interacts with standard HTML syntax in such a way as to allow the designers of HTML pages to easily provide alternate content for those without Java-enabled browsers.

Although this chapter dealt primarily with Netscape 2.0, chances are that by the time you read this there will be at least one other Java-enabled browser available. Sun promises an update of the HotJava browser during the first half of 1996, and Microsoft and AOL, among others, have pledged to include Java applet support in future versions of their browsers.

For those familiar with HTML, placing an applet on a Web page is scarcely more involved than placing an image, and often less complicated than interacting with CGI, the Common Gateway Interface that has traditionally provided much of the Web's approximation of interactivity.

In the next chapter, we'll start writing our own Java programs.

Part Two

The Java Language

JAVA
PROGRAMMING
BASICS

Introduction to Java Programming

What Can You Do with Java?

Applets

The introduction of Java on May 23, 1995, caused quite a stir, particularly among the Internet community. Perhaps the greatest single reason for all this continued excitement is the fact that Java allows programmers to create interactive programs, called *applets*, that reside directly on World Wide Web pages. As we shall see, the enhancements these applets can provide to the Web experience range from the superficial, such as animated images and moving text, to the more substantial, such as continuously interactive educational and business-oriented applications.

Remember that Java is designed as a *cross-platform* language. This means that Java programs can run on *any* machine, using *any* operating system (well, almost. See the sidebar, "Java as a Cross-Platform Language," for details).

Java as a Cross-Platform Language

Is Java really a cross-platform language? The answer is not as simple as the question.

Unlike compilers for traditional languages such as C++, C, Ada, or Pascal, which take source files and translate them into machine instructions for specific hardware, the Java compiler compiles Java source code into instructions for a *virtual machine*. These instructions are stored as *bytecode*. The Java virtual machine can be thought of as an "imaginary" chip, essentially simulated by software.

In order for a given machine to run Java programs, there must be a program on that machine that can interpret the instruction set of the Java virtual machine. This program is called the *Java interpreter*, and its job is to translate the bytecode instructions into machine-language instructions, which are then executed by the actual machine. The instruction set for the virtual machine and the bytecodes through which these instructions are encoded are always the same, regardless of differences in the underlying hardware on which the interpreter is run.

The interpreter itself, however, in order to do its job, needs to know the machine language of the specific hardware on which it is running. Thus, although software written in Java is platform-independent and will behave in essentially the same manner on any platform without the need for porting or recompilation, it is necessary for the Java interpreter itself to have been ported to your platform before you can run these programs on your machine.

The good news is that Java compilers and interpreters have already been made available for Windows NT, Windows 95, and Sun Solaris (Sparc only). Sun has released a beta version for MacOS 7.5, and other companies, including Natural Intelligence, Metrowerks, and Symantec, are producing their own versions for the Mac. Independent ports are also currently underway for Linux (nearly finished at the time of this writing), OS/2, AIX 4.1.3, Windows 3.1, HP/UX, Sony NEWS, and Digital UNIX, as well as Solaris on x86, Nextstep, SunOS 4.1, Amiga, and others.

You may or may not realize it, but if you are using Netscape 2.0 or the HotJava Web browser, you already have a Java interpreter of sorts. These Web browsers are *Java-enabled*, that is, they contain embedded interpreters that allow them to run Java applets (but not stand-alone Java applications). For details on availability of Java-enabled browsers, see the sidebar "Does My Browser Support Java Applets?"

Does My Browser Support Java Applets?

There are currently only two Web browsers that can run Java applets. One is Netscape Navigator 2.0, and the other is Sun's own HotJava browser.

You can obtain Netscape Navigator 2.0 from Netscape's home page at:

```
http://home.netscape.com/
```

Navigator 2.0 supports Java on Windows NT, Windows 95, Sun Solaris, SunOS, SGI IRIX, OSF/1, and HP-UX. Although the current release of Navigator 2.0 for Macintosh does not support Java, Netscape has made available a beta version for the Mac that does.

Navigator 2.0 supports the final version of the Java API and does not support applets written to conform to the alpha or pre-alpha versions of Java. In other words, applets written according to the alpha or pre-alpha specification of Java *will not* run on Navigator 2.0.

Oddly enough, Sun's own HotJava browser does not yet support the final version of the Java API. The current version of HotJava, version 1.0alpha3, will only run alpha or pre-alpha applets. To rectify this situation, Sun provides with the Java Development Kit a program called `appletviewer` that is not a full-fledged Web browser. However, given the URL of a Web page containing an applet, the `appletviewer` will run any applets it finds on the Web page. The `appletviewer` supports the latest version of the Java API, version 1.0, at the time of this writing. Sun has projected that by the time you read this, there will be a version of HotJava that will run applets written to the current API specs.

Things are changing very rapidly in this area. To be sure you have the most current information, you should check both the Java/HotJava home page (`http://java.sun.com`), and the Netscape home page (`http://home.netscape.com`). If you're really serious about Java development, you should check these pages often—at least weekly, if not daily. Needless to say, things change pretty fast on the information superhighway.

Animation

One of the simplest things that Java can add to a Web page is animation. Unlike traditional HTML pages, which can contain only static images, Java-powered Web pages can contain moving images. This is not to be confused with Web pages that allow you to download a video clip, save it as an MPEG file, and use a "helper application" to open and view it. Java provides the ability for an animation to live directly on a Web page, without the need to call an external application. Furthermore, as we shall see, Java applets provide the ability for animations on Web pages to be *continuously* interactive—that is, to respond directly to user input in real time.

Client-Side Interactivity

"Isn't the Web *already* interactive?" you may ask. "I can click on a hypertext link or even a hot-spot on an imagemap and go to a new page of my choice. I can call up an online form and enter data into it, which can be used to query a database that will return a response in a format I can understand."

All this is true. But when you use your browser to access a traditional Web site, all the real processing involved in the "interactivity" takes place on the *server* side. The Web browser (i.e., the *client*) encodes any relevant input you provide (by filling out a form, clicking on an imagemap or hypertext link, etc.) and then transmits that information over the Internet to the Web server. The Web server then processes that information, very likely by executing a CGI program based on your input, and determines what output to send back to you.

When you use a Java-enabled Web browser to access a Java-powered site, the situation is different. The Web page contains the URL of a compiled, executable Java program, a Java applet. When you access this page, the applet is sent to your computer, and it is *your* computer that executes the applet. Thus, much of the processing is shifted to the *client* side—to your computer instead of the remote server. This allows interactivity without the response-time delays that occur when information has to be sent back and forth over the Internet. Your input goes directly to the program responsible for processing it, bringing real-time interactivity to Web pages for the first time.

The developers at Sun bundled Java with an Application Programming Interface (API), which gives the programmer access to classes providing commonly used data structures and routines, including hash tables, file and console input/output, network sockets, graphics and audio, mathematical functions, and constants. What's more, the Java API also comes with prefabricated widgets (such as clickable buttons, scrollbars, check boxes, and pop-up menus) for the construction of Graphic User Interfaces (GUIs). In case you haven't had enough acronyms for one paragraph, the part of the Java API that contains the classes and objects used in constructing GUIs is referred to as the *Abstract Windowing Toolkit*, or AWT.

As we shall see in Chapters 9 and 10, the developers of Java created the applet as a subclass of an AWT element called a Panel, which inherits a great deal of functionality from its various parent classes. This makes it very easy for programmers to create useful, fully interactive applets.

Stand-Alone Applications

The design of Java is not limited to creating applets for use on Web pages. Java is a full-featured object-oriented programming language with which a programmer can create stand-alone applications. Whereas an applet needs to be run from within a Java-enabled Web browser (or a program like Sun's `appletviewer`, which essentially simulates a Java-enabled Web browser), a Java stand-alone application is a full-fledged program in its own right and can be run without the excess baggage of a Web browser.

These stand-alone applications may exist on a single computer, but more likely, people will be using Java to create applications that take advantage of the Internet support built into the Java API. Not only would it be possible, for example, to write a Web browser entirely in Java, but it's been done: Sun's own HotJava browser is a stand-alone application, written entirely in Java.

The uses for Java stand-alone applications extend beyond browsing the Web. Imagine you have a database on a central computer and you want your entire company to have access to this database. You have an office in New York, an office in San Jose, an office in Boston, an office in Dallas, and an office in Chicago. Furthermore, the San Jose office uses primarily Sun workstations, the Chicago office uses primarily Windows 95, the Boston office uses Macs, the Dallas office uses PCs running Linux, and the New York office uses all four platforms. You'd like all the offices to be running the same front-end program to access the database, but do you really want the headache of writing a client application that can be ported and recompiled for all those different platforms? This would be a time-consuming process using a traditional language like C or C++, because there would be a great deal of platform-specific coding, especially when it came to constructing the user interface. Using Java, you would write one client program and compile it once. The same compiled code would run on all those platforms, and the user interface would function in exactly the same way. (For an explanation of how this is possible, see the sidebar, "Java as a Cross-Platform Language.")

Imagine that you want to use a Web-based front end with a standard HTML form interface to access the database. After all, HTML is also platform-independent. But what happens when, for example, you enter an incomplete or improperly formatted query into the form? In order to catch the error, the browser has to send the query over the Internet and establish a connection with the server. Then the server has to pass the query to the database application, which attempts to decode it, only to discover that it's erroneous. The database application sends a message to the Web server, which passes that message back over the Net to your Web browser, telling you that your query was incorrect. This is a great deal of wasted bandwidth for one improperly formatted query. With Java, however, you can create "smart forms," which check the legitimacy of the entries on the client side, eliminating the wasted bandwidth of the previous scenario.

In theory, there is nothing that a stand-alone application can do that cannot be done from an applet residing on a Web page. Why, then, would one write a stand-alone Java application instead of an applet? One reason has to do with security features built into certain browsers. Java makes use of a data structure called the `SecurityManager`, whereby a local machine can enable or disable Java programs from performing certain operations, such as opening a file or automatically downloading program code from an Internet location other than the one from which the original applet was loaded. This is done in order to prevent an unsuspecting victim from downloading a malicious applet, such as a virus or "Trojan Horse," which might do damage to his or her local file system or facilitate unauthorized snooping from the outside. The developers of browsers such as Netscape, in an effort to ensure that their products have no complicity in allowing security breaches, have made implementation decisions to disable applets from taking advantage of certain features of the Java language. Some of these security features are accessible via a dialog box accessible from a Security Preferences menu, but others cannot be changed by the user. The settings of the Security Manager cannot be altered by code loaded from a remote host.

The (understandably) conservative approach taken by Netscape—and likely to be taken by other browser developers in the future—imposes practical limitations on the extent to which applets can take advantage of the full power of Java. It is important to understand that this is not necessarily due to limitations of Java applets per se. Rather, it is due to decisions by browser developers to limit the extent to which the user can relax local security restrictions on applets. Nonetheless, the result is that for some purposes, such as direct user-to-user interaction over the network, it may be necessary to have a stand-alone Java application that implements different security policies from Netscape, perhaps taking specific measures of its own to ensure that security breaches do not occur. It remains to be seen whether the final release of the HotJava browser will allow the user to select a more permissive security policy than Netscape, especially with regard to locally loaded classes. See Chapter 12 for more details about security issues as they relate to Java.

Protocol Handlers

Another type of program that a Java developer can create is the *protocol handler* program that allows a Java-enabled Web browser to interpret a new type of protocol. When you use your Web browser to access an HTML page, you use the HyperText Transfer Protocol (HTTP). To download a file, you use the File Transfer Protocol (FTP). One of the great assets of the World Wide Web is its support for multiple protocols. The problem with traditional Web browsers is that as new protocols come along, developers of these browsers need to release updates that can handle the new protocols, and the browsers themselves, having to contain all the code to handle all the possible protocols they might encounter, end up being huge monolithic programs that eat up large quantities of hard-disk space and RAM.

In contrast, the developers of Java intended Java-enabled Web browsers to be modular and extensible. That is, a browser itself is a streamlined program that uses (rather than contains) a set of protocol handlers that represent the current repertoire of protocols it can interpret. If it encounters a new protocol that is not in its repertoire, it can download a handler that will enable it to handle that protocol. The handler can be downloaded "transparently," so that the user does not have to concern him- or herself with the details; all the user has to do is navigate to the appropriate URL, and the protocol handler can be downloaded in the background so that the browser can receive the data. At any given moment in time, the browser has only loaded into memory those handlers it needs, allowing it to operate in less available RAM.

Currently, however, Netscape does not support protocol handlers. This is partially due to Netscape's overall conservative security policy. Because protocol handlers have more access to the local system than applets do, Netscape currently disallows Java protocol handlers. Another reason that Netscape does not support protocol handlers is that, unlike Sun's HotJava browser, the Netscape browser itself is not written in Java. As a result, it is not as easy to seamlessly integrate incoming Java code with the internals of the Netscape browser. Netscape does provide support for plug-ins, small add-on programs that extend the functionality of the browser and could provide support for additional protocols; however, these plug-ins are written in C++ and thus are not platform-independent in the way that Java protocol handlers would be.

As of this writing, there is no version of the HotJava browser that supports Java 1.0 code. It remains to be seen how upcoming versions of the HotJava browser will deal with the question of protocol handlers and whether the model of the streamlined, modular browser represented by HotJava will supplant the traditional Web browser model represented by Netscape.

Content Handlers

In a traditional Web browser, if one wanted to obtain specialized content from the Web, such as video, audio, or certain types of graphics, it is necessary to first download the files containing the content and then to open a separate application that can interpret the content, such as an audio or video player. Developers of browsers realized that they could determine the type of incoming content by its MIME type and have the browser automatically launch the appropriate "helper application," if it was already present on the user's local machine.

The *content handler* was intended to provide an alternative to the idea of "helper applications," allowing a Java programmer to write code that extends the browser, giving it the ability to interpret the content inline—that is, without the need to rely on an external application. Like a protocol handler, the content handler can be downloaded automatically when the user accesses a Web page containing a new type of content.

The fate of content handlers is also somewhat murky, for the same reasons as that of protocol handlers: Netscape does not support the Java model of the content handler. It does support plug-in content handlers, but these plug-ins are written in C++ and are not innately portable. Furthermore, Netscape's plug-ins do not load automatically, partially because of concerns about the security risks represented by automatically loading executable code. The so-called Field of Dreams philosophy ("If you build it, they will come...") does not always hold true for advances in technology, especially where security risks are involved. It seems that if anyone is going to implement support for Java protocol handlers and content handlers, Sun is going to have to do it in the HotJava browser.

Before You Start...

You're almost ready to try your hand at creating your first Java program. But first, you will need some tools. In order to create Java source code, you need a standard text editor, which you probably already have. (We'll discuss your options for this in more detail later in this chapter.) To create your own Java applets and applications from scratch, you need the Java Development Kit, or JDK, which is included on the CD-ROM bundled with this book. If you have lost the CD-ROM or if Sun comes out with an update, you can download it from Sun's

Web site at `http://java.sun.com` or from its ftp server at `java.sun.com`.

NOTE

If all you want to do is view applets that have been constructed by others, then you don't need the JDK. For this purpose, you can use any Java-enabled Web browser. You only need the JDK if you want to try your hand at writing and compiling your own Java programs, which is the focus of the rest of this chapter.

We will assume that you know enough about Internet basics to invoke your Web browser or begin an ftp session. If you don't, you might consider one or more of the following references:

- *The Whole Internet Guide and Catalog*, second edition, by Ed Kroll (O'Reilly & Associates, 1994)
- *The Internet Starter Kit for Windows*, third edition, by Adam Engst (Hayden Books, 1995)
- *The Internet Starter Kit for the Macintosh*, third edition, by Adam Engst (Hayden Books, 1995)

Downloading the JDK

Using a Web Browser to Download the JDK

If the CD-ROM that came with this book is lost or damaged or if Sun comes out with a new version of the JDK, you may need to download a new copy of it. If you need to do this, the simplest way is to use the Web. Using any Web browser, such as Netscape Navigator, HotJava, or NCSA Mosaic, direct yourself to Sun's Java home page, at the URL:

`http://java.sun.com/`

If you then follow the links labeled **Downloading**, **Java Developer's Kit**, and **How to Download the JDK**, in that order, you should end up at the following URL (if you'd like, you can go there directly, but Sun may change this URL, so if you can't get there directly, try following the links as just described):

```
http://java.sun.com/JDK-1.0/installation.html
```

From there, you can follow links that will allow you to download the JDK for your platform with a click of your mouse on a hyperlink, using the `ftp://` protocol.

Using a Command-Line FTP Client to Download the JDK

If you do not yet have a Web browser or are unable for some reason to use your Web browser to download files via FTP, you may use a standard UNIX-style command-line FTP session to download the JDK. The following are transcripts of FTP sessions to download the JDK. Naturally, where we have printed *user@machine*, you should substitute your complete email address, as is the custom in anonymous FTP.

Windows 95 or Windows NT

```
C:\> ftp ftp.javasoft.com
Name (ftp.javasoft.com): anonymous
331 Guest login ok, send your complete e-mail address as
password.
Password: user@machine
        << informational messages <<
ftp> binary
200 Type set to I.
ftp> cd pub
        << more informational messages <<
250 CWD command successful.
ftp> get JDK-1_0-win32-x86.exe
200 PORT command successful.
```

```
150 Opening BINARY mode data connection for JDK-1_0-win32-
x86.exe (3720379 bytes).
226 Transfer complete.
local: JDK-1_0-win32-x86.exe remote: JDK-1_0-win32-x86.exe
3720379 bytes received in 1.4e+02 seconds (30 Kbytes/s)
ftp> quit
C:\>_
```

UNIX

```
ftp ftp.javasoft.com
Name (ftp.javasoft.com): anonymous
331 Guest login ok, send your complete e-mail address as
password.
Password: user@machine
        << informational messages <<
ftp> binary
200 Type set to I.
ftp> cd pub
        << more informational messages <<
250 CWD command successful.
ftp> get JDK-1_0-solaris2-sparc.tar.Z
200 PORT command successful.
150 Opening BINARY mode data connection for
        JDK-1_0-solaris2-sparc.tar.Z (4595974 bytes).
226 Transfer complete.
local: JDK-1_0-solaris2-sparc.tar.Z remote:
        JDK-1_0-solaris2-sparc.tar.Z
4595974 bytes received in 1.4e+02 seconds (30 Kbytes/s)
ftp> quit
%_
```

NOTE

The names od the files may ahve been updated since this book went to press. To see the available files, use the ls command once you are conected and in the right directory.

Setting up the JDK

After you download the JDK, you will need to decompress and de-archive it. If you're using Windows 95 or Windows NT, then the release is a self-extracting archive, which will unpack itself when you double-click on it. If you're using UNIX, unpack the release using the command:

```
% zcat JDK-1_0-solaris2-sparc.tar.Z | tar xf -
```

Whichever platform you are using, unpacking the JDK creates a directory called **java**. If you're using Windows 95 or Windows NT, you may find it convenient to store the **java** directory at the root level of your hard disk. The path to this directory will thus be **C:\java**. If you're using UNIX, your system administrator may already have the JDK installed someplace where you can access it, or you can install it in your home directory if you have room. If you do this, then the path to the JDK will be **~/java** (where ~ is the standard UNIX alias for the path to your home directory). Wherever you have installed the JDK, we shall refer to this directory in the future as the *Java home directory*. We will also occasionally refer to this directory as **C:\java** or **~/java** in our examples, so if you have them installed elsewhere, make sure you are aware of the path to the Java home directory.

NOTE

One of the subdirectories created within the Java home directory is called **lib**, and it contains a file called **classes.zip**. It is very important that you do not unzip this file. If you do, it may take up an enormous amount of space on your hard disk, and it may cause the JDK tools to function improperly. The JDK tools know how to find the information they need within this file without unzipping it.

If you look in the Java home directory, you should see that one of its subdirectories is called **bin**. This is the directory in which the executable binaries for the Java tools are stored. It contains, among other things, the Java compiler (`javac`), the Java stand-alone interpreter (`java`), and the Java `appletviewer`. It will save you quite a bit of typing if you add this directory to your PATH. In Windows 95 or Windows NT, this is accomplished by typing the following command, or preferably, by adding it to your **AUTOEXEC.BAT** file:

```
C:\> set PATH=%PATH%;C:\java\bin
```

In UNIX, you would type the following command or add it to your **.cshrc** file:

```
% setenv PATH $PATH:~/java/bin
```

Finally, you should set your CLASSPATH variable. This is an *environmental variable* (i.e., a global variable) that identifies the location where the Java tools must look for any classes they can't find as part of the standard set of classes included in the JDK. For details about the CLASSPATH variable and how it works, refer to the sidebar in Appendix A, "About the CLASSPATH Variable and -classpath Options." If you'd just like to get on with writing your first Java program, you can set the CLASSPATH variable as follows, in order to instruct the Java tools to look in the current directory to load your class files.

In UNIX, type the following command or add it to your **.cshrc** file:

```
% setenv CLASSPATH .:~/java/lib/classes.zip
```

In Windows 95 or Windows NT, type the following command or add it to your **AUTOEXEC.BAT** file:

```
C:\> set CLASSPATH=.;C:\java\lib\classes.zip
```

NOTE

In both of the preceding commands, the period (or "dot") is an essential part of the command. This symbol is used in both UNIX and DOS/Windows as the alias for the current directory.

How to Create and Edit Java Source Code

All Java code is encapsulated within definitions of Java classes. Generally, each class that you declare should go in its own source file, preferably named after that class, so if you have a class named `MyClass`, then it should go in a file named **MyClass.java**. (In fact, there may be multiple classes declared in the same source file, as long as no more than one of those classes is declared as `public`. Let's not get ahead of ourselves, though. For now, let's keep things simple: one class, one source file.)

Java source code is simply text. Typically, you use a text editor to create and edit Java source code, and you save the document as a standard text file with a **.java** suffix (i.e., filename extension). To edit the source file, you may wish to use whatever text editor you currently use for C or C++. If your editor has nice syntax-sensitive features, so much the better; Java's syntax is quite similar in many ways to that of C and C++. For those who choose to use `emacs`, there are at least two publicly available Java-sensitive `emacs` modes you can download from the Internet (available at `ftp://java.sun.com/-pub/java/contrib/emacs/` and `http://www.io.org/~mentor1-/java-mode.txt`). If you are using one of the Java Integrated Development Environments (IDEs) that are starting to come out—such as Symantec's Café for Windows 95/NT or Natural Intelligence's Roaster environment for Macintosh (a demo of which is included on the CD-ROM bundled with this book)—then you can use that environment's built-in text editor. These IDEs have the advantage that you can create your source code, compile it, run your program, and debug it all from one central environment. But remember, you don't necessarily need any of these sophisticated tools to create Java source code. You can use any standard text editor, such as the freeware PFE (Programmer's File Editor) for Windows, the vi editor that is a standard part of UNIX; or the SimpleText text editor that comes with MacOS. Mac users may also want to download the shareware Alpha (included on the CD-ROM bundled with this book), the latest version of which (6.12) has a Java mode with syntax-coloring.

NOTE

If you want to get started right away on Windows without downloading a text editor, you can use any text editor that supports long filenames. The standard DOS-prompt **edit** command that comes with Windows 95 supports long filenames, but if you have a pre-95 version, it does not. The Windows 95 Notepad accessory has the rather annoying feature of automatically appending **.txt** to the end of filenames. If you use **Save As...** and specify the **.java** extension at the end of the filename, you should be fine.

Your First Java Applet: "Hello, Internet"

Write an HTML Page to Contain Your Applet

Recall that Java applets are programs that reside on Web pages. In order to run a Java applet, it is first necessary to have an HTML page that references that applet. Like Java source code, HTML source code is composed of text and can be edited with any ASCII text editor, although you may prefer to use an editor specifically oriented toward HTML editing, like HoTMetaL or emacs in HTML-mode.

NOTE

A full discussion of how to compose an HTML page for the Web is not within the scope of this book. If you're interested in learning HTML, you can start by looking online, at `http://www.stars.com/Vlib-/Misc/Tutorials.html`. If you'd rather learn from a book, then you might try John December and Mark Ginsburg's *HTML and CGI Unleashed* (Sams.net, 1995).

Following is the text of the HTML file we will use for our first applet. In whatever directory you use to store your HTML files, you should create a directory called **HelloApplet**. Inside that directory, create a text file called **HelloApplet.html**, type the following text into it, and save the file:

```
<html>
<head>
<title> The Hello Internet Applet </title>
</head>
<body>
<h1>My First Applet:</h1>
<hr>
<b>Behold, it runs:<b>
<p>
<applet code="HelloApplet.class" width=200 height=50>
    <HR>
    If you can read this, then your browser doesn't support
Java.  Perhaps you should check <A HREF="http://java.sun.com/"
</applet>
</body>
</html>
```

NOTE

The `<applet>` tag is described in detail in Chapter 3.

Create Your Java Source File

Next, you need to create the source file for the actual applet. Create a text file called **HelloApplet.java**, with the following text, and store it in the same directory as the HTML file:

```
import java.awt.Graphics;
public class HelloApplet extends java.applet.Applet {
    public void paint(Graphics g) {
    g.drawString("Hello, Internet!", 50, 25);
    }
}
```

Understanding the Source

It's one thing to enter source code into a text editor—and another to understand what it means. Let's take a look at this simple applet and see what's really going on:

```
import java.awt.Graphics;
```

In order to draw to the screen, we are going to rely on some code bundled with the standard Java API. To access the methods for drawing to the screen, we must *import* the class in which these methods are declared. The class we are importing is called Graphics, and it is part of a package called **java.awt**. A *package* is a bundle of related classes. We will talk more about packages in Chapter 5.

```
public class HelloApplet extends java.applet.Applet { ... }
```

An applet is declared as a class. We declare it as a `public` class so that it will be accessible to the Java interpreter built into the Web browser or the `appletviewer`, whichever will be running it. It is important to understand that when our source code is compiled, the name of the output **.class** file(s) are taken directly from the name of the class(es) in the source code, *not* the name of the file that contains the source code. So, if I declare a class `MyClass` and keep it in a file called **OtherName.java**, then the output file will still be called **MyClass.class**. Additionally, if I create three classes, `ClassOne`, `ClassTwo`, and `ClassThree` and write them all in one source file called **BigFile.java**, the compiler will still create *three* output files, called **ClassOne.class**, **ClassTwo.class**, and **ClassThree.class**. You can see from this that, wherever possible, it is advisable to keep one class declaration in each source file. Maintaining parallelism between your source files and your output files makes it easier for you to keep track of where everything is and allows the compiler to automatically recompile needed classes.

```
public void paint(Graphics g) {
    g.drawString("Hello, Internet!", 50, 25);
}
```

We will talk more about the "life cycle" of an applet in Chapter 9, but suffice it to say that the `paint()` method is called from outside your applet, whenever the Java interpreter needs to display or redisplay your applet. Before we move on, though, let's take a moment to notice a few details. When `paint()` is called, it is passed a graphic context object (class `Graphics`) as a parameter. This is why we needed to import the `Graphics` class; otherwise the compiler would not know what it needs to know about the characteristics of this class. Remember the AWT is bundled with the Java language, not built into it. When we call `g.drawString()`, we are calling a method defined in the `Graphics` class, which draws to the graphics context. The first parameter, obviously, is the string we are going to draw. The other two parameters represent the horizontal and vertical coordinates, respectively, of the point at which the baseline of the first character will appear. This point is measured in pixels from the top left of the applet's space on the page. Note that

that means that the y coordinates *increase* as we move *down* the screen.

Compile the Applet with `javac`

Now that we understand what we've written, let's compile it (and hope the compiler understands it). To compile the source file, you use the tool `javac`, the Java compiler. Here's how we do it.

First, make sure that the directory containing the Java binaries is in your PATH. (If you followed our instructions earlier, the Java binaries should be **C:\java\bin** on Windows 95/Windows NT or **~/java/bin** on UNIX, or wherever your system administrator has placed them.)

Next, if you haven't already done so, navigate to the directory containing the source file **HelloApplet.java**. (You don't have to run the compiler from the directory in which your source file resides, but it makes it easier to type the commands if you do. It also helps ensure that the JDK tools will find the files they need if you've set up your CLASSPATH variable as instructed earlier in the chapter.)

Finally, at the command prompt, type:

```
javac HelloApplet.java
```

The Java compiler should run and return you to your command prompt. If you get any error messages, make sure you typed the code in exactly as provided, without any typos, and try compiling it again. If you still have trouble, make sure you are invoking the compiler from the same directory as the source file and that you've set your CLASSPATH variable to include "." ("dot"), the alias for the current directory. Also, make sure you have properly typed the filename with regard to case (`helloapplet.java` is incorrect). If you've done all this, the applet should compile correctly.

That's it—you've compiled your first Java applet! If you look at the contents of the current directory, there should now be three files:

```
HelloApplet.class
HelloApplet.html
HelloApplet.java
```

The **.class** file, as we've discussed, is the executable output of the compiler, containing bytecode instructions for the Java virtual machine. If you're curious to see what your source compiles to, type:

```
javap -c HelloApplet
```

This will show you a representation of the bytecode instructions generated by this file.

Run the Applet

To run your applet, you need either a Java-enabled Web browser or the `appletviewer` tool supplied with the JDK. If you use a Java-enabled Web browser, you will see the entire Web page containing the applet. If you use the `appletviewer` tool, you will only see the applet itself—the appletviewer is not a full-fledged Web browser, and it ignores all of the HTML except the part pertaining to the running of the applet.

If you're using a Java-enabled Web browser, then all you need to do is navigate to the URL of the HTML page containing the applet, which, if you've set up your directories as we have advised is as follows for UNIX:

Where we have printed "…" you should substitute the path leading to your **HelloApplet** directory.

NOTE

```
file:///.../HelloApplet/HelloApplet.html
```

On Windows 95 or Windows NT, you can probably just double-click the HTML file (if "open" is defined to use Netscape for files ending in **.html**). Otherwise, you may need to use the URL:

```
file:///C|/.../HelloApplet/HelloApplet.html
```

If you're using the `appletviewer` and you are invoking it from the same directory as the HTML file referencing the applet, then type:

```
appletviewer HelloApplet.html
```

If you're invoking the `appletviewer` from a different directory, you will need to type the following (again, where we have printed "..." substitute the path leading to your **HelloApplet** directory).

For Windows 95 or Windows NT:

```
C:\> appletviewer file:///C:/.../HelloApplet/HelloApplet.html
```

For UNIX:

```
appletviewer file:///.../classes/HelloApplet/HelloApplet.html
```

NOTE

If you haven't modified your PATH to include the directory containing the Java binaries, then you will need to specify the full pathname of the `appletviewer` command:
```
C:\> \java\bin\appletviewer file:///C:/...<etc.>
% ~/java/bin/appletviewer file:///...<etc.>
```

Notice that the argument of the `appletviewer` is not the **.java** file or the **.class** file, nor is it always simply the filename or path to the HTML file, but rather it is the *URL* of the HTML file, including the protocol used to access that file. In this case, because the file is on the local file system, we are using the **file://** protocol, but we could just as easily use the appletviewer to view an applet on a remote host by using the **http://** protocol. The reason that the filename works on its own if you are invoking the command from within the directory is that in this case, the filename by itself serves as a "relative" URL. If you are familiar with HTML, you will recognize that hyper-references within HTML files also make use of relative URLs when a file is located in the same directory or subdirectory as the referencing file.

A Java Stand-Alone Application: "Hello, Internet (too)!"

Now, having written, compiled, and run a simple Java applet, let's do the same with a simple Java application. Java applications are significantly different from applets in terms of structure. Applets inherit a great deal of their attributes and behavior from a chain of classes within the AWT, and as a result, they are able "right out of the box" to use many of the graphic user interface features provided by the AWT. Java applications can make use of the AWT's graphic user interface routines, but it takes a little more work to set them up. For our first Java application, we will sidestep the AWT entirely and just use standard output, much like a C program running in a text-based terminal window.

Create the Source File

In any directory you choose, create the following text file and call it **HelloApplication.java**:

```
public class HelloApplication {
    public static void main (String args[]) {
        System.out.println("Hello, Internet (too)!");
    }
}
```

Understanding the Code

```
public class HelloApplication { ... }
```

A Java application (or applet, for that matter) is itself a class. Remember that because this class is called `HelloApplication`, the compiler's output will be a file called **HelloApplication.class**.

```
public static void main (String args[]) { ... }
```

An application class must have a method called `main()`, and it must be declared with a return type of `void` (i.e., no return value) and the access specifiers `public static`. We will discuss access specifiers in detail in a later chapter. Notice that the function `main()` takes as a parameter an array of `String` objects. These are passed in from the command line. For example, if I were to invoke an application `myApp.class` as follows:

```
java  myApp thisArg  2   6.5
```

then the array `args[]` would have three elements, the `String` objects `"thisArg"`, `"2"`, and `"6.5"`. The length of this array may be obtained in a program via the variable `args.length`. In Chapter 9, we'll show you how to use methods supplied with the Java API to convert the last two arguments from string form to numerical form.

```
System.out.println("Hello, Internet (too)!");
```

WARNING

Unlike in C and C++, `args[0]` is not the name of the command. Instead, `args[0]` is the first argument to the command.

`System.out.println()` is Java's equivalent of `printf()` in C. `System.out` is essentially equivalent to the `cout` output stream in C++. If this makes sense to you, great; if not, don't worry about it. Put simply, this line is a call to a method that prints text to the console.

Compile the Application

We now have the source code for a Java applet. Before we can run it, we need to compile it into bytecode for the Java virtual machine to interpret. Just as we did for the applet, we navigate to the directory containing the application's source code and type the following at the command prompt:

```
javac HelloApplication.java
```

Run the Application

In a sense, the term stand-alone Java application is somewhat of a misnomer. The application does not exactly stand alone. In order to run it, you must use the Java interpreter, whose command name, simply enough, is **java**. To do this, we type the following command from within the directory in which we compiled the source:

```
java HelloApplication
```

If everything works correctly, the application should print its message to the command line and then exit.

Summary

Perhaps the "sexiest" feature of Java is its ability to create applets, interactive programs that reside directly on pages on the World Wide Web. Applets provide Web pages with animation and client-side interactivity. These programs can be viewed by those using Java-enabled Web browsers, such as Netscape 2.0 and HotJava.

Aside from its usefulness for creating applets, Java can also be used to create stand-alone applications, which do not need to be run within a Web browser. Java is particularly well-suited to creating applications for the Internet, because the API bundled with the language contains built-in networking classes. Another use for Java is to create protocol and content handlers, which can augment the functionality of modular Web browsers, such as the HotJava browser.

Source code written in the Java language is compiled into bytecodes, which are essentially machine language instructions for a "virtual machine." The bytecodes are read in by an interpreter, which translates the bytecode to the native machine language of the machine executing the Java program. As a result of this architecture, Java is innately a cross-platform language, and the same compiled Java programs can run on any machine with a Java interpreter without being recompiled.

To create an applet, you create a Java source file (with the extension **.java**) and an HTML file to reference it. The Java source file contains the definition of a class that `extends` the class `java.awt.Applet`. You then compile the source code into

Java bytecode using the `javac` compiler. The output of the `javac` compiler is one or more **.class** files. To run the applet, you can navigate to the URL containing the HTML file or use the `appletviewer`.

To create a Java stand-alone application, you create a Java source file, which contains the definition of a class with a method called `main()`. You then compile the source code into one or more **.class** files using `javac`. To run your application, you use the Java interpreter, `java`, specifying your new class as an argument to the `java` command.

Congratulations! You can now call yourself a Java programmer. This language hasn't been in existence for very long, and relatively few programmers have learned it yet. Compared to most programmers on the planet, you're a Java expert!

CHAPTER 5

Program Structure

Just like any human language, the best way to learn Java is to use it; that is, to write actual, functioning Java code. However, you must know the rules of the game before you can start. Chapter 5, 6, and 7 are designed to help you to understand the structure of the language (the rules of the game).

Comments

Before we get into the structure of Java programs as a whole, we should introduce one of the most important features of Java—or, for that matter, of any programming language: the comment.

Comments are text that you type into your source code, but are ignored by the compiler. Why is this such an important feature? The answer is that comments are not for the compiler; they are for humans. Programming languages are designed in order for humans to communicate with machines in a way that vaguely approximates a human language. The key word here is "vaguely." Every seasoned programmer has had the experience of writing code at three in the morning, which seemed perfectly logical at the time, but only a week later has become virtually unintelligible. To the programmer who wrote the code, this is a bit of a nuisance, as it may take a while to retrace their steps and recall what they had in mind when they first wrote the code. To anyone else attempting to modify or maintain the code, the situation is a pure nightmare.

Comments to the rescue! Comments are written in human languages, and they serve not only to document the code for future modifcation, maintenance, and reuse, but also—when inserted prior to or during actual programming, rather than as an afterthought—to provide a roadmap for the programmer: a tool for planning ahead, and for backing out of sticky situations when things aren't turning out quite as anticipated.

Java supports three distinct types of comments: Traditional C-style comments, C++-style single-line comments, and a new type of comment unique to Java, the *doc comment* (short for "documentation comment").

Traditional Comments

Traditional C-style comments have the following form:

```
/* comment_text */
```

Very simply, anything between `/*` and `*/` is considered to be part of the comment. Traditional comments can span more than one line, and are useful for paragraph-style comments, as in the following:

```
/*

    This code is a little convoluted,
    but it provides a substantial performance
```

```
        optimization over the more intuitive
        recursive algorithm.
  */
```

As a matter of style, the following version makes it a little easier to see where the comment starts and ends:

```
/*
  *    This code is a little convoluted,
  *    but it provides a substantial performance
  *    optimization over the more intuitive
  *    recursive algorithm.
  */
```

There is no rule that these comments *must* extend over more than one line, but you'll usually want to use the simpler single-line comments for that purpose. Here are some more examples of valid, if a little overzealous, traditional comments, embedded in some Java code:

```
/* Don't divide by zero */
if (denom != 0) {
    frac = num/denom;   /* safe to divide */
}
```

Comments of this kind can even be embedded *within* a single line of code, but it's confusing to read, which defeats the purpose of a comment in the first place:

```
/* Don't EVER do this, even though it's valid: */
myStart = /* We interrupt this line... */ someValue;
```

An important thing to keep in mind about comments is that they may not be *nested* inside one another. The reason is that once the compiler sees comment-start sequence, /*, it ignores everything until it sees the comment-end sequence, */. That means that if you place another comment-start sequence inside the comment, it too will be ignored. The end of the "inner" comment causes the compiler to stop ignoring the text, and the remaining text of the "outer" comment will be interpreted as Java code. Since it's probably *not* Java code, it will produce a compile-time error:

```
/* The comment has begun. This text is ignored.
    /* Comment-start ignored, here comes comment-end: */
The comment is over. This is an error. */
```

Single-Line Comments

Single-line comments are the kind you'll probably find yourself using most often. The rule is simple. Anything after // is a comment, until the end of the line is reached. At the beginning of the next line, the comment is over. They're convenient because you don't have to concern yourself with terminating them, and—for the same reason —they're easy to read. There are two single-line comments in the following example:

```
// Here's some code:
myHome = yourHome;  // cute, no?
```

Doc Comments

Java introduces a new kind of comment called the *doc comment*. Doc comments can be used to automatically generate documentation for your code. The JDK comes with a program called javadoc, which scans your code for doc comments, and collects them into formatted, hyperlinked HTML files. The API documentation that comes with the JDK is in this format, and was generated using doc comments and javadoc.

Doc comments begin with /** and end with */. In between, the programmer can put marked-up HTML text, along with some special *doc tags*, starting with the @ symbol. These tags are useful for including author and version information, and for automatically generating hyperlinked cross-references to related code in the package.

We will not cover the details of doc comments in this book. You can find them in Sun's online documentation for javadoc, at:

```
http://www.javasoft.com/JDK-1.0/tools/index.html
```

Compilation Units

A Java program consists of one or more compilation units. A compilation unit is typically a text file containing Java source code. The text file is saved with the `.java` filename extension. For small-scale programming (ie. writing an applet), one compilation unit (a single `.java` file) is all you need. A Java compilation unit may contain any or all of the following:

- `package` statement
- `import` statement
- `class` declarations
- `interface` declarations

A Typical Compilation Unit

A typical compilation unit may consist of a single `package` statement, multiple `import` statements, and multiple class declarations, one of which may be `public`. Most of the applet examples in this book follow this format.

Most Java code is enclosed in classes or interfaces. As we will see in Chapter 8, an interface may contain method declarations, but the bodies of these methods are left empty.

All methods are implemented in classes. A class definition is composed of variables and methods. In the next chapter, we'll explain the different types of variables and how to declare them. And then, we will revisit variables and methods in Chapter 7.

If a compilation unit contains multiple class or interface declarations, it will compile to multiple output files, one for each class contained in the compilation unit. Thus a single compilation unit, `Car.java`, containing three classes, named `Car`, `Wheel`, and `Body`, will produce three output files, `Car.class`, `Wheel.class`, and `Body.class`.

Packages

What are Packages and Why do We Need Them?

A *package* is a directory that contains classes and interfaces. In other words, classes and interfaces are defined in files residing within the package directory that they belong to. After you have written and tested a class, if you would like to have it available other classes, you should place the class into a package. A `package` statement groups related classes and interfaces to avoid naming conflicts and for better organization. For example, Harry has a class (a `.class` file) named `foo` and Sally has a class named `foo` also. How do you distinguish Harry's `foo` class from Sally's? Harry can package his foo class in a package, say `harryPack`, while Sally puts hers in `sallyPack`. So you can invoke Harry's class by using `harryPack.foo` and Sally's by `sallyPack.foo`, provided that `harryPack` and `sallyPack` are directories in your CLASSPATH (see Appendix A for a discussion of the CLASSPATH variable). This example shows that every class and interface must have an unique name—classes and interfaces within the same package must have unique name; no two packages named the same.

The above solution might still be a problem if more than one person named Sally or Harry has classes on the same host machine. A good way to get around this problem is by naming packages hierarchically, such as `organizationName.division-Name.userName.packageName`. Examples of this convention are `java.net` and `sun.net`. `java.net` contains standard network classes; `sun.net` contains Sun proprietary network classes.

Package names are separated by dots (periods) into *components*. There may, theoretically, be an unlimited number of components in a package name. Each component represents an element in a hierarchical structure, which maps directly onto the directory structure of the file system on which the packages are stored.

The `package` Statement

The syntax of a `package` statement is as follows:

```
package packageName;
```

If you use a `package` statement, it must be the first non-comment, non-white space line in a compilation unit. The `package` statement simply proclaims which package this compilation unit—and all classes and interfaces therein—belongs to.

A compiliation unit can contain multiple classes, but only one `package` statement. Therefore, all classes in a compilation unit are members of the package declared in the `package` statement.

The Default Package

Every class and interface belongs to some package. If a compilation unit has no package statement, the unit is placed in the "default package," which has no name.

If you are hacking, improvising, rapidly prototyping, or otherwise writing code that does not need to be tightly organized, you might want to skip the package statement. On the other hand, if you are developing classes or interfaces intended for reuse by others, it is advisable to place the finished product into packages.

How does Java Find the Right Package?

In environments where Java has access to a file system, each component in a package name is mapped to a directory. If, for example, you have packages myCompany.employeePack and myCompany.clientPack, you should create a directory myCompany under your CLASSPATH. In directory myCompany, create two directories, employeePack and clientPack. Put all classes and interfaces with statements

```
package myCompany.employeePack;
```

under the employeePack directory and, all classes and interfaces with statements

```
package myCompany.clientPack;
```

under the clientPack directory. Figure 5.1 illustrates the directory structure.

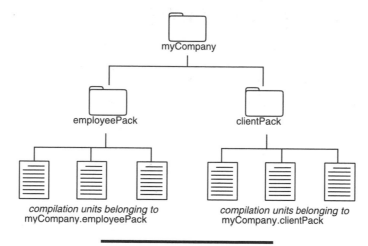

Figure 5.1 Directory structure.

Standard Package Name Conventions

The Java Specification contains a standard for naming packages uniquely. The packages which are part of the standard Java API begin with the component java (in all lowercase). Packages created by other individuals and groups should begin with at least one all-uppercase component, and can be given globally unique names by basing them on the reversed Internet Domain Name (DNS name) of the organization. For instance, if you work for Big Fake, Inc., whose (obviously fictitious) domain name is bigfake.com, then all package names for your company should begin with COM.bigfake. If you work in the system administration department at Big Fake, and your user name is joe_user, then all packages you create should be given names beginning with COM.bigfake.sysadmin.joe_user. Here are some examples of globally unique package names:

```
COM.bigfake.sysadmin.joe_user.WebUtils.HTMLGeneration
COM.bettersoft.AmazingJavaStuff
EDU.nyu.cs.students.phd.jonQstudent.IndependentStudy
GOV.cia.topsecret.blackbox.gk45j90zxf8
```

Import Statements

If a compilation unit intends to refer to any classes or interfaces that are declared in another compilation unit, then it must either qualify all references completely, in the form *packageName.className*, or it must import those classes and interfaces, using an import statement. The syntax of the import statement may be any of the following:

```
import PackageName.ClassName;      // import a class
import PackageName.InterfaceName;  // import an interface

import PackageName.*;       // import all public classes and
                            // interfaces from this package
```

Function of an Import Statement

The import statement allows classes to use abbreviated names to refer to classes and interfaces declared outside their compilation unit. It saves the programmer from having to type the entire package name to qualify references to such classes and interfaces. The resulting code is also much easier to read. The import statement does not really provide any particular advantage in terms of the power of the language, but it does provide an extremely useful syntactic convenience.

Importing a Class or interface

You can explicitly import a single class from a package by using its fully qualified name (*packageName.className*). The following import statement allows a compilation unit to refer to the class Applet, which is defined in the package java.applet.

```
import java.applet.Applet;
```

Once we have placed this statement in our compilation unit, we may refer to the imported class simply as Applet. Without the `import` statement, we would have to refer to it by its fully qualified name, `java.applet.Applet`.

It is important to realize that an `import` statement by itself does not cause a class (or classes) loaded into memory during runtime. It only registers a shortcut for a symbolic name (ie. "`Applet`" for "`java.applet.Applet`") which maps directly to a path by which the class may be found. The class is only loaded when it is referenced.

WARNING

You may be thinking that the `import` statement is something like the `#include` statement in C or C++, which actually includes another file as part of the current compilation unit. This is not the case with the `import` statement. The import statement does not magically "include" the `imported` class as part of this package (the default package). The `import` statement merely provides the programmer with a shorthand for naming classes and interfaces, which are then loaded only as needed. This does not change the fact that the class belongs to a different compilation unit, and probably to a different package as well.

Importing all Classes in a Package

A convenient way to import all classes from package `java.applet` is to use a statement like the following:

```
import java.applet.*;
```

In an `import` statement of this type, the * acts as a "wildcard," causing all classes and interfaces in the package `java.applet` to be imported. This form has the advantage that it's easy to type, and it saves you from having to think in advance about which individual classes from the package you're going to need. Sometimes, you may need them all.

Remember, like any other `import` statement, this statement does not cause all of these classes to be immediately loaded into memory. They are loaded into memory as needed by the compiler and interpreter. Classes which are never referred to in the compilation unit are never actually loaded into memory.

The above `import` statement does, however, cause the compiler or the interpreter to find the appropriate package directory, look at each .class file therein to see if it belongs to the package, and make a note of its name for future reference. This step only needs to happen once for each such `import` statement, but it slows down compilation and execution a bit to have to do it. Thus, once you've finished a compilation unit, and you know which particular classes of a package you actually refer to, you should replace the wildcard-style `import` statement with explicit `import` statements for each class and interface you use.

Another potential problem with importing classes with this style of importing is that it may introduce inadvertent naming conflicts. For instance, imagine you have the following `import` statements:

```
import COM.bigfake.somePackage.*;
import COM.bigfake.otherPackage.*;
```

The above statements import all of the classes from **COM.bigfake.somePackage** and `COM.bigfake.otherPackage`. If there is a class `COM.bigfake.somePackage.ClassA` and another class `COM.bigfake.otherPackage.ClassA`, the above **import** statements will introduce a naming conflict which will cause a compile-time error the first time one of these classes is referenced. This is because compiler is attempting to locally rename both classes with the same name: `ClassA`. It is not an error to *use* both of these classes in the same compilation unit, because we can refer to them by their fully-qualified, unique names; it is, however, an error to try to `import` them both, because the abbreviated names would conflict.

Do *not* get the mistaken impression that the following will import all of the Java API packages:

```
import java.*;              /* wrong */
```

This is because `java.net` and `java.awt` are the names of packages; `java` is not the name of a package. The `*` character may be used in `import` statements as a substitute for class names, but not for package names.

`java.lang.*` **is implicitly imported**

Each Java program automatically imports all of the classes and interfaces in java.lang, the package containing the core set of classes needed to run any Java program. Thus, you do not need to explicitly import classes and interfaces such as `java.lang.Object`, `java.lang.Boolean`, `java.lang.Float`, `java.lang.Runnable`, etc.

Class and Interface Declarations

Although the `package` statement and the `import` statement serve important purposes in a compilation unit, they do not—in and of themselves—cause any code to be generated. The real "meat" of a compilation unit is in it's class and/or interface declarations. For lack of a formal term, we can think of these declarations as the "body" of a compilation unit. In order to concentrate on the broader concept of program structure, we are temporarily sidestepping the issue of describing class and interface declarations in depth. We will go into much greater detail about this in Chapter 8, when we examine how Java implements object-oriented programming.

`public` Classes and the import Statement

Some classes are defined only for use either within the package in which they are defined. This is, in fact, the default case. If you wish for a class to be visible outside the package in which it is defined, then you must declare that class as `public`:

```
public class Beer {

   ...

}
```

Declaring the class as `public` allows it to be referred to within other compilation units. Assuming that `Beer` is in the package `trendy.australian`, a compilation unit in any package may refer to it as `trendy.australian.Beer`. If the programmer of that compilation unit wishes to refer to it simply as Beer, then the following statement may be used:

```
import trendy.australian.Beer;
```

The important thing to remember is that the import statement has no effect on the *visibility* of the class `trendy.australian-.Beer`; it is visible because it was declared as public. Because it is visible, we can refer to it in any compilation unit, and `import` it to make it easier to refer to.

Two Rules Regarding public Classes

Although you can define multiple classes and interfaces within a single compilation unit, there is a restriction that within a compilation unit, at most one class or interface can be declared as `public`. Also, the name of the `public` class or interface must be the same as the name of the file. For example, if the name of the `public` class is `PubClass`, then the name of its compilation unit must be `PubClass.java`.

These two rules are necessary to facilitate a very useful option of the Java compiler which, if set, enables automatic recompilation of any imported classes whose source files have changed since they were last compiled. The one-to-one relationship between public (importable) classes and their source file names allows the compiler to find, check, and recompile the source files—provided they are stored in the appropriate directory. Notice that the class name and file name are case sensitive; i.e., PubClass and Pubclass do not match.

Putting It All Together

To a newcomer—even a programmer with experience in other languages—some or all of these concepts may seem a little unfamiliar and confusing. In fact, the terms *package*, *compilation unit*, *public*, and *import* are found in other computer languages, with different meanings, depending on the language. Figure 5.2 should help sort things out.

Figure 5.2 shows two packages, chap5.comedy and chap4.horror. This means there must be a directory called chap5, containing two subdirectories, comedy and horror. The two subdirectories correspond directly to the two packages. The package directory for comedy contains two files, Abbott.java and Costello.java. Each of these files is a compilation unit, and within each compilation unit there happen to be three classes. Notice, however, that only one class in each compilation unit is declared as public, and that the name of each compilation unit matches the name of its public class (public classes Abbott and Costello; compilation units Abbott.java and Costello.java, respectively).

Package

```
chap5.comedy
```

compilation unit

contents of file: Abbott.java

```
package chap5.comedy;

class Fear {
    // refers to
    //    chap5.horror.Dracula
    //    chap5.horror.Wolfman
}

class Cowardice {
    // refers to Fear
}

public class Abbott {
    // refers to Fear
    // refers to Cowardice
    // refers to Costello
}
```

compilation unit

contents of file: Costello.java

```
package chap5.comedy;

class Impatience {
    // refers to Abbott
    // refers to Fear
}

class Skepticism {
    // refers to
    //    chap5.horror.Dracula
}

public class Costello {
    // refers to Skepticism
    // refers to Impatience
}
```

Package

```
chap5horror
```

compilation unit

contents of file: Dracula.java

```
package chap5.horror;

import chap5.comedy.Abbott;
import chap5.comedy.Costello;

class Hypnosis {
    // refers to Abbott
}

class Fangs {
    ...
}

public class Dracula {
    ...
}
```

compilation unit

contents of file: Wolfman.java

```
package chap5.horror;

import chap5.comedy.*;

class FullMoon {
    // refers to Dracula
}

public class Wolfman {
    // refers to Fangs
    // refers to Abbott
    // refers to Costello
}
```

Figure 5.2 Package Example.

When the four files in this example are compiled, they will produce a total of eleven output (.class) files, one for each class that is declared: `Fear.class`, `Cowardice.class`, `Abbott.class`, `Impatience.class`, etc. The .class files will continue to reside in their respective package directories after compilation, where they can be found and loaded as needed.

Each compilation unit shown above contains a `package` statement, which announces its membership in a particular package. The key point is, a package *contains* compilation units. The compilation units use package statements to announce which package they are contained *in*.

The two compilation units in `chap5.horror` contain `import` statements; the two compilation units in `chap5.comedy` do not contain `import` statements. For this reason, the compilation units in `chap5.horror` may use abbreviated names to refer to `imported` classes, while the compilation units in `chap5.comedy` must fully qualify the names of any classes from outside the package.

Notice that some non-`public` classes are visible in other compilation units, but only compilation units within their package. The non-`public` classes `Fangs` and `FullMoon`, for example, are invisible outside of the package `chap5.horror`. Thus, compilation units outside this package, such as `Abbott.java`, may not **import** or otherwise refer to them. If either of `Abbot.java` or `Costello.java` contained a statement like the following, it would cause a compile-time error:

```
import chap5.horror.Fangs; // can't do it, Fangs is not public
```

Summary

Java programs follow a structural hierarchy such that classes are grouped into compilation units, and compilation units are grouped into packages.

A package's full name may consist of one or more components, which map to the directory path in which the package is stored. This scheme allows classes to be loaded dynamically as needed during compilation and runtime.

Classes may use fully-qualified names to refer to other classes outside of their own package. Alternatively, they may use one or more `import` statements, which allow them to use a more abbreviated name for classes outside the package. Only classes declared as `public` will be visible outside the package.

This chapter focused on a higher-level view of Java program structure. In Chapter 6, we begin to take a more microscopic look at Java, examining the various ways that data can be expressed and manipulated.

JAVA
PROGRAMMING
BASICS

Types, Operators, and Expressions

As you learned in Chapter 4, you must compile your Java source code to bytecode before you can run it. The java compiler, `javac`, will discard comments and whitespace, and reduce the source code to tokens. The five categories of token are: keywords, identifiers, literals, operators, and separators.

Keywords are reserved for use by the language and cannot be used as variable names. An identifier, in general, is the name of a program variable. Literals are the basic representation of any primitive type (integer, floating point, boolean, character, or string value). Operators specify actions to perform on variables and literals. Separators are used to access objects, and to separate expressions or statements.

What is the relationship among types, Operators, and Expressions?

Every identifier and literal has a type (i.e. integer, boolean). The type defines the values an identifier or a literal can hold and the operations which can be performed upon it. For example, if variable i is an integer type and variable b is a boolean type, then i can only hold integer values and b can only hold either `true` or `false`. Furthermore, operators like +, -, *, / can be performed upon i but not b. Similarly, logical operators like && and || can be performed upon b but not i.

An *expression* is a combination of variables, literals, and operators which results in a value. Expressions are separated by separators.

Variables

A *variable* is an identifier which is used to store data. In order to use a variable, you need to declare it with a type. The type of a variable determines the values it can hold and the operations which can be performed upon it. Initialization during declaration is optional. For example,

```
byte b=4;
```

Variable b is declared as a byte. It can hold any valid byte values from -127 to 128 and any integer type operators (these will be explained in the Type section) can perform operations on it. It is initialized to 4.

Naming Rules

The variable naming rules follow the C language standard. Names consist of letters and digits; the first character must be a letter, underscore ("_") or dollar sign ("$"). Letters are the characters "A" to "Z", "a" to "z", and Unicode characters with a character number above hex 00C0. Variable names are case sensitive. abc, Abc, and ABC are three distinct variables. Keywords (explained in the next section) cannot be used as variable names.

Unicode

Most programmers write programs in ASCII (American Standard Code for Information Interchange) format. ASCII is a set of codes to represent characters. Each ASCII code has 8 bits and there are 128 codes. However, most of the non-Latin languages require more than 128 codes to encode their alphabets. Java, a language designed for the Internet, uses Unicode as its character set instead of ASCII. Each Unicode code has 16 bits and there are 2^{16} possible codes. It is sufficient to handle most of the world's languages. Each language encodes its alphabets following The Unicode Standard. For more information on Unicode, check out the http://www.stonehand.com/unicode.html.

Since ASCII is a subset of Unicode, this may not make any difference to you. However, Unicode is great news, for programmers speaking (and writing) in non-Latin languages. With Unicode, they can write Java code in their native languages, though they may need a special editor and font to do so.

Scope Rules

The scope of a variable is an area of a program where the variable is recognized. This area, which is the zone in which the variable exists, runs from the declaration of the variable to the end of the block is in.   For example,

```
class Scope {
    int a;
    // Zone a.
    void scopeMethod1(double c) {
        // Zone c.
        int b;
        // Zone b.
        ......
    }

    void scopeMethod2(int a) {
        // Zone a. Variable a is local to scopeMethod2.
        /* this.a is an instance variable in class Scope.
            It is view as a global variable of class Scope. */
        this.a = a;

    }
}
```

Variable `this` is used to refer to the class itself. It is a built-in variable in every class. In the above example, `this.a` refers to the instance variable declared in class Scope (not the local variable from `scopeMethod2()`).

Keywords

Keywords are special identifiers used by the language. You should not use any of the keywords listed in Table 5.1 as a variable name.

Table 5.1 Keywords for Java 1.0

abstract	boolean	break	byte	byValue*
case	cast*	catch	char	class
const*	continue	default	do	double

Table 5.1 Keywords for Java 1.0 C9continued)

else	extends	final	finally	float
for	future*	generic*	goto*	if
implements	import	inner*	instanceof	int
interface	long	native	new	null
operator*	outer*	package	private	protected
public	rest*	return	short	static
super	switch	synchronized	this	throw
throws	transient	try	var*	void
volatile	while			

*The keywords that are reserved but not used in Java 1.0.

Literal Constants

Literals are the constant representation of any integer, floating point, boolean, character, or string value. Table 5.2 summarizes different forms of literal constant.

Table 5.2 Litetral constants

Integer constant:	
5	integer constant
5L or 5l	integer constant with type long
05	integer constant in octal (base 8) format.
0XaBc	(case insensitive) integer constant in hexadecimal (base 16) format.

Double and Float Fonstant	
5.5 or 5.5D or 5.5d	double constant
5.5E5	double constant with exponent
5.5f or 5.5F	floating point constant

Table 5.2 Litetral constants (continued)

Boolean Constant	
true, false	boolean constant

Character Constant (Escape Characters)	
\	continuation on next line
\n	new line
\t	horizontal tab
\b	back space
\r	carriage return
\f	form feed
\\	backslash
\'	single quote
\"	double quote
\ddd	octal bit pattern (d = digit in octal)
\xdd	hex bit pattern (d = digit in hex)
\udddd	unicode char (d = dight in hex)

String constant:	
"This is a string"	string constant

Types

As mentioned above, the type of an object or a variable determines the values it can hold and the operations which can be performed upon it. The Java language has two categories of types: *base* and *composite*.[1] The base types are "atomic" and cannot be broken down. The four base types in Java are integer, floating point, character, and boolean. Composite types are collections of base types. Java has three kinds of composite

---

[1] Base types are also known as *primitive types*. For reasons we will later discuss, composite types are also known as *reference types*.

types: arrays, classes, and interfaces. Classes and interfaces will be discussed in detail in Chapter 8. This section will focus on the four base types and arrays.

1. Integer Types

NOTE

Don't confuse the integer type, `int`, with the Integer class in package `java.lang`. An integer type is a Java built-in data type, not a class. The following is the declaration of the Integer class.

```
class IntegerClass {   // Contains variables (int) and a set
                       // of methods to act on the variables.

  int MAX_VALUE;    // A variable in the class. This is an
                    // integer type.
  int MIN_VALUE;
  public static String toString (int i)   // A method.
  { ... }


     ......

}
```

Unlike the `Integer` Class, there is no behavior associated with integer types.

The four integer types are `byte` (8 bits), `short` (16 bits), `int` (32 bits), and `long` (64 bits).

WARNING

Unlike C and C++, where the sizes of various primitive types are "machine-dependent," Java is "machine-independent:" primitive types are of fixed size, no matter what hardware the Java virtual machine is running on.

Integer types are "signed", meaning that every variable declared as an integer type must be able to contain positive and negative numbers.

WARNING

Unlike C and C++, there is no such thing as an `unsigned` interger.

All integer types are machine independent. The type determines the range of values and arithmetic properties a variable can hold. If a value is assigned to a variable which is not big enough to hold it (overflow), the value is reduced modulo the range. For example, variable b is a byte type which can hold 256 (28 possibilities) numbers ranging from -128 to 127. If

```
byte b = -129;
```

Then b is equal to -129 - (-256) = 127. If

```
byte b = 128;
```

Then b is equal to 128 - 256 = -128.

This interesting integer property is called *wrap around*. We will show another wrap around example later on in this chapter.

2. Floating-Point Types (defined by IEEE 754)

There are two floating point types (real numbers): `float` (32 bits) and `double` (64 bits) and they are signed. The default of a real number is `double`. For example, the type of 2.60 is `double`.

If an overflow (see previous section) or underflow (a number which is too small to record) is assigned to a floating-point variable, the value of the variable is NaN (*not a number*). We will discuss NaN later in this chapter.

3. Character Types

Unlike C or C++, where each character is 8 bits, each character in Java is represented by 16 bits Unicode. *Unicode* is a character encoding standard based on a 16 bits unit of encoding. See the side bar in the variable section in this chapter for more details.

The keyword for a character type is `char`. The following is an example of its declaration. Variable `a` is declared as a character type with no initialization. Variable `b` is declared as a character type and initialized to 'k'. Variable `c` is declared as a character type and initialized to unicode '\u00c0'.

```
char a,    b='k', c='\u00c0';
```

Notice that a single quote is used for character type initialization.

4. Boolean Types

The keyword for boolean type is `boolean`. To declare a boolean variable, use

```
boolean boolean_variable;
```

A variable of type `boolean` can have one of two values: `true` or `false`. Theoretically, as you probably know, it only takes one bit to represent a Boolean value. In practice, however, computers do not allocate memory one bit at a time, but typically in 8-bit, 16-bit, 32-bit, or 64-bit chunks. For this reason, in many other languages, Booleans are allocated as integers, which is a waste of space, especially if you declare many Booleans. The Java virtual machine does some clever handling of `boolean` values, manipulating individual bits of integer-sized chunks so that if you declare many `boolean` variables, each one only requires one bit of space.

WARNING

In Java, Boolean values are not numbers and cannot be converted into numbers. (The "type-casting" favored by C programmers doesn't work in Java.) The values `true` and `false` are not just aliases for the numbers 1 and 0, and cannot be operated on as integers.

5. Arrays

An array is an ordered list of elements. To create an array, use the `new` operator.

```
int column[] = new int[3];
```

OR

```
int []column = new int[3]; // The bracket can be placed before
                           // or after the array name.
```

Variable `column` has a length 3 (means 3 elements) which indexed from 0 to 2. You can also separate the preceding statement into two.

```
int column[];      // Equivalent to int []column;
                   // Variable column is a handle of an
                   // int array.
```

.....

```
column = new int[3]; // Dynamically allocates memory for
                     // column array.
```

Variable `column` is said to be dynamically allocated if the storage is not assigned during declaration. You should allocate memory dynamically if you don't know in advance how much memory is needed.

Array dimensions must be expressed in integers:

```
int n=2;
double d=2.2;

double dArray1[] = new float[n+1]; // Correct.

double dArray2[] = new float[d];    // Wrong!  Array
                                    // dimensions must be
                                    // expressed in integer.

double dArray3[] = new float[(int)d];     // Correct.

dArray1[0] = 2.3;              // First element of dArray1.
dArray1[1] = 5.5E5;            // Second element.
dArray1[2] = -7;              // Third element.
```

To specify a multi-dimensional array:

```
int matrix[][] = new int[2][4];
```
OR
```
int [][]matrix = new int[2][4];
```

`matrix[0]` is an array of four `int`; `matrix[1]` is an array of four `int`; `matrix` is an array of two elements, each element is an array of four `int`.

For any multi-dimensional array, putting a value in the last bracket([]) is optional:

```
int matrix[][] = new int[2][];
```

But you must define the last dimension of `matrix` before using it.

```
for (int i=0;  i<2; i++) {
   matrix[i] = new int[4];
}
```

To allocate storage for an array, you must use the `new` operator, except you initialize the array elements during declaration. For example,

```
char letters[] = {'a', 'b', 'c'}; // Array letters has length
                                   // 3.
```

 In fact, the `new` operator must be used to create storage on any composite type (arrays, class objects, interface objects). However, explicit storage allocation for the base types are not needed. For example,

```
char a;                  // no need to use the new operator.
char charArray[] = new char[3];
```

During compilation, the Java compiler creates an array class which matches each compiling class. In Java, an array is an object which cannot be explicitly subclassed. In other words, you cannot do the following:

```
class arraySubclass extends int[] {....}
```

Base type arrays are built-in subclasses of Array. The following graph illustrates the relationship

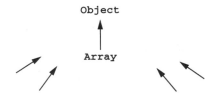

```
                        Object

                         Array


byte[] short[] int[] long[] float[] double[] char[] boolean[]
```

Arrays vs pointers

In C, a *pointer* is the address of a variable. A particular piece of memory can be accessed by providing a pointer. One of the powerful concept in C is pointer arithmetic. Calcuations (ie. +, - , *, /) performed on a pointer result in a pointer and hence, can be used to access memory. Pointer arithmetic, on the other hand, is also a dangerous concept. Accessing a wrongly calculated pointer might result in application errors, or even crash the system. Also, this kind of bug is usually hard to locate.

The Java architects decided to eliminate pointer arithemetic from the language. Pointers in Java are called `handles`. Notice that a Java handle is associated with an object (ie. array), but not an address. The following statement declares variable *column* as the handle of an `int` array. It is refered to as a `null` object because no memory is allocated for its array yet. `null` is a built-in variable for any object. The graphical representation illustrates the idea.

```
int column[];
```

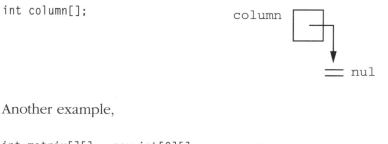

Another example,

```
int matrix[][] = new int[2][];
```

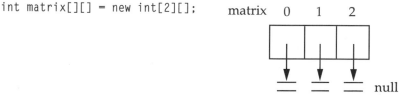

The preceding statement allocates memory for three handles, `matrix[0]`, `matrix[1]`, and `matrix[2]` and each points to null. To dynamically allocate memory for the actual arrays:

```
for (int i=0;  i<2; i++)    {
   matrix[i] = new int[4];
}
```

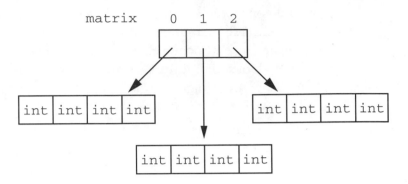

Operators

Operators in Java are very similar to those in the C language. The following is the "precedence and associativity" table. "Precedence" is the order in which operators are interpreted in the same clause. "Associativity" is the direction in which Java evaluates the clause containing the operator. Operators in the same cell have the same precedence.

Operators		Associativity
.	class variables and methods accessor	
[]	array accessor	
()	casting	left to right
++	increment	
--	decrement	
!	boolean negate (not)	
~	one's complement	
instanceof	subclass test	right to left
*	multiplication	
/	division	
%	modulus	left to right

Operators		Associativity
+	addition	
-	substraction (or unuary negate)	left to right
<<	left shift	
>>	right shift	
>>>	zero-fill right shift	left to right
<	ess than	
>	greater than	
<=	less than or equal to	
>=	greater than or equal to	left to right
==	test if equal	
!=	test if not equal	left to right
&	bitwise AND	left to right
^	bitwise XOR	left to right
|	bitwise OR	left to right
&&	AND	left to right
||	OR	left to right
?:	ternary conditional operator	right to left
= += -= *= /= %= &= ^= |= <<= >>=	assignment operators	
a op= b	is equivalent to a = a op b where op stands for operator. eg. a += b is equivalent to a = a + b	right to left

1. Operators on Numeric Types

All binary operations on numeric types obey the following rules:

if   (an operand is a double)
*   the resultant will be converted into a double*

else if   *(an operand is a float)*
                 the resultant will be converted into float
else if   *(an operand is a long)*
                 the resultant will be converted into long
else
                 the resultant will be converted into int

Operators on integers types

Remember that the four integer types are long, int, short, and byte. If a calculation results in an integer type and an operand is long, the result type is long. Otherwise, the result type is int. For example,

```
class intTest {
    public static void main (String args[]) {
        short i=10, j=11, k;
        int m;

        k = i+j;            // Wrong!  Need to cast the
                            // result explicitly.
        k = (short) (i+j); // Correct. k = 21
        m = i+j;            // Correct. m = 21
    }
}
```

If the result is an overflow (exceeds the range of an integer type the variable can hold), the result will "wrap around". For example,

```
class overflowTest {
    public static void main (String args[]) {
        Integer i = new Integer (0);
        int overflowNum = i.MAX_VALUE + 1; // The largest value int
                                            // type can hold
        System.out.println ("Minimum integer value = " +
                            i.MIN_VALUE);
```

```
    System.out.println ("overflow number =  " + overflowNum);
    if (i.MIN_VALUE == overflowNum)
        System.out.println ("overflow number wrap around!");
   }

}
```

The result of the program is

```
Minimum integer value = -2147483648
overflow number =  -2147483648
overflow number wrap around!
```

Operators accepting integer types as operands are "+", "-", "*", "/", "%", "++", "--", and "*op*=". If both operands are integer types, the results will also be integer types (following the rules explained above). Operators "~", "<<", ">>", ">>>", "&", "^", and "|" takes integer types as operands and results in integer types also. They are mainly used for bitwise operation and will be explained in the next section. Operators "<", ">", "<=", and ">=" will takes integer types as operands and result in boolean values.

Integer division truncates any fraction. An `ArithmeticException` will be "thrown" (caused) if you attempt to divide or modulus by zero. Definition of a modulus operator ("%") is a % b = a - (a/b) * b, where a and b are integer types. a++ is equivalent to a = a + 1 and a-- is equivalent to a = a - 1.

Bitwise operators on Integer Types

The seven bitwise operators "&", "|", "^", "<<", ">>", ">>>" and "~" may only be applied to integer types. They are used to test, set, or shift the bits in integer type variables.

Here is a practical example of the use of these operators. Primitive types in Java are stored in big-endian format. Suppose you have a data file in which each chunk of data is a 16-bit `short`, but the machine that wrote the file used little-endian format. After each short is read in, you would need to switch the first 8 bits with the last 8 bits. Here is a method you could call on each short to convert it so that your Java program may use it:

```
short toBigEndian (short littleEndian) {
    byte b;
    short high_byte, low_byte;

    b = (byte) smallEndian;// get the low 8 bits
    high_byte = b << 8;         // shift the bits in b left
                                //      8 places
    low_byte = smallEndian >>> 8; // shift right, with zero-
                                //      // fill

    return high_byte & low_byte;
}
```

Operators on Floating Point Types

All operators that can be applied to integer types can also be applied to floating point types EXCEPT bitwise operators. However, the definition of "%" is different than the one for integer values.

If variable a, b are double or float, then

a % b = a - Math.rint (a/b) * b

Math.rint ( ) converts a double value into an integral value in double format. If the fractional part ends in .5, the number will be converted to an even number. For example,

Math.rint (7.0/2.0) = Math.rint (3.5) = 4

Unlike integer types, overflow (when the number is too big to store) in floating point types generates Inf (infinity), not "wrap around". Underflow (the number is too small to store) generates 0. Divide by zero generates Inf. For example,

```
double oflow = 1.0 / 0.0;          // Overflow
double uflow = 24/0.0;             // Underflow
```

The value of oflow is Inf and uflow is 0.

Although relational operators ">", "<", ">=", "<=", "==", "!="can be applied to floating point types, you should use care when doing comparisons . For example, if a and b are float and a < b is not true, it does not follow that a>=b. Similarly, a !=b does not mean that a>b || a<b.

It is important to be careful of the NaN value in floating point types. A NaN (Not a Number) is any non-meaninful number resulting from a calculation. NaN is unsigned and unordered, meaning that you cannot compare (ic. greater than, less than, equal) between a NaN and anything (including itself). For example,

```
double a = 0.0/0.0;
if (Double.isNan(a))
   System.out.println("a is NaN.");
else
   System.out.println("a is not NaN.");

double b = a;
if (Double.isNan(b))
   System.out.println("b is NaN.");
 else
   System.out.println("b is not NaN.");

if ( a == b)
   System.out.println("a == b");
else
   System.out.println("a != b");
```

The result of this program is

```
a is NaN.
a != b
```

Method `Double.isNaN()` is used to test `NaN` value. To apply relational operators on floating point types safely, you should use it to test `NaN`.

```
double a, b;
.................
if ( (a != b) && !Double.isNaN(a) && !Double.isNaN(b) )
      // a is not equal to b and both numbers are not NaN
```

2. Operators on boolean types

The relational operators or logical operators "!", "<", ">", "<=", ">=", "==", "!=", "&&", "||", "?:" operate on boolean values and produce boolean values.

The preceding GateKeeper example demonstrates the usage of "?:" (known as a "ternary operator") In method IsGateOpen(),

```
return ((mask > 0) ? true : false);
```

is equivalent to

```
if (mask > 0)
  return true;
else
   return false;
```

A ternary operator is just a short hand way to do if-else statements.

3. Operators on arrays

The operator "[ ]" is used to create and specify the size of, or to retrieve, a particular piece of information in an array.

To create an array,

```
type arrayName[] = new type[size];
```

for example,

```
int a[] = new int [3];        // create an array of 3 int type,
                              // range from 0 to 2
```

To access a particular piece of information in an array,

```
arrayName[integer_valued_expression];
```

for example,

```
    a[1];
    a[c+1];                 // c is an int
```

The legal range of an array is between 0 and size of array -1. Trying to access an array with an out of range index will cause an `ArrayIndexOutOfBoundsException` (Evception will be discussed in Chapter 9) at run time.

4. Operators on String Objects

Most of the time, methods are used to operate upon strings. For example, to concatenate two strings, one would use the `String.concat()` method. However, string concatenation is a frequent operation (ie. to compose a print message). Therefore, Java has a short-cut way to concatenate a string by using the "+" and "+=" operators.

5. Operators on Objects

Operator new is used to create a new instance of an object . The binary operator instanceof tests whether the specified object is an instance of the specified class or one of its subclasses. For example,

```
String str = new String();
......
if (str instanceof String)
     ......
```

Type Casting

In Java, any numeric type (integers and floating point) can be cast (transformed) to any other. However, some information might be lost in casting. For example,

```
float f = (float)3.5;
int i;

i = (int) f;            // i = 3
f = (float) i;          // f = 3
```

Casting between base types and composite types is prohibited. Casting between subclasses and superclasses is allowed. An instance may be cast to a superclass, but casting to a subclass will generate a runtime check. The Java interpreter ensures that the subclass is an extension of the casting superclass. If the object is not an instance of the subclass (or one of its subclasses), the runtime system throws a ClassCastException (see Chapter 9).

Expressions

An expression is a combination of variables, literals, and operators which results in a value. For example, if i = 1, then i + 3 is an expression that combines variable i, a literal integer with value 3, and a "+" operator, producing a value 4. You may use a variable to store the value produced by an expression. The process of storing a value is called *assignment* and the assigning variable is called the *lvalue*. For example,

```
int i, j;    // Declares i and j as integer type variables.
i = 10;      // Value 10 is assigned to i.
             // Variable i is the lvalue.


j = i + 10; // Variable j is the lvalue.
```

Expressions are separated by separators. The following are the Java separators:

```
( )  { }    [ ]    ;      ,        .
```

Evaluation Order

Consider the following expressions:

```
int i=1;
int j = (i=0) + i;
```

What is the value of j? Should we evaluate the expression

```
(i=0) + i
```

from left to right (0 + 0 = 0) or from right to left (0 + 1 = 1) ? That's why we need precedence and associativity table (listed in the Operator section) to determine the expression evaluation order. According to the table, operator "+" evaluates expressions from left to right. Therefore, expression (i=0) is evaluated first. And thus, the expression will produce 0 and it gets assigned to variable j. How about this?

```
int i=1;
int j = i=0 + i;
```

First, let's eliminate the lvalue. The statement becomes

```
i=0 + i
```

This expression produces a value 1. Therefore, j = 1.

Summary

For those familiar with C or C++, most of the information in this chapter should look pretty familiar. Java, however, looks at data from a higher level than these languages do. For example, Java does not treat arrays as pointers to memory, and it treats `true` and `false` as distinct Boolean-typed values, rather than as integers.

Java is also much stricter with regard to type-checking. Variables must be treated as members of the type with which they were originally declared, and type-casting is only allowed in a very restricted set of circumstances.

In this chapter, we have focused mainly on data. Chapter 7 brings us to a discussion of action, as we investigate the various types of control-flow you can use to direct the execution of a Java program.

JAVA
PROGRAMMING
BASICS

Control Flow Statements

A *statement* is a high-level instruction. For example, *x=x+1;* is a statement. A pair of curly brackets, {}, typically enclosing one or more statements, is called a *block*. It is used to group variable declarations and statements. Within a method *block*, Java statements are executed from top to bottom unless a *control flow statement* defines the order of execution otherwise.

Label Statement

A *label* serves as a marker for a statement. Declaration of a label is followed by a colon.

```
label :
```

The *scope* of a label is the block in which it resides. A label is an identifier, so it must obey the naming rules described in Chapter 5.

The label statement does not change the flow of execution, but it serves as a marker so that control can jump to the statement marked with a specified label. As we will learn later, `switch`, `break`, and `continue` statements use labels to jump from a normal sequence of execution (top to bottom) to a different sequence.

An important feature of the `if` statement in Java (also true in C, but not in Pascal) is that complex Boolean expressions are evaluated in order, and only as far as necessary to determine the value of the expression. Consider the following code:

```
If ( (a != null) && (a.foobar() ) ) {
    // do something
}
```

Recall that the && operator will only return true if both of its operands evaluate to `true`. Imagine the case in which the first operand is `false`. Having evaluated this operand, we know that the whole expression must be `false`, even before evaluating the second operand. In Java, when this is the case, the second operand is not evaluated.

The Boolcan operator | | is treated in a similar manner. If the first operand of an | | expression evaluates to true, then the other operand is not evaluated.

This is called "short-circuited" evaluation. It is a useful feature, not only because it is more efficient, but because you can use the first expression to "protect" the second expression from being evaluated, particularly if the second expression could cause an error. That is in fact what is done in the preceding code example. We don't want to call `a.foobar()` in the case that a is `null`, because that would cause an error.

Futhermore, if the compiler identifies that the conditional expression in an `if` statement will *always* evaluate to `false`, then the compiler will not output any code for the true branch, and vice versa. For example:

```
if ( 1==0 ) {
    // this statement never makes it to compiled code:
    doThis () ;
} else {
    // this statement goes in unconditionally:
    doSomethingElse () ;
}
```

if **Statement**

The Java `if` statement performs like any other language's `if` statement. If a condition is true, the statement or the statement block beneath it is executed. The syntax is:

```
if (boolean expression) {
    statements;
} else if (boolean expression) {
    statements;
} else {
    statements;
}
```

The curly brackets, {}, are optional if there is only one statement in the block. The `else-if` and `else` statements are optional. An `if-else` compound statement (a group of blocks and statements) is evaluated from top to bottom. If one of the `if` statements is true, the block following it will be executed and then control will be passed to the end of the compound statement. If none of the `if` statements is true, the final `else` block, if present, will be executed.

Notice that an `if` statement can only evaluate a Boolean expression—an expression that results in a `Boolean` data type.

switch **Statement**

A switch statement is an alternative to an if statement. Too many if-else statements make code hard to read. The format of a switch statement is as follows:

```
switch(char, byte, short or int expression) {
    case constant: statements;
        break;

    case constant: statements;
        break;

    ......

    default:    statements;
}
```

The expression for a switch statement must be char, byte, short, or int. The keyword case must be followed by a constant with one of the aforementioned types.

The switch statement expression will be evaluated and compared with each case constant. Each *case* constant is converted to int before the comparison. If a match is found, the statements with the matching case label will be executed. Otherwise, the statement labeled default: will be executed. You should always add a break after each case (this will be explained later in the chapter). Otherwise, execution will "fall through" to the next statement.

Suppose you want to create a simple menu for your program. You can use the switch statement as follows:

```java
import java.io.*;

class AcronymDict
{

    public static void main(String args[])
    {
        char choice;

        System.out.println("Select one of the following
acronyms.");
        System.out.println("a. AWT");
        System.out.println("b. API");
        System.out.println("c. VM\n\n");
        System.out.print("Choice ==> ");
        System.out.flush();

        try
        {
            switch (choice = (char)System.in.read())
            {
                case 'a': System.out.println("AWT - Abstract Windows
Toolkit");
                            break;

                case 'b': System.out.println("API - Application
Program Interface");
                            break;

                case 'c': System.out.println("VM - Virtual
Machine");
                            break;

                default: System.out.println("Invalid Choice (IC)");
            }

        }
```

```
        catch (IOException e)
        {
            System.out.println(e.toString());
        }
    }
    }
```

(The try-catch statement is described in Chapter __.)

`while` Statement

When a `while` statement is executed, its Boolean expression is evaluated. If the Boolean expression is true, the statement or block below a `while` statement will be repeatedly executed until the expression becomes false. Otherwise, the statement or block below the while statement will never be executed. The format of a `while` statement is as follows (the curly brackets, {}, are optional if there is only one statement in the block):

```
    while (boolean expression)
    {
        statements
    }
```

```
    For example,
int i;
boolean isEven = false;

// Keeps generating a random number from 0 - 50. Exits the while
// loop when an even number is generated.
while (isEven == false)
{
    i = (int) (Math.random() * 50);
    if (i % 2 == 0)
        isEven = true;
}
```

do **Statement**

The do statement is somewhat similar to the while statement except the statement or block below a do statement will be executed **at least** once:

```
do {
    statements
}
while (boolean expression);
```

The while statement example can use a do statement instead:

```
int i;
boolean isEven = false;

// Keeps generating a random number from 0 - 50. Exits the do
// loop when an even number is generated.
do {
    i = (int) (Math.random() * 50);
    if (i % 2 == 0)
    isEven = true;
}
while (isEven == false);
```

for **Statement**

Generally, the for statement is used when you know in advance how many iterations you would like a block of code to execute. The general format of a for statement is:

```
for (expression1; boolean expression; expression2) {
    statements
}
```

expression1 initializes the variables of the for statement (ie. loop counter). The *boolean expression* in the middle specifies a condition. If the condition is true, the statement or blocks after the for statement will be executed. `expressionexe2` will be executed after one iteration of the `for` loop. It is often used to increment the `for` loop variables.

Any of these expressions is optional, but the semicolon must be present. For example, if the Boolean expression in the middle is omitted, the `for` loop will become an infinite loop, which is equivalent to:

```
while (true) {
   ......
}
```

The `for` statement is equivalent to:

```
expression1;

while (boolean expression) {
   statements
   expression2;
}
```

except if there is a `continue` statement in the statement block (see the `continue` statement section).

Another difference between the `for` and `while` loop is that any variables declared in the initialization phase of a `for` loop have scope which is limited to the statement block of the `for` loop. It is an error to refer to these variables outside of the `for` loop. A `while` loop does not have any special initialization phase, so it manipulates variables declared outside the scope of its statement block.

Suppose you want to create an animation applet. You need to load several image frames (i.e., gif files). Here is some codes that does the job:

```
public void loadFrames (Image frames[], String frameDir) {
    for (int i=0; i<frames.length; i++) {
        frames[i] = getImage(getCodeBase(), frameDir
            + "/T" + i + ".gif");
    }
}
```

break **Statement**

A break statement changes the flow of execution by jumping from one statement to another. It can only be used in a switch or an iteration (while, do, for) statement block. The format of a break statement is:

break *label*;

where *label* is optional.

If no label is present, a break statement will cause control to exit the switch or the iteration block in which the break statement is located. We have seen an example of this in a switch block.

If a break statement is labeled, control will pass to the statement with the specified label after the associated finally block (see Chapter 9), if present, is executed. The specified label must be placed within an enclosing iteration block. For example, the following code searches a two-dimensional matrix for items in a one-dimensional array. It returns the number of items in the array that are present in the matrix. Notice that as soon as an item is found, the search for that item stops.

```
// search matrix for targets. Returns number of targets found
// in matrix.
public int searchMatrix(int[][] matrix, int[] targets) {
    int numOfMatch=0;    // number of match found.
```

```
    for (int nTarget=0; nTarget < targets.length; nTarget++) {
nextTarget:
    for (int i=0; i<matrix.length; i++) {
        for (int j=0; j<matrix[0].length; j++) {
            if (matrix[i][j] == target[nTarget])  {
            numOfMatch++;
            break nextTarget;
        }
      }
     }
    }


    return numOfMatch;
    }
```

N O T E   Although the code looks a little bit complex, this is what you use labelled break statements for; one doesn't need a labelled break statement unless one has nesting, and nesting is by nature complex. The labelled break statement provides a convenient way to escape from a deeply nested loop without having to introduce additional complexity to the code.

continue **Statement**

A continue statement is similar to a break statement except that it is only used in iteration statements (and not in a switch statement). Also, instead of breaking out from a block, a continue statement passes control to the end of the block in which it is located. The format of a continue statement is:

continue *label*;

The label is optional. However, if no label is presented, control passes to the end of the block in which the `continue` statement is located. If `continue` is located in a try block and followed by a `finally` statement, statements in the `finally` block will be executed before control is passed to the end of the block. (See Chapter 9 for the `finally` statement.)

If a `continue` statement is labeled, the label must be enclosed in the iteration statement. Otherwise, control will pass to the end of the nearest enclosing iteration block.

When a `continue` statement is used in a while or do block, the boolean expression of the while or `do` statement will be evaluated immediately after `continue`. When a `continue` statement is used in a `for` block, the expression$_{exe\_after\_one\_iteration}$ will be executed before the Boolean expression. This is the difference between a `for` and a `while` statement when `continue` is used.

Suppose you are writing a class that randomly generates six lotto numbers. You can make use of the following code:

```
class Lottery {
    int luckyNums[]; // an array (unallocated) of lucky numbers

    // constructor
    Lottery (int nPick) {
        luckyNums = new int [nPick];    // allocates memory
    }

    // randomly generate lucky numbers
    public void pick() {
        int num;

        for (int i=0; i<luckyNums.length; )
        // i will only be incremented if num, generated in the
        // current iteration, has not been picked. Therefore, the
        // third expression is omitted.
        {
```

```
        num = (int) (Math.random() * 53) + 1;
        if (duplicate(i, num))
        {
            // num will not be assigned to luckyNums and i will
            // not be incremented.
            continue;
        }

        luckyNums[i++] = num;

        // continue here.
    }
}

// Return true if num has been picked. Otherwise, return
// false.
private boolean duplicate (int nPick, int num) {
    for (int i=0; i<nPick; i++) {
        if (luckyNum[i] == num)
            return true;
    }

    return false;
}

}
```

return **Statement**

A return statement is used by a method or constructor (see Chapter 8) to return control to its caller. It usually occurs at the end of a method or constructor.

If a method has a return type `void` or a constructor has no return type, a `return` statement is optional. For example, the constructor of the Lottery class in the `continue` section has no `return` statement.

You may also return "early" from a method as a way of preventing the rest of the method from being executed. This saves a level of indentation, allowing for more readable code than embedding the whole body in an `if` clause:

```
void uglyFoo (int x) {
   if (x <= 20) {
      // do stuff with x that assumes (x <= 20)
      // ... now the whole body is indented an extra level
      ...
      return;
   } else return;
}
void betterFoo (int x) {
   if (x > 20) {
      return;    // early return
   }
   // do stuff with x that assumes (x <= 20)
}
```

If a method or constructor is declared with a return type (i.e. ,Boolean, int[]), the `return` statement must return the appropriate type. See the examples in the `break` and `continue` statement sections.

If a `return` statement is enclosed in a `try` (see Chapter 9) block, and followed by a `finally` (see Chapter 9) statement, statements in the `finally` block will be executed before control is returned to the caller.

Summary

Control flow statements allow us to specify actions from a higher-level point-of-view than simply a sequential list of instructions. We need these statements in order to specify conditional, repetitive, and/or noncontiguous execution of our code. Java's control flow constructs are essentially similar to those provided by C, with only slight differences, including labelled break and continue statements, and the lack of a goto statement. These subtle changes are part of Java's overall philosophy of takintg a higher-level, more abstract view of programming than that afforded by C.

We now move on to one of the most powerful and revolutionary aspects of Java: its implementation of object-oriented programming.

JAVA
PROGRAMMING
BASICS

Classes, Variables, Methods, and Interfaces—Object-Oriented Programming in Java

In Chapter 1, we observed that we can analyze real-world systems and problems and model them as a collection of objects. We define general classes of objects, gradually add more specific subclasses that inherit their characteristics, and add specific characteristics of their own.

Once we have analyzed a problem or system from an object-oriented point of view and designed a model of that problem or system, an object-oriented programming language gives us a formalized way of expressing that model and its constituent parts.

This chapter will revisit some of the concepts introduced in Chapter 1, examining Java's own implementation of the object-oriented paradigm.

Classes

When you write a Java program, all your code is contained within class definitions. Recall that in object-oriented parlance, a *class* is a description of a general category of objects that share certain attributes and behavior. In Java, we refer to these attributes as *variables*, and the behavior as *methods*. All variables and methods belonging to a class are declared within the definition of that class. Note that this adheres to the concept of encapsulation discussed in Chapter 1. Here is the general form for the definition of a class:

```
class declaration {
    variable declarations
    method declarations
}
```

Actually, Java allows you to intersperse variable declarations with method declarations, even if the methods make forward references to variables declared later in the class. It is better style, however, to place all the variable declarations first and to follow them with the method declarations, as it makes your code much easier to read.

Parts of a Class Declaration

The *class declaration* denotes the identity of the class. It proclaims not only the name of that class, but also its accessibility and the name of the class that it extends, that is, the class from which it inherits characteristics. (parameters within brackets ([ ]) are optional.)

```
[classModifiers] class ClassName [extends SuperClass]
            [implements Interface1, ... ,InterfaceN] {
    // class body (variable and method declarations).
}
```

classModifiers

One or more *class modifiers* specify the accessibility of the class, as well as information about to what extent the variables and methods defined in this class will be visible in classes derived from it. The class modifiers may be omitted entirely, in which case objects of this class can only be declared and accessed by other classes in the same package, and this class may also be subclassed within this package. There are three possible class modifiers: `public`, `abstract`, and `final`.

public

If a class is declared as `public`, then this class has global accessibility. This means that any class defined in any package may declare and access objects of this class. If a class is not explicitly declared as `public`, then accessibility is limited to within this package.

A class declared as `public` must be the only `public` class declared in its source file. Furthermore, the name of the source file must be the same as the name of the `public` class, with the `.java` extension added. For example, a class declared as:

```
public class MyClass { ... }
```

must live in a source file called `MyClass.java`, and it must be the only `public` class declared within that source file.

You declare a class as `public` when you want that class to be globally accessible. In general, it's a good idea to declare your applets as `public` so that anyone who comes across your Web pages can run your applets. In addition, you may declare packages of related classes, which are intended to provide some general functionality, very likely for reuse by many different programs. In order for these classes to be accessible from outside that package, you must declare them as `public`. Note, however, that not all of the classes in such a package may be intended for use from the outside; some may be intended only for internal use. You would declare those classes with the default access (i.e., you would leave off the `public` keyword), and they would thus be invisible outside the package. Notice how this conforms to the concept of data-hiding, described in Chapter 1, which is central to the object-oriented approach.

abstract

An `abstract` class is a class that contains one or more `abstract` methods. This may sound like a circular definition, but the following explanation should clear things up.

Sometimes you declare a class for which you want to declare a certain method, but you really want the internal details of that method's implementation to be different for each subclass. For example, consider the class `java.awt.Image`. It makes sense to declare a class for displayable bitmapped images that is independent of any particular file format—GIF, JPEG, or some as-yet-undefined standard. There are certain things you need to do with an image regardless of the file format, such as get its width or height. Clearly, however, the implementation of these operations is going to differ for each image format.

In cases like these, it is clear that you need to defer the definition of such methods to subclasses. To do this, you simply leave the definition blank and declare it as an `abstract` method. If a class contains one or more `abstract` methods, then the class itself must be declared as `abstract` or the compiler will flag it as an error.

You cannot directly instantiate an object of an `abstract` class. In order to use an object with the characteristics described in a given `abstract` class, you must create a subclass that includes definitions for the methods left blank in the `abstract` class. You can then instantiate objects of the subclass.

`abstract` classes provide Java with what object-oriented programmers call *pure polymorphism*. In pure polymorphism, there are classes (`abstract` classes) that cannot themselves be instantiated, whose purpose is to serve as a base class for a group of related classes. These base classes are so generic that it is hard, or even impossible, to define the details of their behavior. The details are left to the subclasses, and each subclass may implement these behaviors differently. Thus, we start with no implementation, and we end up with multiple distinct implementations. Hence, the term *pure polymorphism*.

Like any other classes, `abstract` classes may be declared as `public` or with the default access, in which case they will only be visible within the package.

final

Classes declared as `final` may not be subclassed. You may have noticed that this is, in a sense, the opposite of an `abstract` class. The compiler will notice it, too; you may not declare a class as both `abstract` and `final`. If you make such a declaration, it will be flagged as an error by the compiler.

At first glance, it is not obvious why you might want to declare a class as `final`, thereby limiting its ability to take advantage of inheritance, one of the most crucial features of object-oriented programming. There are two very good reasons you might want to do this. One concerns efficiency; as we shall see, it is possible for subclasses to *override* the methods defined in their parent classes. Thus, when a method of a given class is called, it is not possible to determine at compile time which version of that method will be executed: the version of the method defined in that class or an overriding method of a subclass with the same name and parameter types. This must be determined dynamically at run-time, *each time* that the section of code is run, depending on tables generated when the object is instantiated. Each time this determination is made, it is conceivable that it could require the loading of a class not previously resident in memory. There may be a performance cost associated with loading the new class. A `final` class, however, may not be subclassed. Because this guarantees that its methods will not be overridden, the instructions comprising the method may be *inlined* into the compiled code, eliminating the need to make a decision and possibly load a new class while the program is running.

The second reason for declaring a class as `final` concerns both security and quality assurance. If you have specified that a class has certain behavior, you may not want to allow anyone to modify that behavior by subclassing it and overriding its methods. Declaring the class as `final` prevents all subclassing and allows you to guarantee the behavior of your class with respect to both functionality and security.

ClassName

A *class name* is an identifier, and as such it must obey the naming rules specified in Chapter 6. Class names within the same package must be unique. Additionally, if you import classes from another package, the class names you declare in your package must not conflict with the names in the imported package.

By convention, Java programmers capitalize the first character of a class name, as well as the first character of each new word within the name, for example: `ThisClass`, `ThatClass`, and `TheOtherClass`. This convention, while not required by the language or the compiler, provides the convenience of distinguishing class names from variable names, which typically begin with lowercase letters. This makes your code easier to read.

extends *SuperClass*

This clause specifies the class from which this class inherits— that is, its *immediate superclass*, or alternatively, its *parent class*. You can think of the subclass as *extending* the functionality of the parent class, hence the keyword `extends`. Remember, Java has only *single inheritance*, so you can only specify one superclass in the `extends` clause. Recall also that if you have declared a class as `final`, then it cannot be subclassed—that is, it cannot appear in any class's `extends` clause.

If you omit the `extends` clause, your class will inherit by default from a built-in class called `Object`. Class `Object` is the root of all classes and does not inherit from any other class.

Inheritance, as we have pointed out, is one of the central concepts of OOP. Like any good object-oriented language, Java gives you the power to *control* inheritance, that is, to specify, either explicitly or by default, which features of a class will or will not be visible within its subclasses and which methods they may or may not override. By default, a class inherits all fields (variables and methods), except constructors, from its superclass. Other than constructors, all variables and methods are inherited, although as we shall see, those declared as `private` will be invisible to any classes inheriting them. Although constructors cannot be inherited, we shall see later how a subclass can access its parent's constructors.

implements *Interface1, ... , InterfaceN*

Although Java has only single inheritance, the designers of the language were sensitive to the fact that there are times when programmers need the functionality provided by multiple inheritance. In recognition of this, they provided the *interface* mechanism, which provides some of the functionality of multiple inheritance while avoiding the circularity issues and other complexities and dangers that true multiple inheritance incurs. We will discuss interfaces in detail later in this chapter. At this point, the key things to notice are:

- A class can only *extend* one superclass, but it can *implement* as many interfaces as you please or none at all.

- The interfaces are specified in the class declaration, after the `implements` keyword, as a comma-separated list.

- The `implements` clause is optional; if your class does not implement any interfaces, you can omit the `implements` clause entirely.

Variables

Simply put, *variables* hold data. An object-oriented way of expressing this is to say that variables embody the *state* of a given object. Generally speaking, variables come in two flavors: there are *instance variables*, whose data pertains to individual objects of a class, and there are *static variables*—sometimes called *class variables* —whose data pertains to all objects of a given class. Each individual object of a given class is called an *instance*, or an *instantiation*, of that class. When you create a specific object of a class, you are said to *instantiate* an object of that class. When you instantiate an object of a class, space is allocated for that object's instance variables. Each object that you instantiate has space allocated independently for its instance variables.

`static` variables, on the other hand, are created only *once* and are shared by all objects of a given class and any inheriting subclasses. No matter how many objects of that class you create, there will be only one copy of the static variables belonging to that class. For example, in the class `java.lang.Integer`, there is a variable `MAX_VALUE`, which is declared as `static`. This variable reflects the largest value an `Integer` is allowed to have. Because this number is the same no matter how many `Integer` objects you instantiate, it makes sense to allocate memory for only one copy of this variable, and that is in fact what is done.

To refer to the instance variables of an object, you use the name of the specific instantiation, followed by a period, followed by the name of the instance variable. For example, suppose you have a class called `StarShip`, one of whose instance variables is named `powerRemaining`. You have instantiated a `StarShip` object called `excalibur` and another called `meridien`. You can refer to the `powerRemaining` of these instances as `excalibur.powerRemaining` and `meridien.power-Remaining`, respectively.

To refer to static variables, you may either refer to them by the class name, followed by a period, followed by the variable name or you can substitute the name of any instance of that class for the class name; the result will be the same. For example, if we have declared in class `Starship` a static variable called `maxSpeed`, then we may refer to it as `StarShip.maxSpeed`, or `excalibur.maxSpeed`, or `meridien.maxSpeed`. We will get the same value, and any changes we make will affect all objects of class `StarShip`.

Within a class definition, instance variables and static variables belonging to that class can be referred to without qualifying them. For example, within the class `Starship`, we can refer simply to `powerRemaining` or `maxSpeed`. As we shall see, however, we cannot make such references to instance variables from within `static` methods.

The Three Special Variables: `this`, `super`, and `null`

Each object has three built-in variables, represented by the keywords `this`, `super`, and `null`. `this` is an alias to the object itself. Because the code you write within a class is written from the point of view of a single object (except `static` methods, as we shall see) and because there may be many objects of that class instantiated with different names, you need to have a name by which you can refer, within the non-`static` methods of a class, to the current object itself—that is, the object currently performing this method.

Within a class definition, you may refer to the instance variables of that class without specifying an object. For example, within the declaration of the class StarShip, we can simply refer to powerRemaining, although there is an implicit this. in front of the name of the variable (this.power-Remaining). For the most part, you don't need to explicitly type the this. However, there are certain circumstances when you need to use this explicitly.

Consider the example below. this.n is an instance variable of the class, while no dot is a local variable of anyMethod(). The explicit this is necessary to distinguish between the local variable i and instance variable this.i.

super is an alias to an object's immediate superclass (the class named in the extends clause for this class). Typically, because variables in the superclass are inherited by the subclass (unless rendered inaccessible by the keyword private), you simply refer to those variables without qualification as instance variables of the local class. However, it is possible to declare an instance variable in a subclass with the same name as an instance variable in its superclass. The variable defined in the subclass will then mask or "shadow" the variable defined in the superclass. If you want to refer explicitly to the variable defined in the superclass, you use the keyword super, as shown in example below.

```
class SupCls  {
  int i=10;  // i is initialized on instantiation
}

class Cls extends SupCls  {
    int i, j;

      public void anyMethod (int i)  {
        this.i = i; // explicit "this" is needed because there
                    // is a conflict on name.

        j = super.i;    // j = 10

      }

}
```

The keywords this and super can only be used within a non-static method. When we discuss static methods later in this chapter, it will become clear why this is the case.

When you first declare an object, it has no value until it is initialized. Before initialization, the object has the default value of null, which essentially means, "no value." There are times when you will want to explicitly assign the value of null to an object—for example, to terminate dynamic data structures such as trees and lists. Structures like these may grow or shrink in size, with no preset bounds. You use null-valued objects as markers for the endpoints of these structures. Another case in which it is useful to assign null to an object is the case of a Thread. To stop a Thread in Java, you can set its value to null.

NOTE

You can assign the value null to objects of any class but not to methods or variables of primitive data types, such as ints, floats or chars.

Consider the declaration:

```
String str;
```

After this declaration, str is considered to be the *handle* of String object. The concept of a *handle* is similar to the idea of a pointer in C or C++. Unlike a pointer, however, a handle is not a physical address. After the preceding declaration, there is no memory allocation to str, and thus str is considered a *null handle*. Graphically, we represent a null handle using a notation borrowed from electrical circuit design, the symbol for the electrical *ground*:

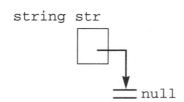

WARNING

When we use the word *handle*, we are not using it in the sense that it is used by Macintosh and Windows C or C++ programmers. This is *not* a "pointer to a pointer," as the word handle often implies on those platforms. In Java, a handle is merely a reference to an object. Again, there is no implied physical address.

Parts of a Variable Declaration

The general form of a variable declaration is:

```
[variableModifiers] type variableName [= initialValue];
```

Variable Modifiers

Variable modifiers specify the accessibility of variables declared at the class level. You do not need to specify variable modifiers if you intend for a given variable to have the default accessibility. By default, a variable defined in a given class will be:

- inherited by and visible within any classes declared *within the package* that extend this class
- accessible to all other classes within the package
- inaccessible outside the package

If you intend otherwise, you can indicate this by specify one of the following: public, protected, private, static, or final.

public

A variable declared as public has the same accessibility as its class. Intuitively, it is clear that a variable's accessibility cannot be wider than that of the class in which it is declared. (Thus, in a class with default access, a public variable will be accessible only within the package, but in a class with public access, a `public` variable will be accessible everywhere.) Variables declared as `public` are inherited by any subclasses derived from the class in which they are declared.

protected

Variables declared as `protected` are accessible by all classes within the package containing the class in which they are declared. However, outside the package, `protected` variables can only be accessed by subclasses of the class in which they are declared. In other words, `protected` variables are relieved of the default restrictions on inheritance, but they retain restrictions with regard to access by unrelated classes outside the package.

WARNING

This is not the same thing as a protected variable in C++. In C++, `protected` variables are only accessible in a given class and its subclasses. Java adds the concept of the package, inside which a `protected` variable is accessible to all classes, even those not derived from the one in which the variable is declared.

private

`private` variables can only be accessed within the class in which they are declared. This restriction extends to derived classes as well. Even in a subclass of the class in which they are declared, private variables are inaccessible.

static

Variables declared as `static` are instantiated only once and shared by all objects of the class in which they are declared and by any inheriting subclasses. Note that there is an important distinction between `static` variables, which belong to the class as a whole, and instance variables, which are separately created for each object of the class that is instantiated and thus "belong" to that object. All variables not explicitly declared as `static` or `final` are instance variables.

The `static` storage class specifier may be combined with any of the access specifiers: `public`, `protected`, `private`, or the default.

final

Variables declared as `final` are, for all intents and purposes, constants. When a variable is declared as `final`, a value must be assigned to that variable immediately, in the declaration. Thereafter, the value of the so-called variable cannot be changed. It is often to declare a constant variable as `final static`.

NOTE

In addition to the modifiers we have described, the Java specification reserves the keywords `transient` and `volatile`. However, these two storage class specifiers are not yet implemented in version 1.0.

type

This simply states the type of this variable, which may be any primitive type or any array or object type, including an object of this class. Types were discussed in detail in Chapter 6.

variableName

The rules for naming variables were discussed in Chapter 6. As a matter of style, it is best to choose a variable name that starts with a lowercase letter, such as `counter`, `smallestValue`, or `myOtherDouble`.

[= initialValue]

As we have pointed out, a variable can optionally be initialized on the same line on which it is declared. It is a good idea to do this whenever possible, because it is an error to try to access the value of a variable that has not yet been initialized. You can initialize a variable to the value of another already-initialized variable or any expression that evaluates to the appropriate type. For example:

```
int myInt = 6;
int yourInt = myInt + 14;
myObject m = new myObject();
int[] foo = {1, 2, 3, 4, 5};
```

Methods

All executable statements in Java are contained within methods (for an exception, see the sidebar, "Static Blocks"). All methods reside inside a class. This is a stricter approach to object-orientedness than that taken by C++, where functions may exist independently from objects if the programmer so chooses.

Static Blocks

There is one exception to the rule that all executable code must reside within methods. Java programmers may use static blocks to specify some code that must occur as a given class is instantiated. Typically, this code is used to initialize static variables that may not be able to be fully initialized on their declaration line, such as arrays.

The static block begins with the keyword static, after which it is enclosed by curly braces—{}. Inside the static block, only static variables may be referenced, although variables local to the block may be declared.

Consider the following example:

```
class Foo {
   static double[] theCosines = new double[100];

   static {         // this is the static block
      for (int i = 0; i < 100; i++) {
         theCosines[i] = Math.cos((double) i / 100.0);
      }
   }

   ...
}
```

Notice that the static block only references static variables and methods. Even the local variable i is implicitly static because it is declared locally within a static block. (Because it is declared within that block, however, it is not accessible outside the block.)

This static block is necessary if we expect there to be specific values in the array Foo.theCosines without necessarily instantiating any specific objects of class Foo.

Argument Passing

When you call a method, you send it information by passing that information as a *parameter* (also called an *argument*) to that method. When the method is called, whatever is passed to these parameters is substituted for them inside the method's execution.

Parameters of primitive types (such as int, float, char, and boolean) are passed by *value*. This means that a local copy is created with the same value as the actual parameter; if you modify the parameter within the method, you only modify the local copy, and the change has no effect on the state of the actual parameter, outside of the method itself.

Object and array types, on the other hand, are passed by *reference.* This means that inside the method, when you refer to that parameter, you are referring to the actual object or array that was passed in—*there is no local copy,* as there would be in a call by value. The result of this is that if you make changes to the state of an object passed in as a reference parameter, then the changes you make will affect the actual object, and therefore those changes will persist even after your method exits.

When you declare a method, you state explicitly what types of parameters it expects to receive. This is done through the method's argument list, the syntax of which will be discussed soon, when we look in detail at the parts of a method declaration.

Note that in object-oriented programming, you don't have to pass a method *all* the information it requires through its parameter list. This is because the method already knows about—and has access to—all the instance variables and static variables of the class in which it is defined. The only items that need to be specified in the parameter list are those to which the method does not already have access, such as the instance variables of other objects or those that may be different each time the method is called.

The following example illustrates several issues of relevance to parameter passing:

```
class Foobar {
   double d = 3.14;

   public void fooMethod (double x, Foobar other) {
      x = x * 2.0;    // no effect outside this method
      d = x * other.d;
      other.d = 0.0;    // has global effects
   }

}
```

```
public class MainClass {
    public static void main(String args[]) {
        double ourDouble = 28.8;
        Foobar ourFoobar = new Foobar();
        Foobar ourOtherFoobar = new Foobar();
        ourFoobar.d = 14.4;
        ourOtherFoobar.d = 19.2;
        System.out.println("Before the call to fooMethod(...)");
        System.out.println("  ourDouble is " + ourDouble);
        System.out.println("  ourFoobar.d is " + ourFoobar.d);
        System.out.println(" ourOtherFoobar.d is " +
        ourOtherFoobar.d);
        System.out.println("");

// Here's the method call of interest...
    ourFoobar.fooMethod(ourDouble, ourOtherFoobar);
    System.out.println("After the call to fooMethod(...)");
    System.out.println("   ourDouble is " + ourDouble);
    System.out.println("   ourFoobar.d is " + ourFoobar.d);
    System.out.println(" ourOtherFoobar.d is " +
    ourOtherFoobar.d);
    }
}
```

The output of this program will be:
```
Before the call to fooMethod(...)
    ourDouble is 28.8
    ourFoobar.d is 14.4
    ourOtherFoobar.d is 19.2
After the call to fooMethod(...)
    ourDouble is 28.8
    ourFoobar.d is 1105.92
    ourOtherFoobar.d is 0
```

When we call ourFoobar.fooMethod(...), we don't need to
pass it a value for d. The object ourFoobar already knows about

d, because d is an instance variable of the class Foobar, and any instantiation of a Foobar knows the value of its own d. What it *doesn't* know is what number we want to pass to x in its fooMethod(...). Nor does ourFoobar know anything about the values of instance variables in ourOtherFoobar, such as ourOtherFoobar.d. This is why we have to pass these items through the argument list of fooMethod(...).

Notice that the changes made to x within the method do not have an effect on ourDouble, because ourDouble is a primitive type and is passed *by value*. The changes we make to other.d, however, have global effects on the state of the object ourOtherFoobar, because, being an object, it is passed *by reference*.

Overloading Methods

The *signature* of a method is defined by its argument list—specifically, by the number, order, and type of each argument. Methods are distinguished by the combination of their name and their signature. In Java, as in C++, it is possible to create *overloaded methods*. These are methods that have the same name but different signatures. It is often useful to provide similar functionality for many different types of arguments and to give the methods that provide that functionality the same name. When the methods are called, there is no ambiguity as to which method will be executed, because methods with the same name are distinguished from one another by their signatures.

For example, in the class java.lang.String, the following two methods are defined:

```
public static String valueOf(int i){ ... }
public static String valueOf(float f){ ... }
```

The method String.valueOf(...) is intended to take whatever primitive data type is passed to it as a parameter and convert that parameter to a `String` representing its value (for example, from the floating-point number `2.4` to the three-character `String` `"2.4"`). It's clear that one needs to go through different steps to make a `String` out of an `int` than to make a `String` out of a `float`. This is where method overloading comes in handy. If you call this function with an `int` as a parameter, it will use the first version listed above; if you call it with a `float`, it will use the second version. The compiler uses the signature to determine which version to execute.

Earlier, we said that abstract methods allow Java to provide pure polymorphism. Method overloading is the mechanism by which Java provides another type of polymorphism, *ad hoc polymorphism.*, in which the compiler decides which version of a method to call based on the signature with which it is called. Contrast this with the pure polymorphism provided by abstract types, where the decision as to which version of a function to use may often need to be deferred until run time.

Overriding Methods

Often, it is useful to have a subclass that defines its own version of a given method, with the same name and signature as that in its superclass. This is called *method overriding*. The new method in the subclass is called the *overriding method*, and the method in the superclass is said to be *overridden*.

Inheritance is useful because it allows the programmer to reuse existing code in defining new classes. Method overriding provides inheritance with needed flexibility. Because of method overriding, you can keep only those methods of the superclass that are appropriate in the subclass and provide a new version of any whose implementation you wish to alter. `abstract` classes rely on method overriding in order to provide pure polymorphism. Not only `abstract` methods may be overridden, however; any non-`static`, non-`final` method in a non-`static`, non-`final` class may be overridden when the class is subclassed.

Constructors

As we have noted, mere declaration of an object does not allocate space for the object's instance variables. When an object is declared, it has a value of `null` until it is instantiated. It is an error to attempt to access the instance variables of an object before it has been initialized. You instantiate an object with the `new` operator. This can be done on the same line as the declaration, for example:

```
Planet p = new Planet();
```

If the use of `Planet()` on the right-hand side of the assignment looks like a method call, that's because it is. It is a call to a special method defined for every class, called a constructor.

A *constructor* is a special method that shares the same name as the class in which it is defined. Its job is to initialize the instance variables of an object when the object is first instantiated. Although in most respects a constructor is like any other method you define, there are certain things that distinguish constructors from other methods:

1. **Constructors have no return types.** A constructor has an implicit return type of `void`. Hence, no `return` statement is required in the body of a constructor.

2. **Constructors are not inherited by subclasses.** Each subclass uses its own constructor, whose name is the same as the class. Although constructors are not inherited, it is possible on the first line of a constructor to explicitly call the constructor of your superclass, by using the `super` keyword as a constructor call. We'll discuss this shortly.

3. **Constructors are invoked differently than ordinary methods.** When you invoke an ordinary method, you qualify it with the name of the object to which you are sending the message to perform that method; for example:

```
str.substring(5);
```

A constructor invocation, on the other hand, needs no
qualification. You simply invoke the constructor with the
constructor name (i.e., the name of the class), typically
preceded by the `new` operator. The `new` operator indicates
that some new storage is being allocated. A constructor is
invoked by the constructor name (i.e., the class name),
usually after the new operator:

```
String str = new String("I am a string.");
```

4. **A constructor may not throw an exception.** If a
   constructor calls a method that could throw an exception, it
   must be caught and handled within the constructor. We will
   cover exception handling in Chapter 9.

In other ways, constructors are like ordinary methods. One very
useful implication of this is that, like ordinary methods,
constructors can be overloaded. Like ordinary overloaded
methods, overloaded constructors are distinguished by the
signature embodied by their argument lists. This allows you to
provide flexibility in constructing objects in your class. For
example, the class `java.lang.String` provides no less than
seven overloaded constructors. Here are a few of them:

`String()`	If given no parameters, the `String()` constructor constructs an empty string.
`String(String)`	Given a `String` as a parameter, this will construct a new `String`, which is a copy of the one passed in. (A constructor like this is called a *copy constructor*, and many classes use them.)
`String(char[])`	This constructs a new `String` from an array of characters.

`this()` as a Constructor

Because constructors can be overloaded, it is often convenient
within a constructor to call another constructor for the same

class. It is a good idea, for example, to provide a default constructor for your class; that is, a constructor with no arguments. Imagine you have already defined a constructor `MyClass(int i, int j)`, and you want the default case to be equivalent to `MyClass(0, 0)`. There is no need to duplicate the code you already provided in `MyClass(int i, int j)`. Instead, you would define your default constructor as follows:

```
MyClass () {        // default constructor -- no arguments
    this(0, 0);     // must be first statement
}
```

The call to `this(0, 0)` invokes the constructor of the same class that has the signature `(int, int)`. The only place you can use the `this` keyword as a constructor call is within a constructor, and it must be the *first statement* of that constructor; otherwise it is an error, and the compiler will catch it.

`super()` as a Constructor

When you declare a derived class, you inherit instance variables from the superclass. Because the constructor for the derived class is not itself inherited, you need a way to initialize the inherited instance variables. You could initialize the inherited variables manually in your constructor—there are times when you may want to do this—but often, it is more convenient and appropriate to let the superclass take care of initializing these variables, especially if you have inherited `private` variables to which you do not have access. Fortunately, you are able to call the constructor for the superclass using the `super` keyword as a constructor call. Just as with the `this()` constructor, the `super()` constructor, if used, must appear as the *first statement* in the body of your constructor method:

```
class MyClass extends MySuperClass {
   double myDouble;
   MyClass(int i, int j, double d) {
      super(i, j);  // calls MySuperClass(i, j);
      myDouble = d; // wasn't initialized by super(...);
   }

   ...

}
```

You can declare a class without specifying a constructor. If your class inherits directly from another class and does not declare any instance variables of its own, then this is the appropriate thing to do. If you omit the constructor from your class, the Java compiler automatically generates a default constructor for that class, which simply calls the default constructor for the superclass:

```
class FinalFrontier extends Space {
   // no constructor supplied

   // compiler automatically generates:
   FinalFrontier() {
      super();  // calls Space();
   }
   ...
}
```

If, however, the immediate superclass does not have a constructor that takes no arguments, then a compiler error will result.

`private` Constructors

You can declare a constructor as `private` and then provide a `public static` method that calls the constructor and returns the constructed object. To create the object from outside the package, you call the `static` method. This is useful for checking the arguments for the constructor and allowing an exception to be thrown if they are incorrect. Remember, constructors themselves may not throw exceptions, but the `static` method described earlier may look at the arguments and, if they are correct, call the constructor; if they are incorrect, then the constructor never gets called, and the `static` method throws an exception instead. Exception handling is covered in Chapter 9.

Parts of a Method Declaration

The format of a method declaration is as follows:

```
[methodModifiers] resultType methodName ([argumentList])
 [Throws Exception1, ... , ExceptionN]
{
    // Method body
}
```

Method Modifiers

The method modifiers `public`, `protected` and `private` have essentially the same meanings as when they are used as variable modifiers. There are also several additional modifiers defined for methods, which we will discuss here. If no method modifiers are defined, then the default access is the same as for variables; methods with no modifiers are:

- inherited by, visible within, and able to be overridden by any classes declared *within the package* that extends this class
- visible to all other classes within the package
- inaccessible outside the package

public

public methods have the maximum accessibility allowed by the class in which they are declared. This means that if the class is declared as public, then any public methods contained therein are accessible everywhere, by every other class, whether in the same package or not. If the class is declared with default access, then public methods are accessible only to other classes within the package. In other words, unless the class is declared as public, declaring its methods as public does not change their access relative to the default.

protected

Again, unless the class is declared as public, the keyword protected does not signify anything other than default access. If, however, the class is declared as public, then protected methods may be accessed by any class within the package and by any derived class, whether in the same package or not. Derived classes, inside or outside the package, may also override these methods. Nonderived classes outside the package, however, may not call these methods. The main reason to declare a method as protected is to remove the default restrictions on the method's inheritance outside the package.

private

Like private variables, private methods are not accessible by classes other than the class in which they are declared, including derived classes.

static

We have seen that some variables are instance variables, and others are static. The same is true of methods. In accordance with the object-oriented notion of encapsulation, instance methods have access to the instance variables of a particular instantiation of an object. Instance methods are invoked using the name of the object as a qualifier, as in the following examples:

```
theObject.itsMethod(anArgument);

yourString = myString.replace('a', 'b');

while (!thisBook.finished()) {
   sleep[tonight++] = 0;
}
```

static methods, on the other hand, like static variables, are instantiated once for all objects of their class. As such, they cannot refer to instance variables, because instance variables belong to specific objects, not to the class as a whole. static methods can, however, access static variables. static methods are implicitly final and cannot be overridden by derived classes.

You can invoke a static method using either the name of the class as a qualifier or the name of any instantiated object of that class as a qualifier; the result is the same. In the following example, the three calls to String.valueOf(int) produce exactly the same results, because that method is defined as static in java.lang.String:

```
String myString = new String();
String otherString = new String();

myString = String.valueOf(4);            // These...
myString = myString.valueOf(4);          // ...are...
myString = otherString.valueOf(4);       // ...equivalent.
```

We mentioned earlier in this chapter that static methods may not use the keywords this and super. Now, it should be apparent why this is so. static methods are shared by all instantiations of the class and thus do not "belong" to any specific instantiation. Clearly, it makes no sense for such a method to make a reference to `this`. There could be a thousand or more objects that are instances of the class, all sharing this one `static` method. If we used the keyword `this` in a `static` method, *which* `this` are we referring to?

The case is similar with `super`. The `super` keyword refers specifically to *this* instance of this class as an instance of the superclass. `static` methods do not belong to any specific instance of the class, so the reference makes no sense. Additionally, the meaning of the `super` keyword presupposes that we know what level of inheritance we are at. Otherwise, what class is the superclass? It makes no sense to distinguish between the superclass and the subclass in a method whose scope spans all levels of inheritance. Thus, in a `static` method, both `this` and `super` are undefined.

A common mistake of a Java beginner is to reference non-`static` fields in a static method. For example:

```
public class Test {
    String str = "I am a string. "; // shorthand - constructor
                                     // is called implicitly

    public static void main(String args[]) {
        System.out.println(str);  // Wrong! str is a
                                  // non-static variable.

        System.out.println(this.str); // This won't work
                                      // either:
                                      // can't use "this" in
                                      // static method

    }
}
```

This mistake is most often made by programmers attempting to convert an applet into an application. We will describe a workaround for this problem in Chapter 11.

Notice that we do not explicitly call the constructor for `string` in creating `str`. The Java language, in order to treat strings more like "normal" types, allows this shorthand initialization for strings.

final

A `final` method cannot be overridden by derived classes. The `final` keyword may be combined with `public`, `private`, `protected`, or `static`, or it may be specified by itself to combine it with the default access specifier.

abstract

We introduced the concept of `abstract` methods early in the chapter, in order to explain `abstract` classes. The concept of an `abstract` class and that of an `abstract` method are intrinsically tied. Recall that an `abstract` method is declared, but no implementation is deferred to the subclasses. Here is an example of what the declaration for an abstract method looks like:

```
abstract void doThatVoodoo(String theMagicWords);
```

Because `abstract` methods only make sense in a context where they can be visibly inherited and overridden, it follows naturally that the `abstract` keyword cannot be combined with any method modifiers that restrict inheritance or overriding; in other words, if a method is declared `abstract`, it cannot be `private`, `static`, or `final`. By the same reasoning, it makes sense that because constructors are not inherited, they cannot be declared `abstract`.

native

As hard as we try to write platform-independent code, there are things that can only be done in a language that compiles to *native code*—instructions for a specific machine. Perhaps we have some interesting hardware device that we need to communicate with, or maybe we need to use a library of C function calls provided by a database package. Perhaps we have a particular method that is very computationally expensive and runs too slowly when interpreted by the virtual machine. We can optimize performance by writing such a method in a language such as C, which compiles to native machine instructions.

A `native` method is essentially a "callout" to a function written in another programming language. Currently, the only other languages for which Java supports `native` methods are C and C++, but it is expected that support for other languages will be provided in the future.

synchronized

Because Java is multithreaded, it is important that the language provide some sort of concurrency control. That is, there are some operations that can be performed in parallel without difficulty, but there are other operations—in particular, when multiple threads are involved in reading and writing the same shared data—that require some delicate handling. You declare a method as `synchronized` when you want a guarantee that only one thread may be executing this method at a given time. We will cover synchronized methods in slighty greater detail in Chapter 10, when we explore threads as part of the Java API.

returnType

All methods, except constructors, must be declared with a return type. If your method does not return any value, you must explicitly declare it with a return type of `void`.

WARNING

This is different from the case in C and C++, where a function that omits the return type from a declaration is implicitly declared with a return type of `int`. In C, it is poor style to omit the return type; in Java, it is an error.

A method may return any type, including object types and primitive types. Unless your method returns `void`, you must include a `return` statement in your method body, and it must match the return type specified in the method declaration. Methods returning `void` may omit the return statement entirely and will automatically return at the close of the method body; alternatively, a `return` statement may be specified within the method body, at which point execution of the method will cease and control will be returned to the calling method.

The compiler is very good at making sure your method returns a value. Even if you include an appropriate `return` statement in your method, the compiler traces any `if...then...else` statements in your method to make sure that there is no branch of control that could lead to the method terminating without a return statement.

```
class ManyHappyReturns {
   void macArthur(String s) {
      if (s.equals("I shall return.")) {
      return;  // early return -- OK
   }

      ... // statements
      return;    // this statement is optional
      }

      int wontCompile(Boolean b, Boolean t) {
      int i;
      double d;

      if (b) {
```

```
...
return;  // error: must return int
} else if (t) {

...
return d;  // error: d is not an int
} else if (i > 0) {
return i;  // OK
} else {

...
// (no return statement in this branch)
// error: all branches must...
// ... lead to a return statement ...
// ... unless return type is void.

   }

  }


}
```

methodName

Method names must follow the naming rules described in Chapter 6. Additionally, as a matter of style, it is a good idea to choose method names that start with lower case letters. This convention helps distinguish ordinary method calls from constructor calls, because constructors will be named after their class, and class names (also by convention) begin with upper-case characters.

```
justStandThere();           // method call, no arguments
doSomething(someArgument); // method call with arguments
Car myPorsche = new Car(java.awt.Color.black); // constructor
                                             // call

myRealCar = herBug.rebuild(); // calling a method with return
                              //  value
```

argumentList

This is a comma-separated list of the *parameters* (or *arguments*) this method expects to be passed. The entire list is enclosed in parentheses—(). The parentheses are required, even if your method takes no arguments. This enables the compiler to distinguish method declarations from variable declarations. Within the argument list, each parameter is preceded by its type. For arrays, you follow the type name with []. (Alternatively, you may use the C style of following the variable name with []. The following example shows both styles, but for consistency, you should choose one style and stick with it.)

```
void doItWith(String s, int[] myIntArray, double myDoubleArray[]) {
    // takes a String, internally called s
    // ... an array of ints, internally called myIntArray
    // ... and an array of doubles, internally called
    // myDoubleArray
}
```

throws Exception1, ... , ExceptionN

Defining the term *exception* is a little tricky. To define it as an error would be incorrect, because an exception and an error are two different things. We will discuss exceptions in Chapter 8, but for now, let's use the rough definition that an exception is an exceptional, and possibly erroneous, condition that arises during the execution of a program. It is generally expected that an exception will occur relatively infrequently. If your method does anything that might generate an exception, you must either handle that exception within your method or state in your method declaration that you do not handle it—that instead, you have chosen to "throw" that exception. The method that called your method must, in turn, choose whether to handle that exception or throw it, and so on.

If a method does not throw any exceptions, the entire `throws` clause may be omitted. If a method throws one or more exception types, the exception types are listed after the `throws` keyword, separated by commas.

Interfaces

An *interface* is essentially a special kind of `abstract` class in which you specify a set of constants and `abstract` methods that can be inherited by any class. A class that is designed to "inherit" an interface is said to *implement* that interface. Perhaps the most important feature of interfaces is that, whereas a class can only *extend* one superclass, it can *implement* any number of interfaces—or none at all. Interfaces thus allow objects to support common behaviors, although their internal implementations may differ greatly. Because they support these common behaviors, interfaces can present themselves as similar and interchangeable to outside entities requesting these behaviors. Their internal differences notwithstanding, their outside appearance with respect to these behaviors is the same; hence, the name interface.

In order to implement a given interface, the implementing class must do two things:

1. include that interface in the `implements` clause of its own class declaration

2. provide non-`abstract` definitions for *all* the methods declared in the interface

All methods declared in an interface are implicitly `abstract`. Thus, it is not necessary to include the keyword `abstract` in method declarations within an interface, although it is not an error to do so. Similarly, all "variables" declared in an interface are implicitly `static` and `final`—because they are conceived as constants—and the inclusion of these keywords in variable declarations is not necessary within an interface, although it is not an error. That said, it is not a bad idea to include these keywords in your variable and method declarations; being explicit improves the clarity of your code.

You can declare an interface that extends another interface. It will inherit all of the methods and variables defined in the interface that it extends. Unlike classes, an interface can extend multiple interfaces, inheriting all variables and methods defined therein. Any class that implements such an interface must provide definitions for all of the methods defined in that interface and all the interfaces it extends:

```
interface Simple1 {
    int a;
    void absMethod1();
}

interface Simple2 {
    String str;
    void absMethod2();
}


interface Combined extends Simple1, Simple2{
    void absMethod3();
}

// ImpClass is required to implement absMethod1(), absMethod2(),
// and absMethod3().  Otherwise, ImpClass would also need to
// be declared as an abstract class.

class ImpClass implements Combined {
    public absMethod1() {
        ...  // definition provided here
    }

    public absMethod2() {
```

```
    ...  // definition provided here
    }

    public absMethod3() {
        ...  // definition provided here
    }

    // other class methods
    ...
}
```

If a class `implements` an interface, then its subclasses inherit, and may override, the implemented methods (subject to any restrictions imposed by the access specifiers for that class). Additionally, if a class `implements` a given interface or set of interfaces, it is not necessary for those interfaces to be explicitly included in the `implements` clauses of any subclasses.

Interfaces as a Substitute for Multiple Inheritance

Multiple inheritance, often referred to as MI by acronym enthusiasts, is one of the most controversial features of many object-oriented languages. This is the idea that one class may be derived from more than one superclass. Java does not support multiple inheritance. In this sidebar we examine the reasons for this, as well as the alternative solution that Java supplies via interfaces.

Multiple inheritance, while providing a certain amount of convenience and flexibility, is also a source of complexity. Furthermore, unless managed very carefully, it is a potential breeding ground for programmer errors that can be hard to trace and debug.

There are two main categories of errors that can result from misuse of multiple inheritance: ambiguity and circularity. *Ambiguity* results when two or more ancestors of a class each define a variable or variables with the same name(s). For example, let's say you're writing in C++ and you declare a class Ancestor_1, in which there is a variable x and a method myMethod(), and another class Ancestor_2, which declares its own variable x and its own myMethod(). You then decide to declare a class Descendant that inherits from both of these ancestors. It therefore inherits two variables, both named x, and two methods, both named myMethod(). How can we know which x or which myMethod() we mean when the Descendant class refers to them? There is no need to go into the specific syntax here, but suffice it to say that the ambiguity in such cases is resolved by the programmer having to specify which x or myMethod() is intended whenever a reference to one of them is made in the derived class. This presupposes that the programmer *knows* there is an ambiguity and is aware of its source. As we shall see, this is not always easy.

Circularity results when a programmer attempts to define a class that inherits, directly or indirectly, from itself. Questions such as "If your ancestor is also your descendant, whose methods override whose?" result in a classic chicken-or-egg game that would destroy the clarity of the inheritance structure.

The problem with multiple inheritance is not that language designers can't deal with these scenarios—either by introducing coping mechanisms that place the burden of resolution on the programmer, as in the ambiguity situation, or, as in the case of the circularity scenario, disallowing them completely. Rather, the problem is for the programmer. If a class is descended from three ancestors and each of those ancestors is descended from three others, etc., and one of these problems somehow creeps into the inheritance structure, the difficulty of isolating the source of the problem becomes exponentially harder with each level of inheritance. If your code is poorly documented, you're in trouble.

Opinion among language experts is by no means unanimous as to whether the advantages of multiple inheritance outweigh its disadvantages. Many object-oriented languages do without it, and indeed, until 1988, even C++ did not support it. Java does not support multiple inheritance, but instead introduces the concept of interfaces.

Interfaces provide a solution for many of the cases in which multiple inheritance is desirable, while avoiding its pitfalls. Because interfaces do not supply implementations for the methods they declare, there is no ambiguity in resolving where the definitions for those methods come from. Because all variables defined in an interface are both `static` and `final`, effectively serving as constants, they too are unambiguous. Finally, because of the distinction between classes and interfaces—in a sense, two separate inheritance chains, each with appropriate limitations—hidden circularities are avoided: there is no way that a class could find itself a hidden ancestor of any of the interfaces it implements.

How Interfaces are Used in Java

A classic example of the type of situation in which interfaces are useful is provided by examining, briefly, the way in which Java implements threads. Recall that a Java applet `extends java.applet.Applet`. However, it is very often the case that you want your applet to run as a thread, allowing other threads to execute simultaneously so as to more efficiently use system resources. However, if your applet `extends java.applet.Applet`, it cannot also extend `java.lang.Thread`, because that would violate Java's restriction against multiple inheritance.

To solve this problem, the designers of Java provided an interface, called `java.lang.Runnable`. If your applet `implements` `Runnable`, you must define a method called `run()` and place the main code for your applet within this method. You then construct a `Thread` within your applet, passing `this` as a parameter to the `Thread()` constructor. The constructor for a `Thread` can take as a parameter any object that `implements` the `Runnable` interface. This constructor is defined as follows:

```
public Thread(Runnable target);
```

This constructor method constructs a `Thread` whose body, when it runs, is the `run()` method you provided in your applet. Notice that the parameter list of this constructor accepts an object of type `Runnable`. Here is the key to understanding how interfaces are used: If your applet `implements` `Runnable`, then your applet qualifies as an object of type `Runnable`. Any method, such as the constructor described earlier, that takes a `Runnable` as a parameter can accept your applet; when it calls the method(s) that are part of the `Runnable` interface—in this case only one method, `run()`—your applet has provided a method consistent with that request. It is as if there were an ordinary class called `Runnable` and your applet were derived from that class.

The `Runnable` interface is an excellent example for someone trying to understand interfaces for the first time, not only because it demonstrates a practical use for interfaces, but also because it illustrates an important concept in interface design, in fact an important principle in all programming, namely: *keep it simple*. There is only one method declared in the `Runnable` interface; thus, it is very easy to implement that interface in any class you design. If an interface were to define 20 methods, it's unlikely that anyone would consider it convenient to implement that interface. On the other hand, if those 20 methods were spread out among several different simpler interfaces, it would be no problem for the programmer to implement just those interfaces whose functionality was really necessary. Remember, you can implement as many or as few interfaces as you please.

Parts of an Interface Declaration

The general form for an Interface declaration is:

```
[interfaceModifiers] Interface InterfaceName
     [extends Interface1, ... InterfaceN] {

  variable declarations
  abstract method declarations

}
```

InterfaceModifiers

If declared without any modifiers, an interface is by default accessible only within the package. Otherwise, it can be `public` or `abstract`.

public

An interface declared as `public` is accessible to all classes everywhere, both inside and outside the package.

abstract

It is redundant to declare an interface as `abstract`, because all interfaces are inherently abstract. It is not, however, an error to explicitly declare an interface as `abstract`.

extends [*Interface1*, ... *InterfaceN*]

As we have pointed out, unlike a class, which can only `extend` one other class, an interface can `extend` as many interfaces as the programmer wants.

Summary

We've covered quite a bit of ground in this chapter. We have focused on bridging the gap between the abstract and the practical—taking the knowledge you gained in Chapter 1 about object-oriented programming concepts in general and bringing that knowledge to a practical examination of the specific ways in which these concepts are integrated into the structure of Java as a language.

We've seen how Java applies the notion of *encapsulation*, grouping data and methods together into classes. Also in the service of encapsulation, Java provides access specifiers (see Table 8.1), which allow the programmer to specify several levels of data hiding. Objects thus see as little as possible of the internal implementations of other objects, calling the other objects' own methods to operate on their instance variables and passing parameters as necessary.

NOTE

In Table 8.1, under **Variable** and **Method**, an assumption is made to save space and preserve legibility. The conditions described for *outside the package* only hold true if the class is `public`. If the class is not `public`, then no variables or methods in that class will be visible outside the package, regardless of their access specifiers.

Table 8.1 Access Specifiers

	Class	Variable	Method
public	• Accessible to all classes, in and out of the package	• Visible to all classes with access to this class, in and out of the package	• Visible to all classes with access to this class, in and out of the package
		• Visible in all classes derived from this one, in and out of the package	• Visible in all classes derived from this one, in and out of the package
			• Can be overridden in all classes derived from this one, in and out of the package

Table 8.1 Access Specifiers (continued)

	Class	Variable	Method
`protected`	Not applicable	• *Inside the package*: visible to all classes • *Outside the package*: visible only to classes derived from this one	• *Inside the package*: visible to all classes and can be overridden by classes derived from this one • *Outside the package*: visible only to classes derived from this one and can be overridden in these classes
`[default]`	• *Inside the package*: accessible to all classes • *Outside the package*: inaccessible	• *Inside the package*: visible to all classes • *Outside the package*: visible onlyto classes derived from this one	• *Inside the package*: visible to all classes and able to be overridden by classes derived from this one • *Outside the package*: visible only to classes derived from this one and can be overridden in these classes
`private protected`	Not applicable	• Visible only to classes derived from this one, both inside and outside the package	• Visible only to classes derived from this one, both inside and outside the package • May be overridden in derived classes
`private`	Not applicable	• Visible *only* within this class	• Visible *only* within this class
`final`	• May not be extended	• Assigned a permanent value in its declaration • Value may not be changed in any class, whether derived from this one or not	• May not be overridden
`static`	Not applicable	• One copy of this variable is shared by all subclasses	• This method is shared by all subclasses • May not be overridden
`abstract`	• Contains one or more abstract methods • May not be instantiated	Not applicable	• No definition (deferred to subclasses) • Must be overridden when subclassed, or subclass is also `abstract`

Table 8.1 Access Specifiers (continued)

	Class	Variable	Method
native	Not applicable	Not applicable	• This method is defined externally in another language (such as C)
synchron-ized	Not applicable	Not applicable	• At a given time, only one thread can tell this instantiated object to execute this method • If static, only one thread can execute this method at a given time, period

Java's *inheritance* mechanism is simple but flexible, again using access specifiers so that inheritance can be controlled and shaped to the application designer's needs. Java avoids the complexity introduced by multiple inheritance, in favor of a simpler, less error-prone *interface* mechanism, which can be applied to many cases where multiple inheritance might have been used in languages such as C++.

Java supports both pure polymorphism (through the use of abstract classes and methods) and ad hoc polymorphism (through the use of overriding and overloading of methods).

At the same time, we have concentrated on the specific syntax for declaring classes, variables, methods, and interfaces. With these fundamentals firmly in place, we are now ready to move on and apply this knowledge, writing true object-oriented software in Java.

Part Three

Programming with Java

CHAPTER 9

Applet Programming Techniques

At this point, you should have a solid understanding of the fundamentals of the Java language. Chapter 5 gave you an overview of Java program structure; Chapter 6 dealt with the basics of how data is expressed and manipulated in Java, and Chapter 7 introduced Java's mechanisms for controlling the flow of program execution. Finally, Chapter 8 outlined the object-oriented features of Java, explaining how the fundamental concepts described in Chapter 1 apply to Java. We are now ready to use Java to build actual functioning applets.

We have said that the best way to learn any programming language is to use it. That's exactly what we'll be doing in this chapter: learning how to write Java applets by example.

Before You Start

Practical Information

All the programming examples in this chapter are included on the CD-ROM bundled with this book, including source code (**.java** files), binary code (**.class** files), and HTML pages (**.html** files).

We assume you know the following:

- How to edit and save a text file
- How to compile a Java program with `javac`
- How to write an HTML file for a Web page containing an applet
- How to put the applet on your Web server, setting file permissions as necessary
- How to view an applet using Netscape or the `appletviewer`

NOTE

If you don't remember how to do these things you can refer to Chapter 4.

TIP

Have the Java API documentation handy while reading this chapter. You can browse the API documentation online at:

`http://java.sun.com/JDK-1.0/api/packages.html`

Or you can download the API documentation in either HTML or PostScript format. Sun has links to these files from the following Web page:

`http://java.sun.com/JDK-1.0/ftp_docs.html`

You can also FTP them from `ftp.javasoft.com` in the directory **docs/**.

If you are intending to put an applet on a Web page or to view it with Netscape, you should not use the -o (optimization) option to javac. Some of the "shortcuts" produced by this option circumvent rules enforced by the bytecode verifier. Although by default, the appletviewer does not use the verifier on locally loaded applets, Netscape uses the verifier on *all* bytecode before passing it to the interpreter. Both Netscape and the appletviewer use the verifier on code loaded from a remote host (see Chapter 12).

Netscape or the `appletviewer`?

You can use either Netscape 2.0 or the `appletviewer` to run the applets described in this chapter. When you write applets for use on Web pages, you'll generally find yourself switching between using the `appletviewer` and a Web browser like Netscape to view your applets during development. There are good reasons to use both of them. The `appletviewer` takes up less memory than Netscape. More importantly, the `appletviewer` can be run with the `-debug` flag, allowing you to debug your applets.

The `appletviewer` does not, however, allow you to see the entire text of a Web page; it only shows you the applet(s). Because other people viewing your applets will be doing so not with the `appletviewer`, but with a Java-enabled Web browser like Netscape, it is in your interests to test your applets with a Java-enabled Web browser. The `appletviewer` may, depending on your settings, have a more relaxed security implementation than Netscape, especially with regard to applets loaded from the local file system (see Chapter 12). If you accidentally compiled your applet with optimization on, then it's likely that it won't run on Netscape because of the verifier. Using Netscape to test your applet will allow you to catch this error before putting your applet on the server. The best way to test your applet, once you think you've gotten all the bugs out of it, is to use a Java-enabled browser like Netscape.

Remember, the `appletviewer` is just a simple tool intended to allow you to test your applets until the new version of the HotJava browser becomes available.

Applet Inheritance

In general, to create an applet, you create a class that `extends` (inherits from) class `java.applet.Applet`. (Recall that `java.applet.Applet` means, "class `Applet` in the package `java.applet`.") Class `java.applet.Applet` is itself descended from a rather long chain of other classes, inheriting a great deal of functionality at each level. (Appendix B summarizes some of the methods inherited by `java.applet.Applet` from each of its superclasses.) Through the power of inheritance, you can take this functionality for granted when writing applets.

Applet Life Cycle

Unlike a stand-alone application, for which the programmer writes a main method that directs the activity of the program from start to finish, an applet does not generally have its own `main()` method. Instead, it is managed by another program—the `appletviewer`, a Web browser, etc.—which tells the applet when to initialize itself, when to start and stop running, and when to purge itself from memory.

`init()`, `start()`, `stop()` and `destroy()`

The underlying main program expects the applet to be able to execute certain methods, namely `init()`, `start()`, `stop()`, and `destroy()`. These four methods define the four stages in the "life cycle" of an applet. They are defined in class `java.applet.Applet`, but they are defined as methods with empty bodies; it is your job to override these methods when you define the functionality of your Applet. Although you provide definitions for these methods, you never have to call them yourself; it is the job of the underlying main program to do that.

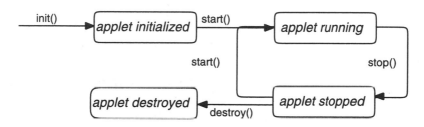

The Life Cycle of an Applet

init()   This method is called when your applet is first loaded. Typically, it is called only once during an applet's lifetime. You use this method to initialize instance variables, set up the width and height of the applet, set its initial foreground and background color, and anything else you might need to do to establish the initial state before the applet actually starts running.

start()   This method is probably the closest thing an applet has to a main method. The system calls `start()` after `init()` to start the applet running. Additionally, if your applet stops running (see `stop()`, below), the `start()` method will be called again to restart your applet. Thus, unlike `init()`, may be called more than once. This method is where you generally instantiate threads to do the main work of your applet.

stop()   When the user leaves the page on which your applet is running, reloads the page, or iconifies (minimizes) the browser, the browser should call the `stop()` method. Typically, you will use this method to terminate your applet's running thread(s).

`destroy()`

When your applet is about to be purged from memory, the browser calls the `destroy()` method. Typically, you don't need to override this method; the Java garbage collector takes care of memory management for you, and the only reason to override `destroy()` is to perform some operation(s) immediately before being unloaded. Keep in mind that because memory allocation is not in your hands, but rather is in the hands of the Java garbage collector, you can't predict when `destroy()` will be called, other than when the user quits the browser application.

WARNING

On Windows 95 and Windows NT, minimizing an applet will not invoke `stop()`, and thus restoring the window will not invoke `start()`. This means that even when you are not looking at the applet, it is still running on the minimized page, taking processor time away from other running processes or threads. A workaround is to make sure you link to a page with no embedded applets before minimizing the browser window. Linking to another page *will* cause the applet's `stop()` method to be invoked.

Remember that the default implementation of each of the four "life-cycle methods" is to do absolutely nothing. Think of each of these methods as an opportunity to specify behavior for your applet at a given point in its life cycle. There is no need to override any method for which you don't need to specify any behavior. For example, if you don't particularly need to initialize any variables when your applet is loaded, you don't need to override `init()`. Another example is `destroy()`, which you will almost never need to override.

paint()

Before we write the first applet of this chapter, there is one more method that we need to discuss, that is of importance to most applets: `paint()`. If you have looked at the API documentation—and we urge you to do so often—you may have noticed that `java.applet.Applet` does not define a method called `paint()`. Instead, the class `java.applet.Applet` inherits `paint()` from one of its ancestors, `java.awt.Component`. Remember, inheritance is cumulative: you inherit everything that your superclass has, including everything that it inherited from it's superclass, and so on.

The browser calls your applet's `paint()` method whenever it thinks that it needs to redisplay the portion of the screen containing your applet. For example, if you move another window partially in front of the applet, it may need to be redrawn, and the browser will call your applet's `paint()` method.

Like the four life-cycle methods, the default version of `paint()` does absolutely nothing. If you want to see anything on the screen when your applet runs, you must override `paint()`.

Example: DrawStar

The following is the code for an applet that will display a red star in a black background. Coding and running this applet should give you a better understanding of the applet life cycle:

```
import java.awt.Graphics;
import java.awt.Color;
import java.applet.Applet;
```

```java
public class DrawStar extends Applet {
   // x and y coordinates of a star
   int x_coords[] = {150, 225, 50, 250, 75, 150};
   int y_coords[] = {25, 250, 100, 100, 250, 25};

// This method is invoked when the applet is first loaded:
public void init() {
   System.out.println("init()");

   setBackground(Color.black);
   setForeground(Color.red);

   resize (300, 300);
}

// This method is invoked when the applet starts running
public void start() {
   System.out.println("start()");
}

// Invoked when the applet is asked to paint itself.
public void paint(Graphics g) {
   System.out.println("paint()");

   // draw the star
   g.drawPolygon(x_coords, y_coords, 6);
}

public void stop() {
   System.out.println("stop()");
}

public void destroy() {
   System.out.println("destroy()");
}

}
```

After creating the source file, you need to create an HTML file so you can view your applet. The following applet tag should appear somewhere in the file:

```
<applet code=DrawStar.class width=400 height=400>
</applet>
```

Create the HTML file and store it in the same directory as the applet.

Notice that the applet includes several calls to `System.out.println()`. If you're running the `appletviewer` from a command prompt, then when you run the applet, you should see these messages on the console. If you are using Netscape to view the applet, you'll need to choose **Show Java Console** from the Options menu in order to see these messages.

Running the Applet

WARNING

There is an inconsistency in Netscape's **Reload** feature. When you use the **Reload** feature to reload a page containing an applet, the browser does not reload the applet itself. As a result, if you want to see a recently visited applet display some newly added behavior, you may need to go to the Options menu, select **Network Preferences...**, and clear your disk cache, and on systems that use a memory cache, clear that as well. Then, when the applet loads, it should display the most recent version.

Once you have the applet running on the screen, try some of these experiments. First, try leaving the page and then returning. What happens on the console? What happens if you try minimizing your browser window? Do you see the evidence of the bug we described earlier? Now, return the browser window to normal, and move the console window in front of the applet, partially obscuring it. Does anything happen on the console? Now move the console window so that it obscures less of the applet than before. What happens on the console? Next, bring the browser window to the foreground with the console still visible in the background, and scroll the page with the applet. Can you see what method this triggers? Can you think of a way to get the browser to call our destroy() method?

Understanding the Code

Let's take this code apart to see what makes it tick:

```
import java.awt.Graphics;
import java.awt.Color;
import java.applet.Applet;
```

These three statements import the classes Graphics and Color from the package java.awt, and the class Applet from the package java.applet. Remember, do not be misled by the implications of the English word import: no additional classes become part of the compilation unit as a direct result of import statements; the import statements do not have any significant impact on the size of the executable code. Nor are the import statements necessary to refer to classes from other packages. If we wanted to type the whole name of each class every time we referred to it in our code, we could simply leave out the import statements. The import statements merely provide a useful syntactic convenience so that we don't have to go around typing fully qualified class names every time we want to refer to these classes. After these import statements, we can just refer to these classes as Graphics, Color and Applet, respectively.

```
public class DrawStar extends Applet { ... }
```

Generally, with each applet that you create, you define a new class. Your new class extends the class java.applet.Applet. This means that the new class is a subclass of java.applet.Applet and thus inherits any variables and methods present in java.applet.Applet. Notice that, thanks to our friend the import statement, we can now use the shorthand Applet, and the compiler will know that we're really talking about java.applet.Applet.

We declare DrawStar as a public class because DrawStar must be referenced from the outside by the application running the applet. If we do not declare this class as public, then the Web browser will not have access to it and will not be able to run it.

```
// x and y coordinates of a star
int x_coords[] = {150, 225, 50, 250, 75, 150};
int y_coords[] = {25, 250, 100, 100, 250, 25};
```

Here, we are initializing two arrays of integers. Notice that we have not used the new operator to create the arrays. This is because when you directly initialize an array during declaration, the compiler allocates space for the array automatically. How many coordinates are in each array? How many points are in the star? We'll come back to this later.

```
// This method is invoked when the applet is first loaded:
public void init() {
    System.out.println("init()");

    setBackground(Color.black);
    setForeground(Color.red);

    resize (300, 300);
}
```

When the browser first loads DrawStar, it calls DrawStar.init(). Notice that init() is public. There are two reasons for this. First, it must be public in order to be called by the browser. Second, an overriding method must have at least as much access as the method it overrides. For the same two reasons, *all* the methods in DrawStar are declared as public.

NOTE

There is no rule that says all the methods in an applet must be public; it's just that this particular applet is so simple that it doesn't declare any methods for local use. Because all of the methods it declares happen to be overridden public methods and because they all need to be called from outside the applet, they are all declared as public.

The method `init()` simply sets up the initial state of the applet. The first thing it does is print an informational message to the console, informing us that `init()` has been called. There is no reason an applet necessarily needs to do this. We put this statement in simply to demonstrate the applet's life cycle.

Next, the `init()` method calls two methods inherited from `java.awt.Component`: `setBackground()` and `setForeground()`. `Color.black` and `Color.red` are both `static` variables from the class `java.awt.Color`. Notice that because they are `static` variables, there was no need to actually instantiate an object of class `Color` to refer to these variables.

Finally, `init()` resizes the applet to 300 pixels wide and 300 pixels high. Depending on whether you are viewing the applet in Netscape or the `appletviewer`, the behavior of this method may differ. If you run `DrawStar` in the appletviewer, you may notice a brief flash as the applet starts because the applet begins at the size specified in the HTML file (400 x 400 pixels) and then is quickly resized to 300 x 300 pixels.

Unlike the `appletviewer`, Netscape needs to keep its page layout static so that it can format text around the applet as necessary. As a result, it does not allow applets to resize themselves on the page. Thus, `resize()` will have no apparent effect in Netscape. There is still a reason to use it, though. When you call `resize()`, you are specifying the area that the applet recognizes as its own. When it redraws its screen, it only updates that area. If you are running an animation, you can get a performance optimization by first calling `resize()` to include only the area you really need to update.

```java
// Invoked when the applet is asked to paint itself.
public void paint(Graphics g) {
  System.out.println("paint()");

  // draw the star
  g.drawPolygon(x_coords, y_coords, 6);
}
```

Running the applet should give you an idea of when the browser invokes your applet's `paint()` method, especially if you try the experiments we recommended. Notice that the browser passes the `paint()` method an object of class `Graphics`. (Look back at our `import` statements to find out what package `Graphics` is in.) The `Graphics` object itself—often referred to as a graphics context—is created, maintained, and owned by the system. Although you need the graphics context of your applet in order to do any drawing, painting, or erasing, you don't have to concern yourself with the details of how to get or create the `Graphics` object. The system simply passes it to you as a parameter whenever it expects you to do any graphics work, such as you do in the `paint()` method.

After announcing to the console that `paint()` has been called, our `paint()` method sends a message to the passed-in Graphics object, `g`, asking it to execute its `drawPolygon()` method. The `drawPolygon()` method (defined in `java.awt.Graphics`) takes three parameters: an array of *x*-coordinates, an array of *y*-coordinates, and a number indicating the number of points in our polygon. Notice that it automatically uses whatever foreground color and background color we previously set for our applet. If we hadn't set these colors, the default would have been black on a gray background.

Notice that our star has five points, but our coordinate arrays specify six points. This is because polygons are not automatically closed; our sixth point is a repetition of our first point, so that we close the star figure. You could specify a polygon that was nothing more than a zig-zagged line on the screen. When the points are connected, they are connected in the order specified by the arrays, even if that means the lines will cross, as they do in our polygon.

The coordinate system may be one with which you are unfamiliar. Ever since you were in grade school, you have probably drawn graphs with the origin in the lower-left corner, with *x* increasing toward the right and *y* increasing toward the top. In Java, as is the case with many other screen coordinate systems, *y* increases towards the *bottom*. This puts the origin in the *upper left* of your applet.

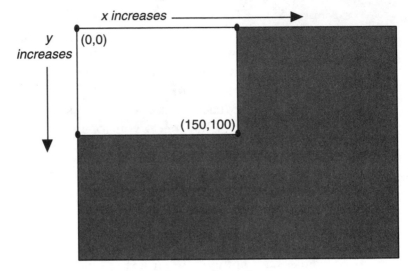

Screen Coordinates

```
public void stop() {
    System.out.println("stop()");
}

public void destroy() {
    System.out.println("destroy()");
}
```

There's nothing special going on here. Remember, there is no rule that an applet must override stop() or destroy(). We only provided these methods so that you could track the applet's life cycle.

Example: `SimpleTickerTapeBad`

You probably didn't decide to learn Java so you could display static pictures on your Web pages. Our next example introduces some animation, in the form of moving text.

WARNING

This example has a deliberate flaw. It keeps running in an infinite loop, never relinquishing control of the CPU. Depending on the nature of your system and the program running the applet, you may not even be able to steal enough processor time to use a menu or quit the applet. This applet is provided to demonstrate what can happen if an animation applet doesn't create an independent thread to run the animation in. If you're running on a system that has preemptive multitasking, then you should at least be able to force a quit. However, on a system like MacOS 7.5, which does not have preemptive multitasking, forcing the quit may render your system unstable until you restart.

```
import java.awt.FontMetrics;
import java.awt.Graphics;
import java.applet.Applet;

public class SimpleTickerTapeBad extends Applet {
    String msg;    // The scrolling message
    int x, y;    // current (x, y) coordinates of the message
    int horizStep;  // step size, in pixels
    int pause;    // number of times to iterate in pause loop
    int msgWidth;  // width of the message with current font

        public void init() {
        msg = "I am monopolizing your CPU!";
        pause = 100000;
        horizStep = 2;

        FontMetrics fm = getFontMetrics(getFont());
         msgWidth = fm.stringWidth(msg);
```

```
    // start x from the right
    x = size().width;

    // start y from just a little above the bottom
    y = size().height - (int)(fm.getHeight()/3);
}

    public void paint(Graphics g) {
        // keep scrolling the message until interrupted
        while (true) {

            // redraw the applet's background
            g.setColor(getBackground());
            g.fillRect(0, 0, size().width, size().height);

            // draw the message in the current position
            g.setColor(getForeground());
            g.drawString(msg, x, y);

            // Advance x position to the left
            if (x > 0 - msgWidth) {
            x = x - horizStep;
            } else {
            // start it over from the right
            x = size().width;
            }

            // pause for some time before the next display
            pauseLoop(pause);

            }
        }

        void pauseLoop(int counter) {
        for (int i=0; i < counter; i++) {
        // wasting my time...
    }
    }
}
```

If you wish to run this example to see what a renegade applet acts like, you can place the following tag in an HTML file:

```
<applet code="SimpleTickerTapeBad.class" width=200 height=50>
</applet>
```

Understanding the Code

We're not going to dissect this applet the way we did the last one, because we don't want to start teaching you bad habits. However, there are a few things in the code worth noting.

In the beginning of the while loop that comprises the `paint()` method, we have the following lines of code:

```
// redraw the applet's background
g.setColor(getBackground());
g.fillRect(0, 0, size().width, size().height);

// draw the message in the current position
g.setColor(getForeground());
g.drawString(msg, x, y);
```

There are a few interesting method calls in these lines. First, there's `g.setColor()`. This method sends a message to the `Graphics` object `g`–the graphics context passed in as a parameter to `paint()`–telling it to set the color of the "pen" that it uses for drawing and/or filling rectangles, polygons, lines, strings, and so on. In this case, we obtain the current background color by calling `getBackground()`, and we set the current foreground color to match it. We then use the background color to create a rectangle that fills the applet's area, thereby "clearing" the applet's area of the screen. Afterwards, we set the current color back to the applet's foreground color in order to draw the message string.

Notice that we obtain the width and height of the applet via calls to a method whose name is `size()`. What is not immediately apparent from the code is the fact that `size()` is a method our applet inherits from `java.awt.Component` and that this method returns an object of type `java.awt.Dimension`. An object of class `Dimension` contains only two variables: a `width` and a `height`. Although there are many things in this applet that are incorrect, this is indeed the correct way to obtain an applet's width and height. Notice that we can access the members of the returned object directly from the method-call, without ever declaring an object of class `Dimension`. If we were going to use `width` and `height` over and over again, it might have been preferable to store the results in an object in order to avoid redundant calls to `size()`. However, because the size of an applet can change over time, the best way to guarantee that you have the most current value is to call `size()` directly. In this case, it really doesn't make a significant difference.

Notice that the preceding code segment redraws the background before each time that it draws the message string. We need to do this partially because of the unorthodox way in which this applet handles animation. It's very atypical to place the animation loop within the `paint()` method. We shall see later that most animation applets use the `update()` method to redraw the background.

Note the use of the `FontMetrics` object. This is used to calculate the width of the message string. Because many fonts are proportional, rather than monospaced, it's useful to have such an object to make these calculations. Also, keep in mind that fonts tend to be pretty system-dependent creatures. Using the `FontMetrics` object helps make sure that your measurements will be appropriate to the system your applet is running on.

Using Threads and the `Runnable` Interface

To avoid the problems caused by our previous example, we need to have our applet perform the animation in a separate thread, allowing other threads to run concurrently with it so that it does not monopolize the CPU. Actually, our applet already runs in a thread, the "main thread." The problem is that this is the same thread that is responsible for handling events, etc. Our goal is to have the animation run while simultaneously returning control to the main thread.

Introduction to Threads

You may (or may not) be familiar with the concept of threads. A *thread* is essentially an independent locus of control in your program. What does that mean? A traditional, single-threaded program essentially executes a list of instructions in order. It may jump from one place in the list to another or loop for a while executing a certain section of the list, but at any given moment during its execution, it is located at exactly one place in the list. This location in the list of instructions is called the program's *locus of control.* A multithreaded program may have several "simultaneous" loci of control. Generally, today's systems use one processor, so they typically simulate parallel execution of these threads by allowing each thread to use the processor for a few microseconds at a time. The actual scheduling algorithm that is used to accomplish this is highly system-dependent.

We're not going to go into advanced multithreading concepts here. Our main intention is to show you how to use a thread to run an animation.

Implementing `Runnable`

The most convenient way to create a multithreaded applet is to implement the `Runnable` interface. Recall from Chapter 8 that we cannot make an applet a subclass of `java.lang.Thread`, because an applet is already a subclass of class `java.applet.Applet`, and Java only has single inheritance. The solution is provided by the `Runnable` interface. Recall also that in order to implement an interface, you must implement all the methods in that interface; the `Runnable` interface only defines one method, `run()`, making it easy and practical to implement. In order to create a `Runnable` applet, we need to do the following:

- Include an `implements Runnable` clause in our applet's class declaration.
- Override the method `run()` from the `Runnable` interface, placing the main execution code of our applet inside this method.
- In our applet's `start()` method, create a thread, passing our applet as a parameter to the constructor, via the keyword `this`.
- In our applet's `stop()` method, include code to stop the thread.

Our next example demonstrates how this is done.

Example: `SimpleTickerTape`

```
import java.applet.Applet;
import java.awt.Graphics;
import java.awt.FontMetrics;
```

```
public class SimpleTickerTape extends Applet implements
Runnable {
    String msg;    // The scrolling message
    int x, y;      // x, y coordinates of the message
    int horizStep; // step size in pixels
    int pause;     // sleep delay (in milliseconds)
    int msgWidth;  // width of the message with current font

    Thread ourThread;  // this thread will handle painting
                       // and scrolling the text

    public void init() {
        msg = "I am a multithreaded Applet!";
        pause = 100;
        horizStep = 2;

        FontMetrics fm = getFontMetrics(getFont());
        msgWidth = fm.stringWidth(msg);

        // start x from the right
        x = size().width;

        // start y from just a little above the bottom
        y = size().height - (int)(fm.getHeight()/3);
    }

    public void start() {
        // create a new thread to execute run()
        ourThread = new Thread(this);

        // invoke run() and return immediately
        ourThread.start();
    }

    // implement Runnable method
    public void run() {
        // scroll the message until the thread is stopped
        while (ourThread != null) {

            repaint(); // calls update() and then paint()
```

```
        // Advance x position to the left.
        if (x > 0 - msgWidth)
        x = x - horizStep;
        else
        // Start over from the far right.
        x = size().width;

        try {
        // Pause for a few milliseconds before repainting.
        // While pausing, free up the CPU.
        ourThread.sleep (pause);
        } catch (InterruptedException e) {
        e.printStackTrace();  // print error log
    }
  }
}

public void paint(Graphics g) {
   // draw the message
   g.drawString(msg, x, y);
}

public void stop() {

   // ourThread is now a candidate for garbage collection.
   ourThread = null;
 }
}
```

Understanding the Code

At this point, most of this applet should look familiar. There's no need to dissect the entire thing, reminding you about the import statements, the life-cycle methods, and so on. What we will focus on is the part of this applet that deals with the creation of the Thread object.

```
public class SimpleTickerTape extends Applet implements
Runnable
```

Notice that `SimpleTickerTape` has only one immediate superclass, `Applet`. However, it also inherits the `abstract` method `run()` from the interface `Runnable`. Like any other inherited `abstract` method, `run()` must be overridden in order to instantiate our applet. Once we have done this, our class may be passed as a parameter to any method expecting to receive a `Runnable` object. This is exactly what we do in our `start()` method:

```
public void start() {
    // create a new thread to execute run()
    ourThread = new Thread(this);

    // invoke run() and return immediately
    ourThread.start();
}
```

The first thing this method does is instantiate an object of class `java.lang.Thread` (remember that because `java.lang.*` is imported implicitly, we can simply refer to this class as `Thread`). The `Thread()` constructor that we use takes a `Runnable` object as a parameter and sets the `Thread`'s `run()` method to call the passed-in object's `run()` method.

Having instantiated `ourThread`, we set it in motion by calling `ourThread.start()`. `ourThread.start()` calls `ourThread.run()` and then returns *asynchronously*. That is, it does not wait around for `ourThread.run()` to complete, the way any normal (*synchronous*) method call would. It just sets it going independently and returns control to us; this means that control returns to `SimpleTickerTape.start()` in the main thread, while the `run()` method has begun executing in parallel, in its own separate thread (`ourThread`). Now, `SimpleTickerTape.start()` completes, returning control to the system so that it can do things like handle events and perhaps eventually call our applet's stop() method.

One tricky aspect of this code has to do with the fact that SimpleTickerTape and ourThread seem to share a run() method, but their start() methods are not equivalent. The similarity in the names of the run() methods is deliberate, but the similarity in the names of the two start() methods is a little confusing, because they don't do the same thing. Remember, SimpleTickerTape and ourThread do not actually *share* a run() method; rather, the Thread is instantiated in such a way that its run() method *calls* SimpleTickerTape's run() method.

After we instantiate the thread and call ourThread.run(), our applet has two threads running: its main thread—the one that handles events and calls the applet's life-cycle methods—and the thread we spawned to run the animation.

```
public void run() {
    // scroll the message until the thread is stopped
    while (ourThread != null) {
        ...
    }
}
```

Our animation thread consists of a loop that runs the animation again and again until the thread is stopped (killed). The condition (ourThread != null) checks to see if ourThread has been stopped. You can stop a thread by setting it to null. Note that because we use a local variable to represent the thread in our run() method, that's exactly what will happen when the run() method terminates; the thread will go out of scope and it's value will become null. This is exactly what should happen. When a thread's run() method terminates, this is synonymous with the thread being stopped.

```
    repaint(); // calls update() and then paint()
```

Recall that in our previous (pathological) example, we needed to redraw the background each time we redrew the message, or each iteration of the message would never be erased from the screen. An applet's built-in `repaint()` method, inherited from `java.awt.Component`, will first call the method `update()` and then call `paint()`. The default version of `update()` simply redraws the applet's background so that `paint()` can do its work on a clean screen. In our case, this is exactly what we want it to do, so we don't need to override `update()`.

```
try {
    // Pause for a few milliseconds before repainting.
    // While pausing, free up the CPU.
    ourThread.sleep (pause);
} catch (InterruptedException e) {
    e.printStackTrace();  // print error log
}
```

One of the most important things a thread can do is yield control to other threads when it does not need to be actively doing anything. Remember that in our previous example, the pause was implemented by means of a 100,000-iteration loop, which accomplished nothing other than wasting the processor's time. This type of loop is called *busy-waiting*. Instead of a busy-waiting loop, it makes more sense to put our thread to sleep for the desired amount of time. We call `ourThread.sleep()` with an integer parameter, indicating the number of milliseconds for which `ourThread` will remain idle, freeing up the CPU.

Notice that we call `ourThread.sleep()` inside a `try/catch` block. We have not discussed exception handling in depth, but we have indicated that a class that does not throw any exceptions must handle any exceptions that may come about as a result of its actions. If you expect that a given operation will throw an exception, you can catch that exception by enclosing the sensitive operation within a `try/catch` block. To maintain the continuity of our focus, we will explain this in more detail after we finish our dissection of this applet's code. For now, all you need to concern yourself with is the fact that ourThread.sleep() might cause an exception. Typically, the appropriate thing to do when faced with an InterruptedException is to simply return. By returning, the run() method terminates, which causes the thread to die naturally.

```
public void stop() {

    // ourThread is now a candidate for garbage collection.
    ourThread = null;
}
```

Recall that an applet's stop() method is called when the user switches to a different page in the browser or when the browser window is minimized (except in the Windows version of Java; see our earlier warning). When this happens, it makes sense to kill the thread, freeing up the CPU to concentrate on other tasks. To do this, we simply set ourThread to null, notifying the garbage collector that it if it wants to, it may reclaim any resources allocated to ourThread. We don't know for sure what the garbage collector will do—or when. Setting the thread to null makes it a candidate for garbage collection.

Note that killing ourThread does not destroy our applet or any state stored in our applet's instance variables. These values persist even after ourThread is killed. Should the user return to this page or restore the browser window, our applet's start() method will be called, and a new thread will be created, continuing ourThread where it left off.

Exception-Handling

A little while ago, we swept the topic of exception handling under the rug promising to get to it later. Having completed our analysis of our first multithreaded applet, we can now devote our attention to introducing exception handling in Java.

What is an Exception?

An *exception*, as implied by the term itself, is an exceptional condition that may come about during the execution of a program. By *exceptional*, we mean that this is a condition that you acknowledge is possible but expect to occur infrequently, if at all. If our definition sounds a little circular, it is perhaps because the term *exception* is very well-chosen to express what it is meant to represent.

The Java language defines a class called `java.lang.Throwable`, used to encapsulate the notion of an exception. Actually, the language defines two broad subclasses of `Throwable`; one is `java.lang.Exception`, and the other is `java.lang.Error`. The idea of this is that an `Error` is conceived as more serious than an `Exception`. An `Exception` may be *caught*, and thereby dealt with in some manner, perhaps avoiding any significant negative impact on the functioning of the program; an `Error`, on the other hand, should typically *not* be caught by a user program and generally leads to the termination of the program. In our discussion of exception handling, we will generally use *exception* to refer to any subclass of `java.lang.Throwable`, whether descended from `Error` or `Exception`.

Your Choice: Catch It or Throw It

When an exception occurs, the method that generates the exception is said to *throw* that exception. In general, when a method `throws` an exception, it terminates its execution, sending a message back to its caller in the form of an exception object, an object of some class derived from `java.lang.Throwable`.

If you call a method that might cause an exception, you generally have two choices: you can either *catch* the exception by placing the "dangerous" method-call inside a `try/catch` block (see below) or you can choose not to handle the exception. If an exception occurs that you do not handle, it is as if you generated that exception; you are said to have *thrown* the exception. Additionally you may catch an exception and handle it by throwing a new exception.

Handling Exceptions: The `try`/`catch`/`finally` Block

You handle an exception using a `try`/`catch`/`finally` block, often just called a `try`/`catch` block. Here's what this looks like:

```
try {

    // put code which might generate an exception here
    ...

} catch (SomeExceptionClass name) {
    // code to handle any subclass of SomeExceptionClass

} catch (OtherExceptionClass name) {
    // code to handle any subclass of OtherExceptionClass
    // ... there may be zero or more such catch blocks ...

} finally {
    // this code gets executed NO MATTER WHAT:
    // 1) If the try block completed normally (no exception)
    // 2) If one of the catch blocks handled an exception
    // 3) If an exception occurred that none of the catch
    //     blocks handled
}
```

The `try` keyword is used to set up a block, within which any exceptions or abnormal exits (`break`, `continue`, `return`; see Chapter 7) are attempted to be handled by the ensuing `catch` blocks, if any.

If an exception occurs, then control immediately leaves the block in which it occurred, and the interpreter falls out to the most immediately enclosing `try/catch` block, looking for a `catch` clause that matches the class of exception that occurred. Only the first `catch` block that matches will be executed, no others. Thus, it is best to deal with the most specific exceptions first, and more general exceptions gradually. To specify behavior that will occur for *any* exception not handled by other `catch` blocks (but not on normal termination of the `try` block), you can make the last `catch` block trigger generally on `Exception`. If no other, more specific, `catch` block handles the exception, you can deal with it here.

NOTE

If you decide to include a `catch` block that triggers on `Exception`, make sure it is the *last* `catch` block of the series. Otherwise it will prevent any other `catch` block from being executed.

To define behavior that absolutely must occur in *all* cases, whether or not an exception has occurred, a `finally` block may be specified. This block is executed whenever the `try` block terminates— either normally or abnormally—and after execution of a `catch` block, if any. Note that as an exception propagates through successive `try/catch` blocks, all associated `finally` blocks, if any, are executed.

Unhandled Exceptions

When an exception occurs in a block that is not a `try/catch` block, or if the `try/catch` block does not have a `catch` clause for the type of exception that occurred, control falls out of the current block, and the interpreter looks in the immediately enclosing block, to see if it is caught there (i.e., to see if *that* block is a `try/catch` block with an appropriate `catch` clause). This continues until an appropriate `try/catch` block is found, in which case the exception is handled as described earlier. If no enclosing `try/catch` block is found within the method block, then the exception is thrown back to the method that called the current method, and so on. If no method handles the exception, then it keeps propagating all the way back to the `main()` method, and the interpreter will exit, printing an error message and a stack trace.

Declaring Methods that Throw Exceptions

If you choose to ignore (and thereby throw) an exception, your method must explicitly state in its declaration that it `throws` this particular class of exception. A method may throw any number of classes of exceptions; you may recall from Chapter 8 that they are indicated in a comma-separated list in the declaration. An important restriction is that an overriding method may not throw any exceptions that its overridden method does not throw.

Run-Time Exceptions vs. Normal Exceptions

Are you ready for a good laugh? The preceding paragraph is only true for "normal" exceptions. If there are normal exceptions, does that imply that there are "exceptional" exceptions?

The opposite of normal exceptions are called *run-time exceptions*. These are exceptions subclassed from `java.lang.RuntimeException`, which might be generated by all sorts of typical run-time activities, such as accessing arrays and performing arithmetic calculations. If a method does not include code to catch these exceptions, it is not necessary to include a `throws` clause in the method declaration. There's actually a good reason to make this distinction. You wouldn't want to have to put a `throws` clause in every method that accessed an array or divided two integers, just because it might generate an `ArrayIndexOutOfBoundsException` or an `ArithmeticException`.

Getting Parameters from an HTML file

Back in Chapter 3, we described how parameters may be passed into applets from HTML files. Until now, however, we have not discussed the technique by which these parameters can be made visible within the applet.

It's actually quite simple. The class `java.applet.Applet` defines the method `getParameter(String name)`. Given a `String` that exactly matches the name of a parameter inside the HTML file, `getParameter()` returns the value that was paired with that parameter.

NOTE

If the parameter cannot be found in the HTML file, `getParameter()` will return `null`. The `String` passed into `getParameter()` must be an exact match—case is not important—for the name of the parameter as specified in the HTML file; otherwise, `getParameter()` will return `null`, because it won't find a matching name.

There's only one thing about getting applet parameters that is tricky. (Isn't there always something?) The tricky part is that `getParameter()` always returns the parameter as a `String`. This means that if you need it to be an `int`, `float`, or `boolean`, you need to do something to convert the `String` to an appropriate value. The good news is that Java makes this process relatively painless through the use of wrapper classes. *Wrapper classes* encapsulate the primitive types but provide—among other things—methods that facilitate conversions between `Strings` and primitive types.

To see how this is done, let's parameterize our multithreaded `SimpleTickerTape` applet, so that the message and sleep delay can be set from the HTML page.

In the `init()` method, where it currently says:

```
msg = "I am a multithreaded Applet!";
pause = 100;
```

we can replace the code with the following:

```
String msg = getParameter("message");
String pause_str = getParameter("pause");
pause = Integer.parseInt(pause_str);
```

Alternatively, we could combine these last two lines into the following:

```
pause = Integer.parseInt(getParameter("pause"));
```

If the parameter is not found, getParameter() will return null. To account for this possibility, you should probably change the whole section to the following:

```
String msg = getParameter("message");
String pause_str = getParameter("pause");
if (msg == null) {
   // not found - using default
   msg = "Put a message parameter in the HTML file!"
}
if (pause_str != null) {
   pause = Integer.parseInt(pause_str);
} else {
   // not found - use default
   pause = 100;
}
```

Having adjusted your code accordingly, try recompiling and running the applet without inserting any <param> tags in the HTML file yet. This way, you can see your defaults in action.

Once you've seen the default values work, try altering the tags in your HTML file as follows:

```
<applet code="SimpleTickerTape.class" width=200 height=50>
<param name="pause" value="250">
<param name="message" value="Why recompile? Just
parameterize!">
```

```
</applet>
```

NOTE

You may notice that all the parameter names and values are enclosed in double-quotes. The double-quotes are only necessary when you have spaces or path-separator characters in the value of the parameter, in which case the double-quotes are needed to group the characters together. As a general rule, however, it can't hurt to include the double-quotes.

You don't need to recompile your applet to see the new parameters work. Just make sure you've placed the `<param>` tags properly between the `<applet>` and `</applet>` tags, and reload the HTML page. Don't forget, though, that in order to see the new behavior in Netscape, you might have to clear your cache, as described earlier in this chapter.

NOTE

Not all of the built-in wrapper classes provide quite as easy a conversion as the `Integer` class. If you wanted, for example, to convert a parameter to a `float`, you could use the following:

```
float f;   // This is where we want to put the value.
String f_str = getParameter("f_param"); // Get the String.
Float f_wrapper = Float.valueOf(f_str); // Convert to Float.
f = f_wrapper.floatValue();   // Get the contained value.
```

Example: ParamParser

It's time to apply some object-oriented dogma. A real object-oriented programmer aims never to write the same code again; instead, he or she reuses the code already written, through inheritance. Perhaps you found yourself looking at the previous section, asking, "Am I going to have to do all this *every time* I want to get parameters in an applet?" To an object-oriented programmer, this feeling is very familiar, and it always generates the knee-jerk response: "Perhaps I can write this code to be general enough so that I never have to write it again!"

This is what we intend to do. We've observed that there are certain types of parameters that are very common for an applet to need, such as int, float, Color, and Font. (The Color and Font classes are defined in the package java.awt, and we'll learn more about them soon.) Rather than rewrite our parameter-parsing code each time we need it, we simply create a class ParamParser that extends java.applet.Applet, and we place the necessary methods in that class. When we want to create an applet that reuses those methods, we simply subclass ParamParser instead of subclassing java.applet.Applet. Because it extends java.applet.Applet, ParamParser inherits all the functionality of java.applet.Applet, and then it adds some of its own.

Following is the code for ParamParser, complete with doc comments capable of being used with javadoc (see Appendix A):

```
package toolBox; // package declaration must be in the first
                 // line of your compilation unit. At most one
                 // package statement per compilation unit.

import java.applet.Applet;
import java.awt.Color;
import java.awt.Font;

/**
 This applet provides functionality to parse parameters
 from an HTML file.
*/
public class ParamParser extends Applet {
   /**
     Should we display error messages to the console if
     a parameter is invalid or not specified?
     Default is true.
   */
```

```java
public boolean displayErrMesg = true;

/**
 Returns a String which is a valid value for the parameter
 (param).
 @param param   Name of the parameter.
 @param defString Default value for the parameter
*/
public String getStringParameter(String param,
   String defString) {
   String str;

   str = getParameter(param);
   if (str -- null) {
     if (displayErrMesg)
       System.out.println("No " + param +
           " specified. Using default.");
     str = defString;
   }

   return str;
}


/**
 Returns an int which is a valid value for the parameter
 (param).
 @param param   Name of the parameter.
 @param min    Minimum value
 @param max    Maximum value
 @param defValue   Default value
*/
public int getIntParameter(String param, int min, int max,
int defValue) {
   int value;

   try {
```

```
        value = Integer.parseInt(getParameter(param));
        if (value < min || value > max)
        throw new Exception();
    } catch (Exception e) {
        if (displayErrMesg)
            System.out.println("Invalid " + param +
                " . Using default.");
        value = defValue;
    }

    return value;
}


/**
 Returns a float which is a valid value for the parameter
 (param).
 @param param   Name of the parameter.
 @param min     Minimum value
 @param max     Maximum value
 @param defValue   Default value
*/
public float getFloatParameter(String param,
    float min, float max, float defValue) {
    float value;

    try {
        String f_str = getParameter(param);
        Float f_wrapper = Float.valueOf(f_str);
        value = f_wrapper.floatValue();
        if (value < min || value > max)
            throw new Exception();
    } catch (Exception e) {
        if (displayErrMesg)
            System.out.println("Invalid " + param +
                " . Using default.");
```

```
            value = defValue;
        }

        return value;
    }


    /**
     Returns a Font object which is formed by valid font name,
     style, and size.
     @param paramName   Name of the font name parameter.
     @param defName   Default font name.
     @param paramStyle   Name of the font style(ie. BOLD)
          parameter.
     @param defStyle   Default font style.
     @param paramSize   Name of the font size parameter.
     @param defSize   Default font size.
     @see java.awt.Font
    */
    public Font getFontParameter(String paramName, String
       defName, String paramStyle, int defStyle, String
       paramSize, int defSize) {
       String fontName = getStringParameter(
          paramName, defName);
       int fontStyle = getIntParameter(paramStyle, Font.PLAIN,
       Font.PLAIN+Font.BOLD+Font.ITALIC, defStyle);
       int fontSize = getIntParameter(
          paramSize, 4, 100, defSize);

       return (new Font(fontName, fontStyle, fontSize));
    }


    /**
     Returns a Color
     @param colorStr   Name of the color.
     @param defColorStr   Default color name.
```

```
    @see java.awt.Color
*/
public Color getColorParameter(String colorStr,
    String defColorStr) {

    return strToColor(getStringParameter(colorStr,
        defColorStr));

}


/**
 Convert a String to a color. The String may
 be the name of any of the thirteen built-in color
 constants; this method is case-insensitive.
 i.e., "Black" will work just as well as "BLACK"
 "bLaCk" or "black"
 @param colorStr    Name of the color
 @see java.awt.Color
*/
public Color strToColor(String colorStr) {
    if (colorStr.equalsIgnoreCase("black"))
        return Color.black;
    else if (colorStr.equalsIgnoreCase("blue"))
        return Color.blue;
    else if (colorStr.equalsIgnoreCase("cyan"))
        return Color.cyan;
    else if (colorStr.equalsIgnoreCase("darkGray"))
        return Color.darkGray;
    else if (colorStr.equalsIgnoreCase("gray"))
        return Color.gray;
    else if (colorStr.equalsIgnoreCase("green"))
        return Color.green;
    else if (colorStr.equalsIgnoreCase("lightGray"))
        return Color.lightGray;
    else if (colorStr.equalsIgnoreCase("magenta"))
        return Color.magenta;
```

```
    else if (colorStr.equalsIgnoreCase("orange"))
        return Color.orange;
    else if (colorStr.equalsIgnoreCase("pink"))
        return Color.pink;
    else if (colorStr.equalsIgnoreCase("red"))
        return Color.red;
    else if (colorStr.equalsIgnoreCase("white"))
        return Color.white;
    else if (colorStr.equalsIgnoreCase("yellow"))
        return Color.yellow;
    else
        return null;
    }
}
```

Understanding the Code

Doc Comments

The doc comments are provided here to give you an idea of
what these comments look like and how they're used. For a
more complete description of these comments and the various
types of special tags used with them, see Sun's online
documentation on javadoc at:

```
http://java.sun.com/JDK-1.0/tools/
```

package **Statement**

This is the first class we've written that contains a package
statement. Recall from Chapter 5 that if a class does not have a
package statement, it goes in the "default package." Recall also
that the name of the package defines a path to the package
directory. ParamParser declares itself to be in package toolBox.

Before compiling `ParamParser`, put the file `ParamParser.java` into a new subdirectory, called `toolBox`.

Compiling `ParamParser`

Next, navigate to the `toolBox` directory and compile `ParamParser`. Remember, `ParamParser` is an applet, even though it doesn't override the life-cycle methods. Once `ParamParser` is compiled, we could conceivably construct a Web page that references `ParamParser` directly and attempt to run it. Indeed, we *could* run it; it just wouldn't be very interesting, because all the life-cycle methods are empty. `ParamParser`, by itself, doesn't do anything. If we really want to test it, we need to subclass it. We shall do this shortly.

Working with Colors

The class `java.awt.Color` is used to encapsulate colors. The class declares 13 color constants, but many more colors can be obtained by specifying numerical values for red, green, and blue components. See the API documentation for more details.

An applet can set its foreground and background colors with `setForeground()` and `setBackground()`, respectively; it can also use `getForeground()` and `getBackground()` to retrieve its foreground and background colors, respectively. All four of these methods are inherited from `java.awt.Component`.

Working with Fonts

The class `java.awt.Font` is used to encapsulate fonts. In an applet, you can set the current font used for drawing strings by calling the method `setFont()`, inherited from `java.awt-.Component`. As you may have guessed, you can also call the method `getFont()` to get the applet's current font.

The following applet may be used to tell you which fonts are available on your platform:

```
import java.awt.Toolkit;

public class PrintFont extends java.applet.Applet {
   String fontList[];

 public void init() {
    fontList = getToolkit().getFontList();
 }

 public void paint(java.awt.Graphics g) {
   int y=10;

   for (int i=0; i<fontList.length; i++) {
   g.drawString(fontList[i], 10, y+=15);
 }

 }

}
```

Class `java.awt.Font` defines three constants to represent font styles: `Font.PLAIN`, `Font.BOLD`, and `Font.ITALIC`. You can represent a combination of bold and italic using `Font.BOLD + Font.ITALIC`.

Example: `SimpleTickerTape2`

Our next example is a new and improved version of `Simple-TickerTape`. We call it `SimpleTickerTape2`. It will make use of `toolBox.ParamParser` to get parameter values from an HTML file. It also shows how to change the font and color of an applet. Before you try to compile and run SimpleTickerTape2, you should read the sidebar, "Setting up the Directory Structure."

Setting up the Directory Structure

All of the applets in this chapter, from `SimpleTickerTape` on, make use of the `ParamParser` utility we created. Because `ParamParser` has been defined in the package `toolBox`, we must make sure that all the applets have direct access to the directory `toolBox`, in which the compiled bytecode file `ParamParser.class` must be stored.

There are several ways to accomplish this, but the simplest way—both for the purposes of getting through this chapter and so that you can easily place these applets on a Web server when you're done—is to place all the applets for this chapter in a single directory and to make `toolBox` a subdirectory of that directory.

If you use this directory structure, you will not have to change your `CLASSPATH` variable or use the `CODEBASE` attribute of the `<APPLET>` tag in your HTML files.

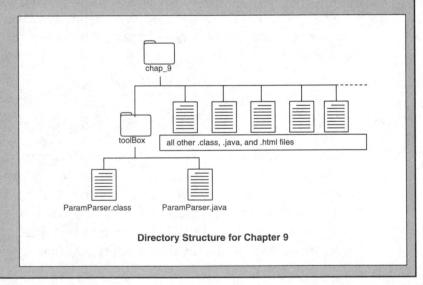

Directory Structure for Chapter 9

A More Comprehensive Directory Structure

The directory structure we chose to use in this chapter was motivated by a desire for simplicity. We wanted to be able to set up the directories on the CD-ROM so that they were organized by chapter, and we also wanted you to be able to set up and run the applets in this chapter with a minimum of housekeeping. As in life, however, if you don't commit yourself to a certain degree of housekeeping, things quickly become an intolerable mess. If you were to use the directory structure we use in this chapter for all of your Java programming, that is what would eventually result. You'd have all of your .class, .java and .html files in a single directory, and it would soon be nearly impossible to find anything in that mess.

In this sidebar, we propose a more generally useful directory structure. The discussion that follows, however, assumes a slightly more advanced level than the rest of the chapter. If you just want to get through this chapter, you can simply ignore this sidebar for now, and then come back and read it at another time. Nothing we do in this chapter as a whole requires the information in this sidebar; in fact, you'd need to restructure some of the instructions in this chapter in order to make them work with this alternate, more comprehensive directory structure. However, as you become a more experienced Java programmer, you will probably want to use a directory structure more like the one proposed below.

The root of the structure is a directory we've called main_dir, in which you place all of your HTML files. You may optionally place the HTML files in subdirectories of main_dir. Beneath main_dir is a subdirectory called classes, which may optionally be a symbolic link to a central classes directory somewhere else on the server. All .class files are stored in the classes directory, or some subdirectory of it, named according to whatever local package-naming conventions are in use. This way, future projects can make use of packages and classes created for earlier projects—such as our `toolBox` package—referencing them and extending them wherever necessary or convenient.

To make this scheme work, you need to make sure that any HTML files with `<applet>` tags include the attribute `codebase="classes"`. (Naturally, any HTML files in subdirectories of `main_dir` should specify `codebase="..-/classes"`.) You should also specify the full path to the `classes` directory in your `CLASSPATH` variable.

Images and audio files are stored in appropriately-named subdirectories of `main_dir`; these may also optionally be symbolic links.

This structure provides several advantages. It keeps the server organized, so that it's more easily maintained, and it allows the reuse of existing code (a key benefit of OOP). Additionally, if you develop applets on a machine other than the server, you can use a parallel directory structure on the development machine, so that when you upload your completed applets and Web pages to their appropriate directories on the server, all of the links will still work.

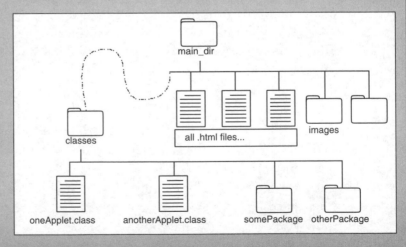

Create the Source File

For the most part, SimpleTickerTape2 is the same as SimpleTickerTape. We need to make only a few changes to SimpleTickerTape in order to have it subclass ParamParser. The easiest way to make the changes is to copy the file **SimpleTickerTape.java**, rename the copy **SimpleTicker-Tape2.java**, and alter the new file as follows.

Change the declaration of the class so that it reads as follows (change the name of the class and add the extends clause):

```
public class SimpleTickerTape2 extends toolBox.ParamParser
implements Runnable {
```

Add the following variable declarations immediately after the declarations for msg, x, y, horizStep, pause, and msgWidth:

```
int width;      // applet's width
int height;     // applet's height
```

Replace the declaration for init() so that it reads:

```
public void init() {

    // show error message to console if parameter is invalid.
    displayErrMesg = true;

    // set the message font. fontsytle 1 is bold
    setFont (getFontParameter("FONTNAME", "TimesRoman",
    "FONTSTYLE", 1, "FONTSIZE", 20));

    // get the message
    msg = getStringParameter("MESSAGE",
    "I am a multi-threaded applet!");

    // get the font metrics of the applet
    fm = getFontMetrics(getFont());

    // get the width (in pixel) of the message
```

```
msgWidth = fm.stringWidth(msg);

// set applet's width longer than the message's width
width = x = msgWidth + 60;

// get the height (in pixel) of the selected font
int fontHeight = fm.getHeight();

// set applet's height taller than the message's height
height = fontHeight + 60;

// vertically center the message
y = fontHeight + 30;

// set the scrolling message step.
horizStep = getIntParameter("STEPSIZE", 1, msgWidth, 2);

// smaller the number, faster the text scroll
pause = getIntParameter("PAUSE", 100, 10000, 100);

// set color of the message -- default = red
setForeground(getColorParameter("MSG_COLOR", "RED"));

// resize the applet size to the size of the message.
resize (width, height);
}
```

Create the HTML File

Create an HTML file, called `SimpleTickerTape2.html`, and place the following tag group in it:

```
<applet code="SimpleTickerTape2.class" width=600 height=200>
<param name=MESSAGE value="Welcome to Java Basics!">
<param name=PAUSE value="100">
<param name=STEPSIZE value="2">
<param name=FONTNAME value="Helvetica">
<param name=FONTSTYLE value="1">
<param name=FONTSIZE value="30">
<param name=MSG_COLOR value="green">
</applet>
```

Naturally, if you want, you can change the values of these parameters to suit yourself.

Understanding the Code

Most of this code is recycled. There's very little new here, other than a combination of various things we've already learned.

One thing that deserves some attention, though, is that this is the first working applet we've created that uses a package of our own design. When we design our own packages, we have to make sure they are stored in a place where they can be accessed when they need to be used. Some packages are created for local use only. Others, however, are needed by applets on Web pages and must be put where the client can download them; otherwise, they will not be able to run applets that depend on these packages.

When the Java runtime system needs to load a class, it searches each location specified in the CLASSPATH, looking for a directory whose name matches the first component of the class's package name (or just the class name, if it's in the default package). If it finds such a directory, it uses the package name to reconstruct the path to the appropriate .class file. Otherwise, if it is an applet that needs to load the class, then the next place the system will try to locate the package is in the location specified by the CODEBASE; that is, the location in which the applet's .class file resides. Recall that if no CODEBASE is specified in the <applet> tag, then the CODEBASE is set by default to the directory in which the HTML document resides.

Thus, the simplest way to make a custom package available to clients running your applet is to put the package directory in the same directory as the applet.

Documenting Applet Parameters

It's not uncommon for an applet to define many parameters. This makes the applet more customizable and reusable. The problem with this is that it's hard to memorize a large number of parameters. To make it easier for those using your applets, you can override the method `getParameterInfo()` defined in class `java.applet.Applet`. If you do this, then anyone using the `appletviewer` to test your applet can pull down a menu allowing them to see the parameters of your applet, among other information.

NOTE

If you are using Netscape, you should document your applet parameters in some other form, such as HTML, because the current version of Netscape does not support this feature.

The following example shows how we can override `getParameterInfo()` for `SimpleTickerTape2`:

```
public String[][] getParameterInfo() {
    String[][] info = {
        {"MESSAGE", "String", "Displayed Message"},
        {"PAUSE", "int", "Pause Duration."},
        {"STEPSIZE", "int", "Step size"},
        {"FONTNAME", "String", "Font Name"},
        {"FONTSTYLE", "int", "0=Plain, 1=Bold, 2=Italic." +
        "Can be combined for mixed style."},
        {"FONTSIZE", "int", "Font Size"},
        {"MSG_COLOR", "String", "Color Name"}
    };

    return info;
}
```

There are a few things worth noticing about this code. First, the method returns an array of arrays of `String`s. (That's not a typo; it *is* an array of arrays.) Notice how the local variable `info` is initialized during its declaration. Arrays of arrays are initialized just as one-dimensional arrays are, only each element is itself an array.

Notice that if a `String` is too long to fit on one line, you must close the double-quotes on that line and then continue on the next line, using the `String`-concatenation operator `+`. You cannot simply hit the `Return` key and continue the string on the next line. If you do this, the compiler will complain that you have an unterminated `String`.

WARNING

Recall that as a rule Java does not have operator overloading. The use of `+` as the `String`-concatenation operator is one of several built-in exceptions to this rule. The fact that the arithmetic operators `+`, `-`, `*` and `/` can be used on `int`, `long`, `float`, `double`, etc., is in and of itself a kind of operator overloading. Java does not, however, allow the programmer to define new meanings for operators, as can be done in C++.

Example: `SimpleAnimator`

Our experience with the `SimpleTickerTapeBad` example taught us that any applet that is going to be updating the screen constantly should spawn a separate thread in which to run the animation. This is equally true of animated images and animated text, . Images, after all, need to be loaded from somewhere, typically the disk of the network. Since disk I/O, and especially network I/O, requires some wait time (*latency*), it makes a great deal of sense to be able to share the processor so that CPU cycles do not go to waste during this latency period.

Animation is done by displaying one static image (i.e., a *frame*) at a time, typically in an infinite loop. The idea is to display the frames in sequence, making the switch from frame to frame fast enough that our natural perceptual processes blend them into a coherent whole, which looks like a moving image.

Following is the code for SimpleAnimator. Before you type it in, notice that SimpleAnimator extends toolBox.ParamParser. The easiest way to make sure ParamParser can be loaded is to follow the directory structure laid out in the sidebar, "Setting up the Directory Structure."

```java
import java.awt.Image;
import java.awt.Graphics;

public class SimpleAnimator extends toolBox.ParamParser
    implements Runnable {
    // Maximum number of frames to load
    public final static int MAX_FRAME = 40;

    Image animationFrame[];
    int currentFrame=0;
    int numFrames;
    int pause;
    Thread myThread;
    int priority;

    public void init() {

        // get parameters from HTML file
        // (use methods inherited from ParamParser)
        String imageDir = getStringParameter("IMAGE_DIR", ".");
        String imageName = getStringParameter("IMAGE_NAME", "T");
        String extension = getStringParameter("EXTENSION", "gif");
        numFrames = getIntParameter("NUM_FRAMES", 1, MAX_FRAME, 1);
        pause = getIntParameter("PAUSE", 100, 2000, 200);
        setBackground(getColorParameter("BG_COLOR", "lightGray"));

    priority = getIntParameter("PRIORITY", Thread.MIN_PRIORITY,
        Thread.MAX_PRIORITY, Thread.NORM_PRIORITY);

        // Allocating memory for image HANDLES, not image
        animationFrame = new Image[numFrames];

        // load images
```

```
      for (int i=0; i<numFrames; i++) {
      // construct the file name of the image
      String imageFileName = imageDir + "/" + imageName +
      (i+1) + "." + extension;

      // animationFrame[i] is a handle to an Image object
      // returned by getImage().
      animationFrame[i] = getImage(getDocumentBase(),
      imageFileName);
    }

  }

public void start() {
   // allocate and run the thread
   myThread = new Thread(this);
   myThread.start();
}

public void run() {
   myThread.setPriority(priority);

   while (myThread != null) {
   repaint();
  currentFrame = (currentFrame + 1) % numFrames;
  try {
     myThread.sleep(pause);
     } catch (InterruptedException e) {
     System.out.println(myThread.toString() +
     " interrupted.");
     return;
  }
 }
}

public void paint(Graphics g) {
   g.drawImage(animationFrame[currentFrame], 0, 0, this);
}
```

```
public void stop() {

   myThread = null;
 }
}
```

Here are some HTML tags that will allow you to run this applet:

```
<applet code="SimpleAnimator.class" width=75 height=75>
<param name=image_dir value="images/globe">
<param name=num_frames value=8>
<param name=pause value=400>
<param name=bg_color value="lightGray">
</applet>
```

N O T E

For these tags to work, you will need to make sure that the HTML file is in the same directory as `SimpleAnimator.class` and that you have a copy of the directory **globe** in this directory as well. The **globe** directory contains eight images that comprise an animation of a spinning globe. It can be found on the CD-ROM, in the directory containing the `SimpleAnimator` example code.

Dynamic Memory Allocation and Arrays

When an array is declared in Java, it has no value. As we have discussed, we express "no value" in Java by the value `null`. Furthermore, if it is an array of object types (as opposed to primitive types), then instantiating the array does not, in and of itself, allocate memory for the individual objects that comprise the array. Instead, the array is instantiated as a collection of `null` handles. In order to fill the array with meaningful objects, we must either instantiate objects for the handles to point to or assign already-instantiated objects to the individual handles comprising the array.

In the animation applets presented in this chapter, we store our animation frames in an array of objects of class `java.awt.Image`. We declare the array as follows:

```
Image animationFrame[];
```

What we now have is a `null` handle called `animationFrame`. Not only does `animationFrame` have no value, but there is as yet no indication of how many items will be in the array when it is instantiated.

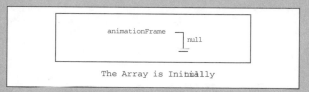

The Array is Initially null

Later, we instantiate the array as follows:

```
animationFrame = new Image[numFrames];
```

Now `animationFrame` is no longer a `null` handle. It is a handle to an array of exactly `numFrames` handles to `Image` objects. Although `animationFrame` has now been instantiated, we have *not* instantiated the individual `Image` objects in the array yet, so the individual values of `animationFrame[0]`, `animationFrame[1]`, etc., are still `null`.

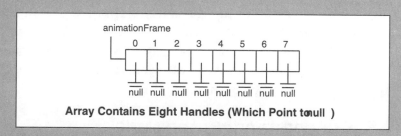

Array Contains Eight Handles (Which Point to null)

When the individual elements of the array are instantiated, memory is allocated for them individually and dynamically in the garbage-collected heap. They may or may not be contiguous in memory. We use a loop to instantiate all the elements in the array. Here is what our diagram becomes after the first three iterations of the loop:

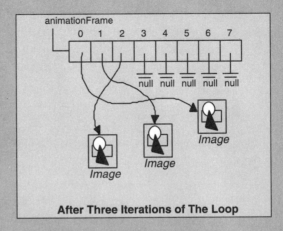

After Three Iterations of The Loop

Nothing we have said here about dynamic memory allocation is in any way specific to images. Java uses this dynamic memory allocation scheme for all objects (but not for primitive types such as `float`, `int`, and `char`). Primitive types are allocated statically.

Try changing the parameters in the HTML file. What happens if you increase the pause time? What happens if you change the PRIORITY parameter? What happens if you change the background color, and what does this tell you about the kind of image being used? What happens when you specify invalid parameters? What kinds of invalid parameters "break" the code, and what kinds do not?

Understanding the Code

Note the strong similarity between this code and the code for our ticker-tape applet. The only real difference between the two is that this example animates images, and the ticker-tape applet animates text. Other than that, the basic idea is the same: use a thread to run an infinite loop, displaying one frame at a time and pausing for a given number of milliseconds before moving on to the next frame.

There are, however, a few snippets which deserve closer attention.

Using the `abstract` class `java.awt.Image`

```
import java.awt.Image;

...

Image animationFrame[];

...

  animationFrame = new Image[numFrames];
```

Do not confuse the class `java.awt.Image` with the package `java.awt.image`. Remember, package names are case-sensitive. The class `java.awt.Image` is in fact an `abstract` class. Does it seem odd that we have declared an object that is of an `abstract` class? Remember, you cannot directly instantiate an object of an `abstract` class; you must subclass it and instantiate objects of the subclass. Notice that in our code, we never use the `new` operator to directly instantiate any objects of class `Image`. We do instantiate an array of *handles* to class `Image`, but we never instantiate individual elements of that array (see the sidebar "Dynamic Memory Allocation and Arrays"). Instead, we call `Applet.getImage()`, which constructs an object of a platform-dependent subclass of `java.awt.Image` and returns us a handle to that object. Because that object is a subclass of `java.awt.Image`, it is compatible with `java.awt.Image`, and so it can be assigned to an element of our array.

Loading the Images

```
for (int i=0; i<numFrames; i++) {
    // construct the file name of the image
    String imageFileName = imageDir + "/" + imageName +
        (i+1) + "." + extension;

    // animationFrame[i] is a handle to an Image object
    // returned by getImage().
    animationFrame[i] = getImage(getDocumentBase(),
        imageFileName);
}
```

The method `java.applet.Applet.getImage()` returns *asynchronously*. This means that it spawns a thread to do its work—which is to load an image—and then returns without waiting for the thread to complete. It returns a handle to an `Image` object, but the thread that loads the image is typically still in the process of loading the image when `getImage()` returns. Thus, even though we initiate the loading of all the images during our `init()` method, they are most likely still in the process of loading—in parallel—when we begin the loop that paints them to the screen.

This is why, if you watch the applet starting up for the first time, you will initially see a blank background and then a succession of partially loaded images, followed by a mixture of fully and partially loaded images, until finally, all images are loaded and you see the complete animation. We actually begin drawing the images on the screen before they are fully loaded. Our next example will demonstrate how we can solve this problem.

Notice that we use a call to `getDocumentBase()` in order to specify the root directory from which the images are to be loaded. The method `java.applet.Applet.getDocumentBase()` returns the URL of the directory containing the HTML file referencing the applet. When combined with the relative path to each image file, this gives us the complete URL from which the images are to be loaded.

NOTE

There is also a similar method, `java.applet.Applet.getCodeBase()`, which returns the URL of the directory containing the applet's **.class** file. Remember that there is no rule that the applet and the HTML file must live in the same directory—or even on the same server.

Drawing the Images

```
public void paint(Graphics g) {
    g.drawImage(animationFrame[currentFrame], 0, 0, this);
}
```

The method `java.awt.Graphics.drawImage()` takes as parameters an `Image`, an (*x, y*) coordinate pair—indicating the position to draw the image relative to the applet's upper-left-hand corner—and a handle to an object of class `java.awt.image.ImageObserver`. In truth, `ImageObserver` is not a true class, but rather is an interface. Recall from Chapter 8 that an interface allows objects from different class hierarchies to present themselves as if they belong, at some level, to the same class, thereby simulating multiple inheritance. Because `java.applet.Applet` implements `ImageObserver`, we can pass an applet to any method expecting an `ImageObserver`.

NOTE

Actually, `java.applet.Applet` does not *directly* implement `ImageObserver`. Rather, it inherits the implemented methods from `java.awt.Component`, which `implements` `ImageObserver` directly.

We pass `this` in as the `ImageObserver` so that `drawImage` can notify the applet i.e., `this`) when it has finished constructing the image.

In this chapter, because we're doing fairly simple things, graphically speaking, our `paint()` methods have generally included a single method call, like `drawImage()` or `drawString()`. Keep in mind that, in general, you can call as many graphical methods as you wish in an applet's `paint()` method. You can, for example draw an image and then a string on top of that, followed by a polygon, another image, and so on. As long as you don't clear the background, each item that you draw to the screen will get drawn on top of what is already there. In fact, as we've already seen, clearing the background is not a special operation; it's a normal case of drawing a rectangle on the applet's screen area, obscuring anything beneath it.

Thread Priority

In our discussion of threads, we did not mention thread priority. The priority level of a thread may range from `Thread.MIN_PRIORITY`, which is 1, to `Thread.MAX_PRIORITY`, which is 10. Higher-priority threads are given more CPU time— and therefore execute faster—than lower-priority threads. In addition, depending on your system, higher-priority threads may be allowed to pre-empt lower-priority threads, essentially kicking them off of the processor and making them wait while the higher-priority threads finish what they need to do.

Try changing the priority parameter of the HTML file. Does it have any noticeable effect on the speed of the applet's execution? Try adding two `<applet>` tags to the HTML file, one that specifies a low priority and one that specifies a high priority. Does one of them execute noticeably faster?

Reducing Image "Flicker"

You may notice a bit of "flicker" in the animation, especially if you replace the small globe animation with an animation consisting of larger images. This is rather annoying to look at.

Both our ticker-tape applet and our image animation applet suffer from this problem. Fortunately, there are ways to reduce flicker.

Whenever you call `repaint()`, the system will invoke your applet's `update()` method, which is inherited from class `java.awt.Component`. The source code for the default version of this method looks basically like this:

```
public void update(Graphics g) {
    g.setColor(getBackground());
    g.fillRect(0, 0, width, height);
    g.setColor(getForeground());
    paint(g);
}
```

All this does is clear the applet's portion of the screen and then call the applet's `paint()` method. Because the applet is clearing its screen each time it draws an image, we are seeing that blank background for a brief moment before each image is drawn; this is partially responsible for the flicker in the animation.

Because in this case the image is just drawing over itself again and again, we really don't need to redraw the background every time. We can therefore reduce the flicker by overriding the `update()` method so that it no longer redraws the background:

```
public void update(Graphics g) {
    paint(g);
}
```

This trick cannot be applied to our ticker-tape applet. In the case of the ticker-tape applet, we need to clear the screen at each iteration; otherwise, the new text will be drawn right over the old text, and the screen will soon be a jumble of intertwined and unintelligible characters. This trick is also inappropriate for animations in which the image changes its position on the screen. Additionally, you may have trouble if you use this trick on images stored in "transparent interlaced" format. This is because the initial low-resolution versions of the image will leave artifacts around the edges. As the edges become more clear, artifacts residing in the transparent portion of the image are not erased unless we redraw the background.

However, this is still not a perfect solution. If you make the preceding change in the code and then recompile the applet, you can still see some flicker. To fully solve the problem, we need to apply a technique called *double-buffering*.

Example: DoubleBufferAnimator

In order to understand double-buffering, you need to have some idea of how graphics contexts work. Imagine that the screen is a whiteboard on which I can draw graphics or text with a pen. To draw a new picture on the whiteboard from scratch, I have to take out the pen, put it to the whiteboard, perhaps think a little, and then draw. All of this takes time. If you want to see what I'm drawing, you have to wait, watching me go through the motions of drawing the picture.

Imagine, on the other hand, that I have *two* whiteboards. I let you look at one of them while I draw a new picture on the second one. This way, I show the new picture to you only when it's fully ready to be displayed; you will not have to look at the whiteboard in an inconsistent state while I draw the new picture. You only look at completed pictures.

The whiteboard in this analogy represents a *graphics context*, a data structure that the system uses as its interface to drawing on the screen. In double-buffering, we keep an invisible graphics context around, and we do all drawing to that context. When we are done drawing, we tell the system to swap in our invisible—or "off-screen"—graphics context and make it visible.

Making an already-prepared graphics context visible on the screen takes less time than the actual drawing operations we did behind the scenes.

We can add double-buffering to our animator by overriding update(). Here's a version of the animator that extends the previous version, inheriting all its fuctionality, but overriding the update() method:

```java
import java.awt.Graphics;
import java.awt.Image;

public class DoubleBufferAnimator extends SimpleAnimator {
    private Image offScreenImage;
    private Graphics offScreenGC;

    public void update(Graphics g) {
        if (offScreenImage == null) {
        // offScreenImage not yet created; create it
        offScreenImage = createImage(size().width,
            size().height);

            // get the off-screen graphics context
        offScreenGC = offScreenImage.getGraphics();

        // paint the background on the
        // off-screen graphics context
        offScreenGC.setColor(getBackground());
        offScreenGC.fillRect(0, 0, size().width, size().height);
        offScreenGC.setColor(getForeground());

    }

    // first, draw the current frame to the off-screen GC
    paint(offScreenGC);

    // draw the image to the on-screen Graphics object g
    g.drawImage(offScreenImage, 0, 0, null);
    }
}
```

Understanding the Code

The inherited code from the previous example sets up the animation frames during `init()`. The inherited `run()` method then calls `repaint()`, which calls `update()`, passing in the on-screen `Graphics` object g; i.e., the graphics context of the applet itself.

Declaring the Off-Screen Graphics Context

```
private Image offScreenImage;
private Graphics offScreenGC;
```

We use these two variables for our off-screen graphics manipulations. Notice that they are declared as `private`. The double-buffering scheme we use is part of our applet's implementation and need not be known from the outside. We count on the fact that no other entity will be altering these objects, so we declare them as `private` to ensure that is the case. In general, it's good object-oriented programming practice to declare as `private` any data that doesn't need to be accessed from the outside.

Creating the Off-Screen Graphics Context

```
if (offScreenImage == null) {
   // offScreenImage not yet created; create it
   offScreenImage = createImage(size().width,
     size().height);

     // get the off-screen graphics context
   offScreenGC = offScreenImage.getGraphics();

   // paint the background on the
   // off-screen graphics context
   offScreenGC.setColor(getBackground());
   offScreenGC.fillRect(0, 0, size().width, size().height);
   offScreenGC.setColor(getForeground());
}
```

The first time `update()` is called, it sees that the off-screen graphics context has not yet been created, so it first calls `createImage()`, inherited from `java.awt.Component`, to create an off-screen `Image`. As before, the created object is actually a system-dependent subclass of `java.awt.Image`. A graphics context cannot be created directly with the `new` operator, so in order to get our off-screen graphics context, we call `getGraphics()`, asking the system to return us a handle to the off-screen image's graphics context. Once we have that, we can draw to `offScreenGC`, and anything we draw will be imprinted on `offScreenImage`. Right away, we draw the background to the off-screen context. This sequence of steps only needs to be done once.

Drawing to the Off-Screen Graphics Context

```
// first, draw the current frame to the off-screen GC
paint(offScreenGC);
```

To draw to the off-screen graphics context, we call our inherited `paint()` method. It does just what it used to do, which is to draw the current animation frame to the passed-in graphics context. The only difference is that we have "tricked" it into drawing to our off-screen graphics context, by passing `offScreenGC` in as a parameter.

Remember, `paint()` takes a `Graphics` object as a parameter, but there is no hard-and-fast rule that it must be the visible `Graphics` context representing that applet. If that were the case, it wouldn't need to take a parameter in the first place.

Switching the Off-Screen Image to the Visible Graphics Context

```
// draw the image to the on-screen Graphics object g
g.drawImage(offScreenImage, 0, 0, null);
```

At this point, we have an off-screen graphics context, with an image painted on it. We now send a `drawImage()` message to the applet's graphics context—the "real" graphics context passed in to `update()` as g–telling it to draw the image that we have constructed off-screen. Because we know the image is fully constructed, we pass in `null` to the `ImageObserver` parameter, indicating that we do not need to be notified when the drawing is complete. We already know it is complete, because we were notified the first time when we drew the image to the off-screen graphics context in the call to our inherited `paint()` method.

MediaTracker

Now the flicker has been eliminated and the globe is rotating smoothly. But there is still one problem. As the applet starts up, it displays partially loaded images until it finishes loading everything. If you find this unattractive, there is a way to keep track of the loading images, so that you can wait until some or all of them are loaded before beginning to display the animation.

To address this problem, the API provides a class called `MediaTracker`. `MediaTracker` is used to keep track of media objects, such as images and sound files, as they are loaded, so that we don't get the kind of half-baked media displays that we've just described.

The MediaTracker is simple to use. You just tell it to register each media item you'd like to track, and then you wait for it to notify you that either a certain number or all of items have loaded. Here's the code:

```
import java.awt.MediaTracker;

public class TrackerAnimator extends DoubleBufferAnimator {
    MediaTracker tracker;

    public void init() {
        tracker = new MediaTracker(this);
        super.init(); // same init
```

```
        for (int i=0; i < animationFrame.length; i++) {
        // register the image with the tracker. And also
        // assign an id (not necessary unique) to the image.
        tracker.addImage(animationFrame[i], i);
    }
}

public void run() {
    try {
        // wait until all images are loaded
        tracker.waitForAll();
    } catch (InterruptedException e) {
    return;
    }
    super.run(); // Run our animation.
  }
}
```

Understanding the Code

Having already created such a well-rounded animator applet, adding the MediaTracker into the picture is fairly trivial. In fact, there are only a few lines of code in this file that are any different from anything we've already done. We only need to override two methods: init(), where we create the MediaTracker object and register the images in it, and run(), in which we implement the part where the applet waits for all media to load.

```
  super.init(); // same init
```

Notice the call to super.init(). This demonstrates an important point mentioned in Chapter 8 that bears repetition: Even an overriding method need not do from scratch what was done in the overridden method. If everything in the overridden method still applies, all you have to do is use the super keyword to uncover it, as we have done here, significantly decreasing the size of the code and increasing its legibility. We have done the same in the `run()` method, calling `super.run()`.

To instantiate a `MediaTracker` object, you simply pass a `Component` object for the `MediaTracker` to notify. In our case, it is the applet, so we pass in `this`.

```
// register the image with the tracker. And also
// assign an id (not necessary unique) to the image.
tracker.addImage(animationFrame[i], i);
```

As we begin loading each image, we tell the `MediaTracker` to register the image and assign it an ID number that we specify. The ID numbers are used if we later want to wait for a specific image to load. The ID numbers need not be unique. This way, we can choose to wait for a specific group of items with the same ID to load.

```
// wait until all images are loaded
tracker.waitForAll();
```

Finally, at the beginning of our `run()` method, we *block* (that is, wait) until all the items have loaded. This way, when we actually start drawing on the screen, we are guaranteed to have complete images.

That's all there is to it.

NOTE

The current version of `MediaTracker` does not support audio; thus, you cannot register an audio clip in a `MediaTracker` object. However, future versions are expected to support audio.

Audio

The Java API class `java.applet.AudioClip` deals with the playing of audio files. In this version, audio capability is limited.

As you just learned, `MediaTracker` does not yet support audio. Also, Sun currently only supports the **.au** audio file format through its proprietary packages (`sun.audio`). Furthermore, even the limited audio capabilities of the current Java release are somewhat buggy on the Windows and Mac platforms.

Audio data in Java is handled very similarly to image data. There is a method `getAudioClip()`–very similar to `getImage()`– that loads an audio clip. Once an audio clip is loaded, there are only three methods you can use to control it: `play()`, `loop()`, and `stop()`. These methods are fairly self-explanatory.

Summary

Because an applet is managed by an underlying application, such as a Web browser or the `appletviewer`, its life cycle is defined by the methods that provide that application's interface to the applet. The basic life-cycle methods of an applet are `init()`, `start()`, `stop()`, and `destroy()`. These methods are defined in `java.applet.Applet`; one typically creates an applet by subclassing `java.applet.Applet` and overriding the life-cycle methods.

Animation applets provide an excellent training ground for discovering multithreading, exception handling, and many other techniques that are an essential part of a Java programmer's repertoire. The object-oriented nature of Java provides a mechanism by which these techniques may be introduced in a modular fashion, reusing existing code and adding functionality via subclassing and inheritance.

In Chapter 10, we will build on our understanding of applet programming techniques, exploring various aspects of the Java API, including the Abstract Windowing Toolkit for constructing graphical user interfaces in Java.

JAVA
PROGRAMMING
BASICS

Exploring the Java API

Introducing the Java API

What is an API?

API stands for Application Programming Interface, a set of commonly used functions and data types, or in the case of an object-oriented language like Java, commonly used classes. The purpose of an API is to minimize your development and debugging time by providing a standard set of commonly used code.

The Java API is a set of standard packages—each containing several classes—that come with the JDK. This chapter serves as a basic and general guided tour of the packages in the Java API, concentrating on the most frequently used classes in each. It is by no means exhaustive, and it is expected that you will refer often to the HTML documentation Sun supplies for the Java API.

Knowing the API can help shorten your development time, because you will find that a great many commonly used classes have already been defined for you; why implement your own stack, hash table, or resizable array if the API has already provided one? Additionally, you will often find that the API provides multiple ways of accomplishing the same task, but that one way in particular is well-suited to the application you need; knowing your way around the API is a good way to ensure that you use it to your own advantage. Finally, much of the API is actually written in Java; studying the source code for the API classes can help increase your understanding not only of individual classes and how they behave but also of how to use the language as a whole.

NOTE

To find out how to download the source code for the API, go to http://java.sun.com/source.

Sun has promised the public that the interface for the standard API is frozen. This means that developers are safe to create software using the standard API, without worrying that their code will be rendered nonfunctional and obsolete by future versions of Java. Code written to the specifications of Java API 1.0 can always be used in future releases of the JDK.

Besides the standard Java API, you are likely already using some proprietary APIs. For example, when you use Netscape, you are using not only the standard Java API, but the Netscape Java API and Sun's proprietary API for audio support. The Java debugger (jdb, see Appendix A) also uses a proprietary API from Sun. Unlike the standard API, proprietary APIs are written with specific software and/or hardware in mind and are custom-tailored to the platform for which they are written. Unless specifically promised, vendors may change these APIs in future versions. Finally, you are unlikely to be allowed to see the source code for a proprietary API.

The compiled `.class` files for the Java API are stored in a zipped file called `classes.zip`, typically in the `lib` subdirectory of the Java home directory. The Java compiler and the interpreter can read the classes directly from the zipped file. *Do not unzip the file*; it takes significantly more space to hold individual `.class` files, and it actually takes longer to access them in unzipped format.

What's in the Java API?

The Java API consists of eight packages. Some of them we've already used in this book; some will be explained in this chapter; some are mainly used by the system, and unless you are porting Java to a new platform, you don't need to worry about them (we won't cover these).

Before we look at individual classes from each package, let's take a quick overview of what each package provides.

java.applet

This package contains mostly interfaces that are used to build an applet viewer. These interfaces are rarely used by applet programmers. The only true class in `java.applet` is class `Applet` itself, which we have already discussed. This chapter will not elaborate further on the package `java.applet`.

java.awt

AWT stands for Abstract Windows Toolkit. This package contains all the widget, graphics, and layout classes you use for building GUIs in Java. Using the AWT will be a major topic of this chapter.

java.awt.image

This package contains classes to manipulate images (i.e., filtering, compression, etc.). You would typically use these classes to implement support for a new image format in Java. If you are not writing this sort of sophisticated code, you'll rarely use classes in this package. We will not discuss it further in this chapter.

java.awt.peer

If you compare this package and `java.awt`, you will find that they are very similar. Classes in `java.awt.peer` are the native "peer" of the classes in `java.awt`. Scrollbars, buttons, menus, check boxes, etc., all have a distinctive look and feel on each different platform. Each platform provides native support for the construction and maintenance of these elements. By implementing the interfaces in the peer classes, one provides a sort of translation mechanism between the generic Java widgets and their native counterparts, allowing Java programs to have the same GUI look and feel as other programs on the native platform. Unless you are porting Java to a new platform, you don't need to concern yourself with this package at all.

java.io

This package contains classes to do sequential and random file I/O. In addition, it contains various types of input and output stream classes, which facilitate all sorts of specific I/O applications, including networking, console I/O, and interthread communication via "pipes." Later in this chapter, we will discuss some commonly used classes in `java.io`.

NOTE

For security reasons, applets are forbidden to read, write, create, or check the accessibility or existence of files and directories. This type of functionality is reserved for stand-alone applications. See Chapter 12 for a more detailed explanation.

java.lang

This package contains basic functions necessary for any Java program. (Recall from Chapter 5 that every Java program explicitly imports `java.lang.*`.) It contains the wrapper classes for primitive data types (such as `Integer` and `Boolean`). It also contains the classes `String` and `StringBuffer`. It contains the class `Math`, which provides commonly used mathematical functions. Also contained in this package are the class `Thread` and the `Runnable` interface. This chapter will examine some of the classes in this package.

java.net

This package contains classes to handle network connections. The most commonly used classes are `URL`, `Socket`, and `ServerSocket`. We will discuss these classes in this chapter; in the next chapter, we will provide a client-server example using both `Socket` and `ServerSocket`.

java.util

This package contains some useful data structures that will be discussed later in this chapter, such as `Stack`, `Hashtable`, `StringTokenizer`, and `Vector`.

Frequently Used Classes

In this section, we take a slightly more detailed look at some of the more frequently used classes in four of the packages described earlier: `java.lang`, `java.util`, `java.io`, and `java.net`.

Package `java.lang`

String **and** StringBuffer

We have used the `String` class often in this book. We have converted objects to `String` representations, printed `Strings`, passed `Strings` as arguments to methods, and assigned values to `Strings`. Having created a `String` object, however, we never actually change its size or contents. The reason for this is that objects of class `String` are *immutable*. Once you instantiate a `String` object with a set of characters, you cannot change its size or replace its characters; in effect, the `String` becomes a constant.

Why make `Strings` immutable? It is cheaper (in terms of memory overhead) and safer. Because a `String` has a constant length, the virtual machine doesn't need to put aside extra space for the `String` to expand into or worry about wasted space due to fragmentation, should the `String` contract. Passing `Strings` to methods is safer this way, because you can be sure that the contents will not be changed without your knowledge.

Sometimes, of course, you need to change the size or contents of a string variable. In these cases, you use a `StringBuffer`. A `StringBuffer` is more mutable than a `String`. To change the contents of a `String`, you first convert it to a `StringBuffer` by passing it as a parameter to the `StringBuffer` constructor. Then you operate on the `StringBuffer`. Finally, having made whatever changes you need to, simply use the `StringBuffer`'s `toString()` method to convert it back into a `String`.

You can append characters to the end of a `StringBuffer`, or insert characters at any point, causing the `StringBuffer` to grow in length. You can overwrite individual characters of the StringBuffer. You can decrease the length of the `StringBuffer` with its `setLength()` method, deleting characters from the end. You cannot, however, delete characters from within the

`StringBuffer`. In order to do this, you need to construct a new `StringBuffer` and copy into it the characters you wish to keep.

Note that the class `StringBuffer` overloads its `append()` and `insert()` instance methods, so that you can append or insert any primitive data type to a `StringBuffer`. You can also append or insert any object to a `StringBuffer`. The object's `toString()` method—either an overridden version or the version inherited from `Object`—will be used to convert the object to a `String`, the characters of which will be inserted or appended to the `StringBuffer`.

NOTE

Most of the classes defined in the API override the method `toString()`, inherited from `java.lang.Object`, the mother of all classes. It's a good idea to override this method in any class you define to facilitate printing a meaningful representation of an object's value. This way, you can append and insert it into strings and easily print its value by placing it in a `println()` call.

We have actually been using `StringBuffer` implicitly throughout this book. Consider the following line of code:

```
String imageFile = imageFileName + "." + imageType;
```

During compile time, this line is actually translated into the following:

```
String imageFile = new
StringBuffer().append(imageFileName).append(".").append(imageT
ype).toString();
```

Incidentally, converting between `StringBuffer`s and `String`s is computationally very inexpensive. When you call a `StringBuffer`'s `toString()` method, it does not create a new copy of the character array, but rather the returned `String` and the `StringBuffer` share the character array. Only if the

`StringBuffer` is altered will a new copy be made, so that the `String` can remain unchanged.

Thread

When you run an applet, whether or not you explicitly create any threads, there are at least three threads running: the system thread, the main thread of your applet, and the garbage collector. If your applet `implements` the `Runnable` interface, you can add one more to that count. One of the goals of Java was to make threads so lightweight that they cost nearly nothing to use. (This is a goal that has not translated well to UNIX versions of Java but has been fairly successful in Windows versions.)

Notice that spawning a thread is not the same as spawning a *process* with `fork()` in UNIX. `fork()` actually creates a separate process, each with its own independent execution stack, program counter, and separate memory space. Processes do not share variables with other processes; not even with the process that spawned them.

Like a separate process, each thread has its own execution stack and program counter. Unlike processes, however, threads may share access to some of the same variables. This requires careful programming. Imagine two threads whose job is to read a variable, "think" about it for a little while, and then write a new value back to the variable. If thread A is thinking about the variable while thread B writes it back, then we have two problems: thread A is thinking about a value that is no longer current, and thread B's change will be undone when thread A writes the variable back.

The solution is provided by the keyword `synchronized`. In Chapter 8, we mentioned briefly that a method declared as `synchronized` may only be executed by one thread at a time. Computer scientists call this sort of concurrency control a *monitor*, or a lock. The terminology comes from the idea of a watchful monitor, who ensures that when one thread begins executing the method, all others are locked out (forced to wait) until that thread has completed the method, at which point the lock is released, and another thread may enter the critical section.

To make use of the concurrency control features provided by Java, you first isolate those areas of your program—called *critical sections*—where shared data is being accessed in a way that could cause an inconsistency, such as the one described above. Having isolated the critical sections, you place these parts of your program in synchronized methods or blocks, thereby ensuring that only one thread may execute them at a time.

synchronized Methods

There are two ways to do synchronization. The first way is to synchronize an entire method, as in the following:

```
synchronized int updateCounter () {
    return ++counter;
}
```

synchronized methods which operate on instance variables (that is, synchronized, non-static methods) need only require protection from other threads belonging to the same instantiation. Therefore, there is one lock per instantiation of the object. When a thread is executing a synchronized method in that object, no other threads may access that object's variables or call its methods. They must wait until the synchronized method has completed.

Methods which are both synchronized and static, however, do not operate on instance variables, but on static data. Since static data is essentially global in scope, synchronized static methods must ensure that *no* object of this class, or any derived class, is executing this method simultaneously. Thus, for synchronized static methods, there is one lock *per class*, and that one lock affects all derived classes as well. When a thread is executing a `synchronized static` method, no other thread may access the variables or call the methods of *any object* of that class, nor access any `static` method or variable of that class.

synchronized Blocks

Sometimes you don't need to declare an entire method as . It is often sufficient to find the specific statements that form the critical section, and create a "`synchronized` block," for example:

```
public void aMethod() {

    ...

    // beginning of critical section
    synchronized (myTable) {
    myTable.data[++myTable.numRecords] = myRecord;
    System.out.println("Record #" + myTable.numRecords +
            " has been added to the myTable.");
    }
    // end of critical section


    ...


}
```

The expression in the parentheses after the word `synchronized` must evaluate to an object or array. Whatever object or array it evaluates to may not be modified by any other thread while the `synchronized` block (or statement) is being executed. You can use this same approach to synchronize a single statement:

```
synchronized (myTable) myTable.numRecords++;
```

WARNING

Although using synchronized blocks (instead of synchronizing entire methods) is attractive because it allows programs to run more efficiently, it can also create more room for error. It is easy to miss parts of a method that should be synchronized, and these errors can be difficult to trace.

Putting critical sections in `synchronized` methods or blocks is a basic technique for making your programs *threadsafe*; it provides a thread with a guarantee that the shared data it is reading and/or writing cannot be altered when it expects that data to remain stable. Building threadsafe programs is of critical importance, especially for large projects, in which it often makes sense to use as many threads as you can, dividing the various tasks of the program so that while one thread is waiting for I/O and has nothing to do, another thread can use the processor to perform a computation.

Package `java.util`

Hashtable

A hashtable object can be thought of from a high level as a heterogeneous associative array of objects. In English, this means that it is a collection of key/value pairs, where the keys—unlike normal array indices—are not necessarily numbers, and the values in the array are not necessarily objects of the same class. If you insert a key/value pair into a given `Hashtable` h using `h.put(key, value)`, then you can later retrieve the value using `h.get(key)`. Not surprisingly, you can also remove a key/value pair from the `Hashtable` using `h.remove(key)`.

Properties

Class `Properties` is subclassed from `Hashtable`, providing efficient mapping of a key `String` to a value `String`. To add a key/value pair to some `Properties` object `myProp`, you call the method `myProp.put(key, value)`, which is inherited from `java.util.Hashtable`. You can use any class of object for `key` and `value`, although what you get back when you execute the retrieval method `getProperty(key)` will be a `String` representation of the value.

`Properties` objects are useful when you want printable representations of key/value pairs.

Enumeration

`Enumeration` is an interface that may be implemented by any class representing a collection of objects. The `Enumeration` is used to step through the elements in the collection. The only two methods in the `Enumeration` interface are `hasMoreElements()` and `getNextElement()`. The `Enumeration` interface makes no guarantees about the order in which elements are returned, although one can certainly implement `Enumerations` that do make such guarantees. Those familiar with object-oriented programming will recognize the `Enumeration` interface as embodying the familiar concept of an abstract *iterator* over a collection of objects.

One does not generally instantiate an `Enumeration` object directly. Typically, you ask an object representing a collection (such as a `Hashtable`, a `Properties` object, or a `Vector`) to create an `Enumeration` for you and return it. You can then use the returned `Enumeration` object to step through the items in the collection. Note that there is no way to go backwards in an `Enumeration`; it is considered to be *consumed* as you step through it. If you want to go back to a previous object in the `Enumeration`, you either have to keep a reference to it or ask the collection object to create another `Enumeration` for you and step through the new `Enumeration` from the beginning again.

Do not confuse the `Enumeration` interface with the concept of an enumerated type (using the `enum` keyword) found in ANSI C and C++. These are two fundamentally different concepts. Java does not have enumerated types, although `static final` variables can be used to provide a reasonable simulation of the functionality enumerated types provide.

StringTokenizer

This class implements interface `Enumeration`. The constructor for a `StringTokenizer` takes three parameters: a `String` that you want to split into tokens, a second `String` comprised of the characters that you wish to be the token delimiters, and finally, a `boolean` value indicating whether or not you wish the delimiters to be included as the last character of each token. Having constructed the `StringTokenizer`, you can step through the elements using `nextToken()`, and each element will be the next token extracted from the `String`. For example, you could break up an English sentence into words by using spaces and punctuation as delimiters:

```
String theSentence = "Frankly, my dear Scarlett, I don't give " +
        "two hoots of a Spotted Owl!"
StringTokenizer theWords = new StringTokenizer(theSentence,
        "., !", false);
```

Here is another, more practical example, illustrating the use of `Properties` and `StringTokenizer`. The class `java.lang.System` maintains a `Properties` object, which stores information about the local system. To see what these properties are, you can run the following program. Because applets are not allowed access to all the properties, you may notice that you get different results, depending on whether you run the program as an applet or a stand-alone application; it can be run as either. When you call the method `java.lang.System.getProperties()`, you are returned a `string` object containing a list of name and value pairs, separated by commas, and surrounded by curly braces. It makes the output much more readable if we take out the commas and curly braces and put each element of the list on a separate line. This is where the `StringTokenizer` comes in handy.

```java
import java.util.StringTokenizer;

public class PrintProperties extends java.applet.Applet {
 String propString;

 public PrintProperties() {
  java.util.Properties p = System.getProperties();
  propString = p.toString();
 }

 public static void main(String args[]) {
  PrintProperties app = new PrintProperties();
  StringTokenizer st = new StringTokenizer(
   app.propString, "{,}", false);

  while (st.hasMoreTokens()) {
   System.out.println(st.nextToken());
  }
 }

 public void paint(java.awt.Graphics g) {
  StringTokenizer st = new StringTokenizer
          (propString, "{,}", false);
  int y = 10;

  while (st.hasMoreTokens()) {
   g.drawString(st.nextToken(), 10, y+=15);
  }
 }

}
```

Notice that because `StringTokenizer` is an `Enumeration`, we can only read through the values in `st` once. This is why each time the applet is repainted with `paint()`, we create a new `StringTokenizer` and extract the values anew so that we can paint them on the screen.

Vector

A `Vector` is an array with adjustable size. A `Vector` array can hold objects but not primitive-type data. It is, however, fairly trivial to wrap primitive-type data in the wrapper classes supplied in `java.lang`. You can use `Vector` to optimize storage management by dynamically adding and deleting objects from a `Vector`. A good example of the use of `Vector` is the class `java.util.Stack`. We'll also use the `Vector` class in our GUI example later in this chapter.

Stack

Generally, a *stack* is a list of objects, with certain well-defined operations: you can *push* a new object onto the top of the stack, thereby adding it to the list, or you can *pop* the top object off the stack, thereby deleting it from the list but returning a reference to it so you can use it. All adding and deleting happens at the top of the stack, so if you push, say, five items on the stack, then you have to pop off the last four before you can get at the first one again. A stack is an example of what is called a *FILO* (First-In-Last-Out) data structure. Stacks are very useful for implementing nested or recursive control and data structures; every modern run-time system uses a stack to keep track of local variables.

`Stack` is a subclass of `Vector` that provides a `push()` method; a `pop()` method; a `boolean` method called `empty()`, which tells you if the stack is empty; and a method aptly named `peek()`, which returns the top item from the stack *without* deleting it.

Package `java.io`

`InputStream` **and** `OutputStream`

What is a stream? A *stream* is an imaginary path that carries data between two points—a source and a destination. The source and the destination are simply endpoints of the communication. The endpoints could be any entity that can give our program input or receive its output—such as a file, the console, the keyboard, a network socket (see `java.net`), etc.

At the most general level, there are two kinds of streams— input streams, from which our program may read data, and output streams, to which our program may write data. These two general kinds of streams are represented by the `abstract` classes `java.io.InputStream` and `java.io.OutputStream`, respectively. The bulk of the `java.io` package consists of 10 classes subclassed from `InputStream` and 7 subclassed from `OutputStream`.

A particularly powerful feature of the stream classes is that they may be chained together, so that you can use the combined functionality provided by several different stream classes to process the same stream of data.

We won't cover all the stream classes here, but we will go over some of the most commonly used.

N O T E

Nearly any operation involving input or output has an inherent unreliability; it is dependent on hardware and system conditions that are beyond the control of the programmer. As a result, virtually every method defined in any of the classes in `java.io` is declared with the clause `throws IOException`. `IOException` is not a subclass of `RuntimeException`. As we have discussed, when you call a method that might throw an exception—other than a `RuntimeException`—you have a choice: either catch it or throw it (see Chapter 9). To concentrate on the topic at hand, we have chosen to ignore (throw) these exceptions in most of the examples that follow.

FileInputStream **and** FileOutputStream

You can use these two classes to read or write files, respectively.

```
// to open a file for reading
FileInputStream fis = new FileInputStream("InputFile");

byte b[] = new byte[100];
// read the first 100 byte of data into b
int numByteRead = fis.read(b);
System.out.println(new String(b, 0, 0, numByteRead));
System.out.println(numByteRead + " bytes read.");
```

If the file is not found in this example, a FileNotFound-Exception will be thrown by the FileInputStream() constructor. If the file exists but is not readable, an IOException will be thrown. When a FileInputStream is constructed from a String, the parameter to the constructor may optionally be the simple name of a file in the current working directory or a full or relative path to the file.

```
// to open a file for writing
FileOutputStream fos = new FileOutputStream("OutputFile");
```

If the file is not found when the FileOutputStream constructor is called, it will be created. If the specified path is not valid, the constructor will throw FileNotFoundException. If the file exists but may not be written, an IOException will be thrown.

N O T E

The file path is somewhat system-dependent. If you try to open a file on UNIX using the Windows style path, using the backslash ("\") as a separator, you will get an IOException. The solution is to always use the forward slash ("/") because Java guarantees to treat this character as a file separator, translating it when necessary to maintain system independence.

You don't necessarily need to use a `string` to construct `FileInputStream` or `FileOutputStream` objects. You can optionally pass in a `FileDescriptor` or `File` object to the constructor. These two classes are explained later.

Once you have constructed the `FileInputStream` or `FileOutputStream` object, you can access the file using the methods implemented in the class. If you read the API documentation, you will find that these two classes have very limited functionality. For example, you cannot read or write `strings`, `Objects`, or most primitive data types to or from these stream classes; you can only read or write `bytes`. That's why you need to chain the `FileInputStream` or `FileOutputStream` to some other stream with more functionality.

DataInputStream **and** DataOutputStream

Typically, you will want to look at input and output streams from a higher level than as a stream of bytes. In general, you will want to think of them as streams of characters or of primitive or object types. This way, you can read and write integers, characters, or even lines of text at a time. If you only use `FileInputStream` and `FileOutputStream` to read or write to files, you will need to perform all these conversions yourself.

The classes `DataInputStream` and `DataOutputStream` allow you to read and write data at a slightly higher level than simple streams of bytes. Data is read from a `DataInputStream` or written to a `DataOutputStream` as a binary representation of its primitive type. Thus, a `DataInputStream` has instance methods such as `readInt()`, which reads 32 bits of data and returns an interpretation of them as an `int`; `readDouble()`, which reads 64 bits of data and returns an interpretation of them as a `double`, etc. A `DataOutputStream` provides instance methods such as `writeInt()`, which takes an `int` as a parameter and writes its 32-bit binary representation to the stream; `writeDouble()`, which takes a `double` as a parameter and writes its 64-bit binary representation, etc.

For the most part, `DataInputStream` and `DataOutputStream` follow a parallel design. However, of the ways in which they are not parallel, one is of particular importance. `DataInputStream` provides a method `readLine()` for which there is no counterpart in `DataOutputStream`. As you would expect, `readLine()` reads a line of one-byte ASCII characters from the stream, stopping when it sees an end-of-line (\n) or end-of-file character, returning the characters in a `String`. This provides a convenient way to read lines of text from an ASCII file or from the standard input.

N O T E

`readline()` reads 8-bit ASCII characters, not 16-bit Unicode characters. The `String` that it returns contains the Unicode counterparts of the ASCII characters read from the stream.

There is no analogous method defined in `DataOutputStream`. For writing `Strings` to a stream, you will want to use a `PrintStream`. Thus, `DataInputStream` is optimized for text input, whereas `DataOutputStream` is not.

N O T E

Although the standard output stream, `System.out`, is declared as a `PrintStream`, which is optimized for text output, the standard input, `System.in`, is declared simply as an `InputStream`, meaning that you need to chain it to a `DataInputStream` in order to facilitate text input with calls such as `readLine()`.

PrintStream

`PrintStream` is a class of output stream optimized for text output. This stream does not come in a pair because a `PrintStream` is by nature an output stream.

`PrintStream` provides methods such as `print()` and `println()`, which will print to the stream a `String` representation of any object or primitive type. You can chain a `FileOutputStream` or a `DataOutputStream` to a `PrintStream` in order to add the ability to use `print()` and `println()`. The standard output stream `System.out` and the standard error stream `System.err` are both examples of class `PrintStream`.

NOTE

The characters put to a stream by `print()` and `println()` are output using their 8-bit ASCII representation, rather than the 16-bit Unicode representation. The top 8 bits of each character are simply discarded, leaving the lower 8 bits. Recall that the ASCII character set is a strict subset of the Unicode character set. Thus, for characters in the ASCII character set, this does not present a problem. For characters in non-Latin character sets, however, the standard `print()` and `println()` methods will generally not be appropriate.

`BufferedInputStream` **and** `BufferedOutputStream`

Rather than reading and writing data one item at a time, it is more efficient to read and write data in large blocks. This is called *buffered I/O*, and it provides much more efficient use of memory and processor time.

`BufferedInputStream` and `BufferedOutputStream` provide support for this kind of I/O. Thus, when you read a single item of data from a `BufferedInputStream`, a large block of data will be read into a memory buffer. Subsequently, instead of reading one item at a time from disk, which is (relatively) slow (or, for that matter from the network, which is *very* slow) you read data from the buffer, which is significantly faster. The same applies for output to a `BufferedOutputStream`. When you write data to the stream, it is actually written to a buffer in memory; when you have filled the buffer, the entire buffer is written at once to the stream's destination. The default buffer size for both of these classes is 1024 bytes, but other sizes can be specified as parameters to their constructors.

An additional advantage of buffered input is that you can go back to any position on the data stream that is still in the buffer. To facilitate this, BufferedInputStream provides the methods mark() and reset(). These methods allow you to mark() the current position in the stream, and later reset() your stream position pointer back to the marked position, so that you can reread the data.

PipedInputStream **and** PipedOutputStream

These streams are useful for thread-to-thread communication. The idea is borrowed from the UNIX pipe utility, where output of one program is sent to the input of another. The difference is that the UNIX pipe is for interprocess communication, while these streams are for interthread communication.

These two classes must be used in a pair to facilitate the connection. For example:

```
PipedInputStream lucyInput = new PipedInputStream();
PipedOutputStream rickyOutput = new
PipedOutputStream(lucyInput);
```

After this relationship has been set up, you can instantiate a Thread ricky, which can send data to another Thread lucy. When ricky writes data to rickyOutput, lucy can read that data from lucyInput. As usual, you can chain these streams to other streams to provide additional functionality.

StreamTokenizer

As you might have guessed, a StreamTokenizer is an Enumeration class, virtually identical to StringTokenizer, except that instead of extracting tokens from a String, it extracts them from an input stream. Other than that, the functionality is exactly the same.

File

A `File` object allows you to check and perform various operations with files (other than reading or writing to them—for that you need to construct a stream from the `File` object). You can check the accessibility of a `File` with `exists()`, `canRead()`, `canWrite()`, etc.; you can create a directory with `mkdir()`, rename files with `renameTo()`, obtain a list of files in a directory with `list()`, and more.

RandomAccessFile

The `RandomAccessFile` object allows you to read and write a file at the same time without opening two separate input and output streams. You can also specify the opening file accessing mode (i.e., `"rw"`). The class comes with methods to read primitive data types and more. You can also set the file pointer using seek. An example using `RandomAccessFile` is presented in the next chapter.

FileDescriptor

File descriptors are used to uniquely identify files. In addition, they are used to uniquely identify the standard input, standard output, and standard error.

You can't do anything to alter a `FileDescriptor`; it is, for all intents and purposes, opaque. You can, however, use it to construct an object of type `File`, `FileInputStream`, `FileOutputStream`, or `RandomAccessFile`. These classes all provide a `getFD()` method, by which you can obtain the `FileDescriptor` object that uniquely identifies the `File` to which they are attached. The file `FileDescriptor`s of two such streams may be compared to see if the streams are attached to the same file. Additionally, you can call a `FileDescriptor`'s `valid()` method to get back a `boolean` value indicating whether it is a valid `FileDescriptor`.

The `FileDescriptor` class defines three constant `FileDescriptor` objects: `FileDescriptor.in`, `FileDescriptor-.out`, and `FileDescriptor.err`. You can, therefore, compare a stream's `FileDescriptor` to ascertain if it is connected to these standard stream endpoints.

Chaining Streams Together

We have said several times that it is possible to chain streams together. You typically do this by creating a stream designed to attach to a certain endpoint, such as a `Socket` or a `FileInputStream`, and then passing it as a parameter to the constructor of another class of stream, designed to filter the data in some way. By *filter*, we mean that the stream class either alters the flow of the data, as in the case of `BufferedInput-Stream` and `BufferedOutputStream` or that it provides us with methods that let us view the data in a way that is convenient, such as `DataInputStream` or `PrintStream`.

Very often, you will read a text file using a `DataInputStream` or write to a text file using a `PrintStream`, in order to take advantage of the text-centered methods provided by these classes. Because these streams do not directly create, read, or write to files, we need to first create a `FileInputStream` or `FileOutputStream`. We then chain these streams, typically with nested constructor calls as in the following:

```
// create a FileInputStream and wrap a DataInputStream around it.
DataInputStream dis = new DataInputStream(
  new FileInputStream("MyInFile"));
```

```
// create a FileOutputStream and wrap a PrintStream around it.
PrintStream ps = new PrintStream(
  new FileOutputStream("MyOutFile"));
```

As we have discussed, it is usually preferred to use buffered I/O for files. The idea is to have a stream that deals with the file, a stream connected to that to handle the buffering, and a stream connected to that to give us the ability to look at the data from a higher-level point of view. Thus, we use doubly nested constructor calls:

```
// Create a FileInputStream, wrap a Buffered InputStream
//    around it, and then wrap a DataInputStream around that.
DataInputStream dis = new DataInputStream(
    new BufferedInputStream(
    new FileInputStream("MyInFile")));
```

```
// Create a FileOutputStream, wrap a BufferedOutputStream
//    around it, and then wrap a PrintStream around that.
PrintStream ps = new PrintStream(
    new BufferedOutputStream(
    new FileOutputStream("MyOutFile")));
```

If these nested constructor calls look confusing, try keeping two things in mind:

- **The *innermost* constructor is invoked *first*.** Typically, the stream that is most directly in touch with the endpoint of the data flow should be constructed first (in our examples, the endpoint is a file). Thus, if you're opening a stream to a file, then the first stream you need to construct is one that deals directly with files. The last stream constructed is typically the one to which you'll be talking most.

- **Make sure you are familiar with the types of streams we have presented and that you know what they "buy" you.** If you know what functionality you need from a stream, then you'll have a better idea of where it should lie in the flow of data. This chapter provides a good introduction to commonly used stream classes and what their advantages are. Don't be afraid to look at the API documentation, though. It can be extremely helpful.

We'll see examples of stream-chaining in action in the next chapter, when we build a client-server application.

Package `java.net`

`Socket` **and** `ServerSocket`

You need to use these two classes to create sockets for transferring data between a client and server. The client-server example in the next chapter demonstrates the use of these two classes.

URL

You can also use a URL (uniform resource locator) object to open a connection between a client and a server. The string of characters that defines a URL encapsulates the protocol, network address, and port via which the data is transmitted and received. You can construct a URL directly from a `string`; often, however, you call a method that returns a URL, enabling you to use that URL to open a connection. In such a case, you don't even need to know the protocol or type of data you are transferring; it's all contained within the URL.

We have already used the URL class to good advantage in our animation examples from the previous chapter. To get animation frames from the server, we used the following:

```
Image theImage = getImage(getDocumentBase(), "image1.gif");
```

The method `getDocumentBase()` returns a URL. Thus, the preceding statement is equivalent to:

```
Image theImage = getImage(
  new URL("http://some_site.com:80/some_dir/image1.gif"));
```

(assuming the HTML file was loaded via the HTTP protocol on port 80).

GUI Construction with `java.awt`

This section consists largely of a single major applet example. This example uses most of the `Component` widgets provided by the AWT, including `Button`, `Canvas`, `Checkbox`, `Choice`, `Panel`, `Label`, and `Scrollbar`. It is meant to give you a very basic and easily comprehensible introduction to the manner in which GUIs can be constructed in applets.

Example: `GUIExample.java`

Our `GUIExample` is a very simple drawing program. It allows you to draw one type of object, namely, rectangles. You can decide what color each `Rectangle` object will be drawn in and whether or not it will be filled with that color. As simple as the program is, it illustrates the difference between a bitmapped painting program and an object-oriented drawing program. A *painting program* puts bits on the screen and then conceives of the whole thing as a collection of bits, making no distinction between individual objects that the viewer sees as comprising the image. Our drawing program is *object-oriented*, in that each rectangle, visible to the user as an object, is also modeled in the program as an object. It would not be too difficult to modify the code—or to extend it through inheritance—to allow different types of objects to be drawn and to allow individual objects to be selected and manipulated.

NOTE

If you are using a beta Mac version of Java, your interpreter may not handle the `Scrollbar`-generated events properly, if at all. At the time of this writing, the `appletviewer` in the Mac version of Sun's JDK doesn't deal properly with horizontal `Scrollbar` drags, and Roaster (release DR1.1) doesn't respond to `Scrollbar`-generated events at all. In addition, if you're using this release of Roaster, the mouse-drag coordinates may be inappropriately translated on the `Canvas`. The developers are working on these problems, however, and by the time you read this, there may already be updates in which these problems are fixed.

Scrollbars have been known to be buggy in a few other implementations of the AWT as well.

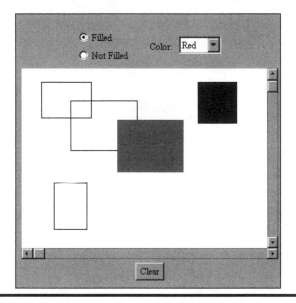

Figure 10.1 A screenshoot of GUIExample.java in action.

```
import java.applet.Applet;
import java.awt.*;          // we're using just about
everything
import java.util.Vector;

// A class for drawable rectangles
class DrawableRect extends Rectangle {

    Color color = Color.black; // What color am I?
    boolean filled = false;    // Am I filled, or not?

    // constructs a drawable rectangle with the indicated
    // dimensions and attributes
    DrawableRect(int x, int y, int width, int height,
```

```
        Color color, boolean filled) {

        super(x, y, width, height);
        this.color = color;
        this.filled = filled;
    }

    // draws a rectangle taking into account the specified
offset
    void draw(Graphics g, int offset_x, int offset_y) {

        Color temp = g.getColor();
        g.setColor(color);
        if (filled) {
            g.fillRect(x - offset_x, y - offset_y, width,
height);
        } else {
            g.drawRect(x - offset_x, y - offset_y, width,
height);
        }
        g.setColor(temp);
    }
}

class CheckboxPanel extends Panel {

    // A CheckboxGroup enforces mutual exclusion
    CheckboxGroup myGroup;

    // Two checkboxes in the group
    Checkbox filledBox;
    Checkbox notFilledBox;

    CheckboxPanel() {
        // new java.awt.Panel()
        super();
        setLayout(new BorderLayout());

        myGroup = new CheckboxGroup();
```

```java
        filledBox = new Checkbox("Filled", myGroup, false);
        notFilledBox = new Checkbox("Not Filled", myGroup, true);
        myGroup.setCurrent(notFilledBox);

        add("North", filledBox);
        add("South", notFilledBox);
    }

    // Return the state of our checkbox group
    boolean isFilled() {
        return (myGroup.getCurrent() == filledBox);
    }
}

class RectCanvas extends Canvas {
    // mouse down point
    int orig_x;
    int orig_y;

    // where the canvas has scrolled to
    public int offset_x = 0;
    public int offset_y = 0;

    // current settings for new rectangles
    boolean filled = false;
    Color rectColor = Color.black;

    // the collection of rectangles
    int numRects = 0;
    Vector rects = new Vector(100, 10);
    DrawableRect currentRect;   // just for convenience

    // create a drawable rectangle and add it to the list of rects
    DrawableRect addRect(int x, int y, int width, int height) {

        DrawableRect r = new DrawableRect(x, y, width, height,
                                rectColor, filled);
        rects.addElement(r);
        numRects++;
```

```
        return r;
    }

    // disposes of all rectangles and starts a new list
    void clearRects() {
        numRects = 0;
        rects = new Vector(100, 10);
        repaint();
    }

    // set the color for adding new rectangles
    void setRectColor(Color c) {
        rectColor = c;
    }

    // set the filled attribute for adding new rectangles
    void setFilled(boolean b) {
        filled = b;
    }

    // respond to mouseDown events
    // ... called by inherited handleEvent()
    public boolean mouseDown(Event evt, int x, int y) {

        // set the mouse-down point
        orig_x = x;
        orig_y = y;

        // start a new rectangle
        currentRect = addRect(orig_x + offset_x,
                              orig_y + offset_y, 0, 0);
        return true;
    }

    // respond to mouseDrag events
    // ... called by inherited handleEvent()
    public boolean mouseDrag(Event evt, int x, int y) {

        // how far have we dragged in x and y?
```

```java
        int x_diff = x - orig_x;
        int y_diff = y - orig_y;

        // Rectangles can't have negative height and width.
        //    We want the Rectangle to follow the mouse.
        //         Which is the top left corner?
        int x_val = (x_diff > 0)?
                orig_x + offset_x :
                x + offset_x;
        int y_val = (y_diff > 0)?
                orig_y + offset_y :
                y + offset_y;

        // Height and width determined by drag length.
        int width_val = Math.abs(x_diff);
        int height_val = Math.abs(y_diff);

        // Interactively reshape the rectangle
        currentRect.reshape(x_val, y_val, width_val,
height_val);

        // Show the results as the user drags
        repaint();
        return true;
    }

    // Draw all rectangles on the canvas
    public void paint(Graphics g) {
        DrawableRect r;

        for (int i = 0; i < numRects; i++) {
            r = (DrawableRect)rects.elementAt(i);

            // draw each rectangle, offset by the scroll amount
            r.draw(g, offset_x, offset_y);
        }
    }

}
```

```java
public class GUIExample extends Applet {

    // the top panel and its subitems
    Panel topPanel = new Panel();
    CheckboxPanel checkboxPanel = new CheckboxPanel();
    Label colorLabel = new Label("Color: ");
    Choice colorChoice = new Choice();

    // the middle panel and its subitems
    Panel middlePanel = new Panel();
    RectCanvas rCanvas = new RectCanvas();
    Scrollbar x_scroll = new Scrollbar(Scrollbar.HORIZONTAL);
    Scrollbar y_scroll = new Scrollbar(Scrollbar.VERTICAL);

    // the bottom panel and its subitem
    Panel bottomPanel = new Panel();
    Button clearButton = new Button("Clear");

    public void init() {
        // create a layout manager and set our applet to use it
        this.setLayout(new BorderLayout());

        // SET UP THE TOP PANEL...

        topPanel.setLayout(new FlowLayout());

        // the color choice
        colorChoice.addItem("Black");
        colorChoice.addItem("Blue");
        colorChoice.addItem("Red");
        colorChoice.addItem("Green");
        colorChoice.addItem("Cyan");
        colorChoice.select("Black");

        // ... add all items to the top panel
        topPanel.add(checkboxPanel);
        topPanel.add(colorLabel);
        topPanel.add(colorChoice);
```

```
        // ... add the top panel to the applet
        this.add("North", topPanel);

        // THE MIDDLE PANEL...
        middlePanel.setLayout(new BorderLayout());

        // ...set up the middle panel's RectCanvas
        rCanvas.setFilled(checkboxPanel.isFilled());
        rCanvas.setRectColor(getSelectedColor());
        rCanvas.setBackground(Color.white);

        // ...add all items to the middle panel
        middlePanel.add("South", x_scroll);
        middlePanel.add("East", y_scroll);
        middlePanel.add("Center", rCanvas);

        // ... add the middle panel to the applet
        add("Center", middlePanel);

        // THE BOTTOM PANEL...
        bottomPanel.add(clearButton);
        // ... add the panel to the applet
        this.add("South", bottomPanel);

        resize(350, 350);
    }

    public void paint(Graphics g) {
        // make sure the canvas gets repainted

        rCanvas.repaint();
    }

    // Read the currently selected color
    //  from the Choice item
    Color getSelectedColor() {
        if (colorChoice.getSelectedItem().equals("Black")) {
            return Color.black;
        } else if (colorChoice.getSelectedItem().equals("Blue"))
{
```

```java
                    return Color.blue;
                } else if (colorChoice.getSelectedItem().equals("Red"))
{
                    return Color.red;
                } else if
(colorChoice.getSelectedItem().equals("Green")) {
                    return Color.green;
                } else if (colorChoice.getSelectedItem().equals("Cyan"))
{
                    return Color.cyan;
                } else {
                    return Color.black;
                }
            }
            // overrides java.awt.Component.handleEvent()
            public boolean handleEvent(Event evt) {

                if (evt.target == colorChoice) {
                    rCanvas.setRectColor(getSelectedColor());

                } else if (evt.target instanceof Checkbox) {
                    rCanvas.setFilled(checkboxPanel.isFilled());

                } else if (evt.target == x_scroll) {
                    switch (evt.id) {
                        case Event.SCROLL_LINE_UP:
                        case Event.SCROLL_LINE_DOWN:
                        case Event.SCROLL_PAGE_UP:
                        case Event.SCROLL_PAGE_DOWN:
                        case Event.SCROLL_ABSOLUTE:
                            // evt.arg holds the value that
                            //    the scrollbar has scrolled to
                            rCanvas.offset_x = ((Integer)
evt.arg).intValue();
                            break;
                    }
```

```java
        } else if (evt.target == y_scroll) {
            switch (evt.id) {
                case Event.SCROLL_LINE_UP:
                case Event.SCROLL_LINE_DOWN:
                case Event.SCROLL_PAGE_UP:
                case Event.SCROLL_PAGE_DOWN:
                case Event.SCROLL_ABSOLUTE:
                    // evt.arg holds the value that
                    //    the scrollbar has scrolled to
                    rCanvas.offset_y = ((Integer)
evt.arg).intValue();
                    break;
            }
        }
        // the canvas has been scrolled, so...
        rCanvas.repaint();

        // make sure other events are handled by
        // ... the overridden event handler
        return super.handleEvent(evt);
    }

    // Respond to ACTION events
    // ... called by java.awt.Component.handleEvent()
    public boolean action(Event evt, Object what) {
        if (evt.target.equals(clearButton)) {

            // clear the rectangles
            rCanvas.clearRects();

        }

        // ...just in case our parent needs the event
        return super.action(evt, what);
    }

    // Overrides java.awt.Component.reshape()
    // This method is called when the user resizes the applet
```

```
public void reshape(int x, int y, int width, int height) {

    // allow java.awt.Component.reshape()
    //    ... to do the real work
    super.reshape(x, y, width, height);

    // Adjust the scrollbars:
    //   values, visible amounts, and ranges
    int canvasWidth = rCanvas.size().width;
    int canvasHeight = rCanvas.size().height;

    // ... use 1000 pixel "virtual" canvas
    x_scroll.setValues(rCanvas.offset_x,
              canvasWidth,
              0, 1000 - canvasWidth);
    y_scroll.setValues(rCanvas.offset_y,
              canvasHeight,
              0, 1000 - canvasHeight);

    // repaint the canvas
    rCanvas.repaint();
  }
}
```

Understanding the Code

The example consists of four classes, one of which is, of course, the `GUIExample` applet itself. `DrawableRectangle` is an extension of `java.awt.Rectangle`. We need to extend this class because `java.awt.Rectangle` by itself is aimed at modeling a rectangular area of the screen in general; we want a class of rectangle that knows how to draw itself, including state information about whether it is a filled rectangle and what color it is. The other two classes are extensions of AWT `Component` widgets: `RectCanvas` is a canvas that maintains and displays a collection of `DrawableRectangles`; `CheckboxPanel` gives a convenient way to encapsulate our `CheckboxGroup` widget—it's not a fully fleshed-out class, but it helps modularize some of the initialization code.

Widgets

A good deal of the functionality of our applet is not shown in our code, because it already programmed into the various "widgets" that we use and subclass—scrollbars, buttons, checkboxes, etc. Nowhere are the advantages of object-oriented programming more clearly demonstrated than in GUI design. It is an immensely complicated task to correctly implement graphical widgets, but they represent fairly simple abstractions. Object-oriented programming allows us to bury the complexity of these widgets in a hierarchy of classes that present a relatively abstract and simple interface. This is what an application programmer's interface (API) is really for: to reduce the complexity of development and provide the programmer with the abstractions they need to get things done.

What kind of complexity is hidden from us by the AWT Components? Quite a bit. For example, the Checkbox components have built into them the capability of being grouped into a CheckboxGroup, enforcing mutually exclusive selection. The Checkboxes themselves automatically respond to mouse clicks by graphically selecting themselves and, if the programmer has designated a group for them, deselecting the others in the group. Choice widgets automatically pop up a menu of choices and select one choice, which you can then query with the getSelectedChoice() method.

You don't have to respond to the mouse clicks on these components. This is, in fact, the reason that there is a handleEvent() method built into each component. The components that naturally respond to mouse clicks, keyboard presses, and other events override handleEvent(), catching these mouse clicks and then generating new events, typically some kind of ACTION_EVENT. In short, whatever functionality defines the basic nature of each widget is already built into it, so that you don't have to do it. In a little while, we'll go into more detail about how Components handle events.

The Component Hierarchy

At the most general level, we can say that there are two kinds of Components:

- "basic" Components, such as Canvas, Scrollbar, Button, Checkbox, etc., and

- Containers, or Components that can *contain* other Components, such as Window (and its subclasses, such as Frame), and Panel (and its most familiar subclass, Applet). Containers are subclassed from java.awt.Container (which is a subclass of java.awt.Component).

Because Containers can contain other Components (including other Containers), they form the branches of a hierarchical tree of Components. This hierarchy, which we'll refer to as the "Component hierarchy" is quite important for understanding both Component layout and event handling.

The Component hierarchy for our GUIExample applet is essentially the following:

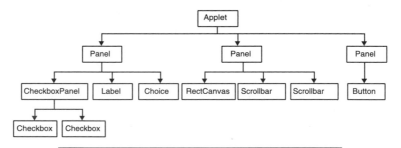

Figure 10. Component hierarchy for GUIExample.

NOTE

Don't confuse the `Component` hierarchy with the class inheritance hierarchy. The structure of the `Component` hierarchy has nothing to do with inheritance; rather, it has to do with which `Components` "belong" to which `Containers`. The arrows in the diagram above point downward in the tree, and can be thought of as representing the word "contains." (By contrast, the arrows in an inheritance diagram typically point upward in the tree, and represent the word "extends.") It is important to understand that these two hierarchies describe fundamentally distinct sets of relationships.

The class `java.awt.Container` includes a method called `add()`, by which one adds `Components` to a `Container`. For instance, in our example above, we used the following code to add three items to the `Panel topPanel`:

```
// ... add all items to the top panel
topPanel.add(checkboxPanel);
topPanel.add(colorLabel);
topPanel.add(colorChoice);
```

LayoutManagers

In order to layout `Components` on the screen, the AWT uses an object that implements the interface `LayoutManager`. A `LayoutManager` controls the rules by which a given `Container` will lay out its constituent `Components`. You typically instantiate a new `LayoutManager` object for each `Container` you create, using that `Container`'s `setLayout()` method to specify that it will use that `LayoutManager`, for instance:

```
middlePanel.setLayout(new BorderLayout());
```

There are several `LayoutManagers` defined in the standard AWT package, including the following:

FlowLayout

Perhaps the simplest LayoutManager to use, but also the one over which you have least control, is FlowLayout. FlowLayout arranges Components in rows in the order that they are added to the Container, flowing from left to right. When it runs out of space in the current row, FlowLayout creates a new row below the current row, and so on. If you do not specify a LayoutManager for a Panel or and Applet, it uses FlowLayout by default.

BorderLayout

Almost as easy to use as FlowLayout, but allowing a slightly higher degree of control, BorderLayout divides its allotted space into five regions, identified by the Strings "North," "South," "East," "West," and "Center." These regions are laid out essentially as shown in the following diagram:

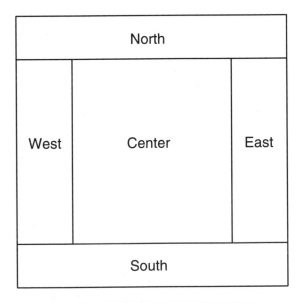

Figure 10.3 BorderLayout regions.

We used a `BorderLayout` in order to add `Scrollbars` and a `Canvas` to the `middlePanel` in our example:

```
middlePanel.setLayout(new BorderLayout());

...

// ...add all items to the middle panel
middlePanel.add("South", x_scroll);
middlePanel.add("East", y_scroll);
middlePanel.add("Center", rCanvas);
```

The following diagram shows how we used a combination of `FlowLayout` and `BorderLayout` to manage the display of the various components in our `GUIExample` applet.

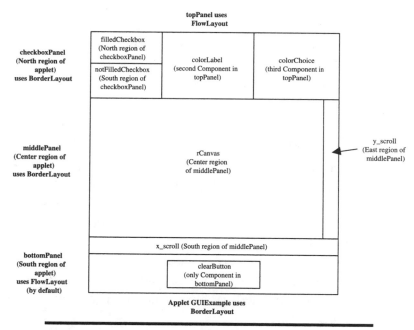

Figure 10.4 Use of LayoutManagers in GUIExample applet.

CardLayout

In a Container set up to use CardLayout, only one of the constituent Components is visible at a time. CardLayout provides methods such as first(), last(), next(), previous(), and show(), for selecting the Component to be made visible. Typically, each component added to a CardLayout will be a Container containing other components. This is useful for designing "tabbed" screens, where each screen presents a set of related controls, and the user can flip through the screens either in order, or by clicking on some sort of control, often made to simulate the index tabs on the tops of file folders.

GridLayout

GridLayout subdivides a component into a number of rows and columns (specified in the constructor). Components are placed into the cells of the grid in the order in which they are added to the Container. The cells expand and contract as necessary to fit the preferred size of the Components. Do not confuse GridLayout with its more complicated cousin, GridBagLayout, described below.

GridBagLayout

The queen of LayoutManagers, GridBagLayout offers the most flexibility and control to the programmer, but is also the most complex to use. As with GridLayout, the Container is divided into a grid of cells, but there the similarity ends. Each Component managed by a GridBagLayout may take up one or more cells, may be weighted so that it takes up a certain amount of space relative to other Components, and may also have its display area internally padded to allow some empty space between it and other components.

For each Component it manages, a GridBagLayout maintains an instance of GridBagConstraints, which contains specific information about how that particular Component is to be laid out. You can set this information by constructing an object of class `GridBagConstraints`, setting its fields appropriately, and then passing it to the `GridBagLayout`'s `setConstraints()` method, along with a reference to the `Component` whose constraints you are setting, as follows:

```
gb = new GridBagLayout();    // we need to keep a reference to gb
                             // ... so we can call its methods
c = new GridBagConstraints();
myContainer.setLayout(gb);
c.weightx = 2.0; // specify a horizontal relative weight of 2.0
gb.setConstraints(myComponent, c);
myContainer.add(myComponent);
```

In the above example, the call to `gb.setConstraints()` causes gb to create a *copy* of the `GridBagConstraints` object c and use it to manage `myComponent`; the `GridBagLayout` does not use the original object c. This makes it easy to create a single instance of `GridBagConstraints`, set its fields as desired, and use it to add multiple `Components` to the layout with the same characteristics.

`GridBagLayout` is, as we have said, rather complicated, but it is documented fairly thoroughly in the API documentation. We will not go into it further here.

Event Handling

One of the things that makes AWT code a little opaque the first time you look at it is that there is apparently no event loop. There are methods to handle events, but there is no loop that catches them. There actually *is* an event loop, but this functionality is built into Java at a lower level. You don't need to write this loop, because it's already there. Remember, we're object-oriented; there's no need to rewrite what's already written, unless we wish to modify it.

When an event occurs, the system creates an object of class `java.awt.Event`, determines the `Component` that should get the event, and calls that Component's handleEvent() method, passing the Event object in as a parameter.

Event Handling and the Component Hierarchy

What if the event could pertain to more than one Component, such as a mouse click on a Canvas contained by a Panel contained by an Applet? How does the system decide which Component should get the event first? The rule is as follows: it starts with the lowest Component in the Component hierarchy. (Remember, when we refer to the Component hierarchy, we are referring to the one established by Components and their Containers, *not* the inheritance hierarchy.) If the lowest Component's handleEvent() method returns true, then this signifies that event has been handled by that Component, and nothing further need be done. If, on the other hand, it returns false, then the system calls the handleEvent() method of the next Component up in the hierarchy: the Component's Container. The event continues to propogate up the hierarchy in this manner, until either some Component returns true from handleEvent(), or there are no Components left to which the Event pertains.

Components that Handle Events by Generating New Ones

Some Components, such as Checkbox, Button, and Choice, that have a certain degree of inherent functionality respond to events by generating additional events, often Event.ACTION_EVENT. Scrollbars generate various types of events, shown in our example; Lists (listboxes) generate Event.LIST_SELECT and Event.LIST_DESELECT, in addition to Event.ACTION_EVENT.

`java.awt.Component.handleEvent()`

Several types of events, such as `Event.MOUSE_DOWN`, `Event.MOUSE_DRAG`, and `Event.ACTION_EVENT`, are handled by the method `java.awt.Component.handleEvent()`, which responds to them by calling `mouseDown()`, `mouseDrag()`, and `action()`. In a generic `Component`—and particularly in `Applet`, `Panel`, and `Canvas`—these methods, by default, do nothing. If you want a `Component` to respond in any particular way to these particular events, then you subclass it and simply override `mouseDown()`, `mouseDrag()`, `action()`, etc., to add in the specific functionality you desire. This is what we have done in our `RectCanvas` class.

The default version of `handleEvent()`, however, does not respond to all of the `Event` types defined in `java.awt.Event`. If you need to respond to events not caught by the default `handleEvent()`, then you need to go one step further and override `handleEvent()`, as we have done in our applet class. Notice that we only use our version of `handleEvent()` to respond to those events we need that are *not* caught by the default version; once we have finished checking for those, we call `super.handleEvent()` to let the default version handle the `Events` it has already been programmed to handle, such as `ACTION_EVENT`. There's no need to *rewrite* `handleEvent()`, even when we *override* it.

To see which `Events` the default `handleEvent()` method responds to, you need to look at the code for `java.awt.Component.handleEvent()`:

```
public boolean handleEvent(Event evt) {
  switch (evt.id) {
    case Event.MOUSE_ENTER:
      return mouseEnter(evt, evt.x, evt.y);

    case Event.MOUSE_EXIT:
      return mouseExit(evt, evt.x, evt.y);
```

```
    case Event.MOUSE_MOVE:
      return mouseMove(evt, evt.x, evt.y);

    case Event.MOUSE_DOWN:
      return mouseDown(evt, evt.x, evt.y);

    case Event.MOUSE_DRAG:
      return mouseDrag(evt, evt.x, evt.y);

    case Event.MOUSE_UP:
      return mouseUp(evt, evt.x, evt.y);

    case Event.KEY_PRESS:
    case Event.KEY_ACTION:
      return keyDown(evt, evt.key);

    case Event.KEY_RELEASE:
    case Event.KEY_ACTION_RELEASE:
      return keyUp(evt, evt.key);

    case Event.ACTION_EVENT:
      return action(evt, evt.arg);
    case Event.GOT_FOCUS:
      return gotFocus(evt, evt.arg);
    case Event.LOST_FOCUS:
      return lostFocus(evt, evt.arg);
  }
  return false;
}
```

Fields of `java.awt.Event`

The `Event` object contains several fields. The most important of these include the following:

- `id` contains the `Event` type, such as `Event.ACTION_EVENT` or `Event.MOUSE_DOWN`. You can find a list of all these types in the API documentation for `java.awt.Event`.

- `target` contains the widget that generated the event.

- `when` contains a time stamp indicating when the event occurred (only used for mouse and keyboard `Event`s).

- `x` contains the *x*-coordinate of the `Event` (only used for mouse, keyboard, and `WINDOW_MOVED` `Event`s).

- `y` contains the *y*-coordinate of the `Event` (only used for mouse, keyboard, and `WINDOW_MOVED` `Event`s).

- `key` contains the ASCII code for the key that was pressed in a keyboard event.

- `modifiers` contains an indication of which modifier keys (**Shift**, **Ctrl**, etc.) were down when a keyboard or mouse event occurred (not used for `MOUSE_ENTER` or `MOUSE_EXIT` `Event`s). Note that the modifier keys themselves do not generate events. Each possible modifier key is represented by a nonoverlapping set of bits in this field, so that you can use masking constants provided in the `Event` class to determine whether a given modifier was down during a keyboard or mouse event.

- `arg` contains an `Object` that varies for the particular type of event. For `ACTION_EVENT` (generated when a `Button` is pressed, a `Choice`, `Checkbox`, or `MenuItem` is selected; a `List` item is double-clicked' or the user hits the `Return` key in a `TextField`) this field generally contains a `String` with the label of the selected item. In the case of the `TextField`, the `String` contains the text that was entered in the field. For the various `Scrollbar` `Event`s, all of which are listed in our example, this field contains an `int` indicating the position to which the `Scrollbar` has moved. Finally, when the user single-clicks in a `List`, generating either a `LIST_SELECT` or `LIST_DESELECT` `Event`, the `arg` field contains an `int`, which is the index of the list item that was clicked.

Some Details

offset_x **and** offset_y

We have designed our applet to include a scrolling Canvas. Remember that screen coordinates grow from the upper-left corner of the screen. A vertical Scrollbar is at zero when it is in its top position; a horizontal Scrollbar is at zero when it is at its leftmost position. However, when you move a vertical Scrollbar *down* (from 0 to 1, for example), the items on the screen appear to go *up*! This is natural-looking when it happens on the screen, but it requires one to think a little harder in programming.

We chose to have the offset_x and offset_y values map directly to the values of the Scrollbars, because this is the place from which they are controlled. As you look through the code and see that we have sometimes subtracted and sometimes added the offset to our coordinates, remember that these are Scrollbar values, and things should become clear.

reshape()

Our applet overrides java.awt.Component.reshape(), which is called whenever a component is resized. We need to do this because our applet contains Scrollbars, and when their size changes, we need to reset their ranges and "visible" amounts to accurately model a constant-sized "virtual canvas" that is 1000 pixels square. Typically, you will not need to override reshape(). If you do, however, it's important that you call super.reshape(); the default method does a lot of housekeeping, and you will get unpleasant results if that housekeeping is not done.

Things to Try

The version of the applet listed earlier does not use double-buffering. As a result, there's quite a bit of screen flicker, especially as the number of rectangles increases. It could easily be modified to use double-buffering, but we found that the double-buffered version crashed every beta version of Java for the Mac that we could get our hands on. If you're running on Windows or UNIX, it should work fine. See if you can use the techniques described in Chapter 9 to add double-buffering to the applet. If you want to see the solution, it's included on the CD-ROM.

How would you alter the code if you wanted to include circles as well as rectangles? What about other objects? Would you need to use separate lists? How can inheritance help you manage this? (*Hint:* What type of data is stored in an object of type `Vector`?)

How would you modify the code to allow the user to select objects on the screen by clicking on them with the mouse? (*Hint:* The `Rectangle` class includes a method called `inside()`). How would you decide which object to select if two objects were overlapping?

If one object partially obscures another, how could you implement code to bring the partially obscured object to the front? (*Hint:* Look at the API documentation for `Vector`.)

Summary

Object-oriented programming has many advantages, which we have discussed at every opportunity. One disadvantage often pointed out is that while OOP makes it relatively easy to reuse code that has already been written and to increase the functionality of a program without breaking its fundamental design, it requires a great deal of extra work to do OOP from scratch. Creating classes that are broadly generalizable takes careful design. This is why it is virtually essential to have a good API if you're going to do meaningful programming in an object-oriented manner. Programmers should spend their time and effort designing programs to achieve the functionality they desire, not agonizing over the details of creating generalizable data structures at the most basic level.

The Java API rises to the challenge. Classes such as `Stack`, `Vector`, and the various subclasses of `InputStream` and `OutputStream` allow the programmer to concentrate on the task at hand, rather than rebuilding commonly used classes from the ground up. This makes it practical to write software in an object-oriented manner, because the programmer defines objects at a higher level of abstraction, either including the classes from the API within new classes or subclassing them to add functionality more specific to the application being designed.

This chapter presented a brief overview of some of the most commonly used classes in the Java API. What we have provided here, however, is by no means exhaustive coverage. There is a great deal more in the API, which is best discovered by reading the HTML documentation provided by Sun. Additionally, there is much that a programmer can learn by looking at the source code for the API classes, which can also be downloaded from Sun's Java Web site.

One part of the API of particular interest to applet programmers is the Java AWT package. An `Applet` itself is a subclass of the AWT class `java.awt.Panel`, providing a way to construct programs that are both simple and compact. Applets are relatively simple, because much of the work of constructing usable GUI widgets has already been done for the programmer. Applets are compact, because anyone with a Java-enabled browser already has the basic AWT classes on their machine; to run a given applet from the Internet, only a small quantity of additional executable code needs to be transferred. By no means, however, are the AWT classes for exclusive use by applet programmers. Any Java program may use these classes.

For security reasons, which we will discuss in more detail in Chapter 12, there are certain facilities provided by the API, such as file I/O, which applets are typically restricted from using. Additionally, there are some classes, such as the network I/O classes, that applets may use, but only to a limited extent.

For this reason, many programmers will want to develop Java stand-alone applications, which can take full advantage of the functionality offered by the API. In the next chapter, we discuss techniques that are useful in programming Java stand-alone applications.

JAVA
PROGRAMMING
BASICS

CHAPTER 11

Application Programming Techniques

Java is a General-Purpose Language

As we have said, Java is a general-purpose language. It is not limited to creating applets that run on Web pages. Instead, it promises to change the way programmers write software for the Internet. In truth, Java application development is in its infancy, and you are getting in on the ground floor.

In this chapter we introduce the basic techniques you need to know in order to write a stand-alone Java application. We show how you can transform a Java applet into a stand-alone application (in those cases where it is possible and practical to do so). Finally, we show how to develop a simple networked client-server application.

main()

All Java stand-alone applications must have a method called `main()`, defined in the following format:

```
public static void main(String argv[]) {
// method body
}
```

It must be defined with exactly this name, signature, return type, and access specifiers, because the `java` interpreter searches the `.class` file for a method that matches these specifications. Of particular importance is the fact that it is declared `static`. This has two important ramifications, which we will deal with several times in this chapter:

- The interpreter does not instantiate an object of the class in order to run your `main()` method; `static` methods, as you recall from Chapter 8, may be called without instantiating an object of the class in which they are defined.

- You cannot call instance methods or access instance variables from the `static` method `main()` unless you qualify them with the name of a specific object of the class in which `main()` is defined. If you have declared any instance variables, you need to provide a constructor and call the constructor from `main()` to create a specific object of the class. You can then refer to that specific object's instance variables and methods.

Note also that `main()` has a return type of `void` and takes a single parameter, which is an array of `string` objects.

WARNING

Unlike C and C++, where `main()` has an implicit return type of `int`, you must specify the return type of a Java `main()` method, and it must be `void`. If you need your main program to return a value, you can do so with `System.exit()`.

How the Interpreter Runs Your Program

You invoke your program using the command `java` to start the interpreter and specify on the command line the name of a Java class containing a main method.

```
% java MyApplication
```

The interpreter finds the class whose name you specified and looks for a method called `main()`. If this method is not present or is incorrectly declared, then the interpreter exits with an error. Otherwise, it executes your `main()` method.

Note that the interpreter does not instantiate an object of your class when it runs your `main()` method. If for some reason, you have declared instance variables or non-`static` methods in the class containing your main method, then you must explicitly instantiate an object of your application's class within `main()`. We will discuss this further when we investigate transforming applets into applications, later in this chapter.

Command-Line Arguments

`main()` takes one parameter. This is an array of `String` objects that represent the command-line arguments to your program. Consider the following command:

```
% java DataEntry makower dave 5 4.75 2 26 true
```

When the `main()` method for the program `DataEntry` is called, the array `argv` will have the value `{"makower", "dave", "5", "4.75", "2", "26", "true"}`. Thus, `argv[0]` holds the value of the first parameter, `"makower"`, `argv[1]` holds the value of the second parameter, `"dave"`, and so on. As with any array, `argv.length` will tell you the number of elements in the array, which is the number of command-line arguments.

WARNING

A reminder of an important fact we pointed out in Chapter 4—in Java, `argv[0]` holds the first command-line argument to the program, *not* the name of the program itself, as is the case in C and C++. The name of a Java program is the name of the class in which `main()` is declared, and the `Strings` in the argument to `main()` consist only of the command-line arguments.

Like an applet, an application's parameters are passed in as `Strings`, so you need to do some processing on them if you'd like them to have values of another type, such as `int`, `float`, or `boolean`. Unlike an applet, however, the parameters are not read in from an HTML file, but from the command line. (Not that your application couldn't read `Strings` from an HTML file if you programmed it that way, but you'd have to include code to read the file yourself.)

Even if you do not need any input from the user to run the program, you still need to declare `main()` with the proper signature, or the interpreter will not recognize it.

N O T E

A method's signature is defined by the type, number, and order of parameters, *not* by the names of the parameters. Thus, you may occasionally see `main()` defined with a parameter named something other than `argv` (such as `args`). This is not incorrect, as long as it is of type `String[]`. For those familiar with C programming, however, `argv` is the more comfortable and familiar name for this parameter, so you will see `argv` more often.

Example: SimpleMath

Here's a simple example to demonstrate command-line argument processing in Java. `SimpleMath` computes the total and average of integers input on the command line. It deals with invalid entries by simply ignoring them.

```java
public class SimpleMath {

    public static void main(String argv[]) {
        int total=0;      // sum of arguments
        int invalid=0;    // number of invalid arguments
        int thisNum;     // current argument

        // for each argument
        for (int i = 0; i < argv.length; i++) {

            try {

                // get int value from String argument
                thisNum = Integer.parseInt(argv[i]);

            } catch (NumberFormatException e) {

                invalid++;   // count invalid args
                continue;    // go on to next arg
            }

            // valid arg; add it to total
            total = total + thisNum;
        }

        // subtract invalid entries from number of arguments
        int validNums = argv.length - invalid;

        // Report number of valid entries (use correct English)
        System.out.println(validNums + " valid entr" +
            ((validNums == 1) ? "y." : "ies."));

        // calculate and print total and average
        System.out.println("The total is " + total + ".");
        System.out.println("The average is " +
            ((validNums > 0)? (total/validNums) : 0) + ".");
    }
}
```

Understanding the Code

The code for SimpleMath is relatively straightforward. It looks almost exactly like a C program.

Note the use of the wrapper class Integer to obtain an int from a String:

```
thisNum = Integer.parseInt(argv[i]);
```

Note also that the call is placed in a try/catch block, so that if the String is improperly formatted to be read in as an integer, it is not included in the total. The continue statement is used to jump immediately to the next iteration of the for loop without adding the current argument to the total.

To those unfamiliar with C, there is one bit of C-derived syntax that we discussed in Chapter 4 but haven't used in a while. This is the *ternary conditional operator*, ?:. Recall that the ?: operator allows an expression to return one of two values, based on a key value. Thus, the output from the following statement will include the word *entry* in the case of one valid entry, and *entries* in the case of either zero or multiple valid entries.

```
System.out.println(validNums + " valid entr" +
    ((validNums == 1) ? "y." : "ies."));
```

It is true that there is nothing the ?: operator can do that can't be done by an if/else statement, and it is cryptic to look at until you get used to it, but the syntactic convenience is considerable. Had we used an if/else statement for this code, it would have had to look something like this:

```
if (validNums == 1) {
    System.out.println(validNums + " valid entry.");
} else {
    System.out.println(validNums + " valid entries.");
}
```

Whether to use the ternary operator or an `if/else` statement is ultimately a matter of style. (Incidentally, on the topic of style, the curly braces used in the preceding code are superfluous, but as a matter of consistent and error-resistant style, they're a good idea.)

Note that the ternary operator is used again, to prevent division by zero in the following statement:

```
System.out.println("The average is " +
    ((validNums > 0)? (total/validNums) : 0) );
```

Running the Application

To run the program, simply type `java SimpleMath`, followed by some integers:

```
% java SimpleMath 10 2 30
```

If you type this, the output will be:

```
3 valid entries.
The total is 42.
The average is 14.
```

When the data is passed to your program, the values in `argv` will be as follows:

```
argv[0] == "10"
argv[1] == "2"
argv[2] == "30"
```

Remember, `argv` is an array of `Strings`; each element of the array is a string. You don't need to worry about allocating memory for the strings or for `argv`; the system does this before calling your `main()` method.

Things to Try

- Try entering invalid data (alphabetic strings, floating-point numbers, etc.) to the program.
- What happens if you change the first line of the `for` loop to the following and recompile your program? Does the compiler catch the error or can you run the program? *Could* the compiler catch the error?

```
for (int i = 0; i <= argv.length; i++) {
```

- Can you modify the program to accept floating-point values?

Running an Applet from a Stand-Alone Application

It should come as no surprise that a stand-alone Java application can run an applet; after all, the HotJava browser is such an application, as is the `appletviewer`. Running an applet is not quite as simple as calling its life-cycle methods, however. To provide comprehensive support for applets, a Java-enabled browser (or an applet viewer) must implement the methods defined in three interfaces from the package `java.applet`: `AppletContext`, `AppletStub`, and `AudioClip`. In addition, it must implement its own `SecurityManager`. The list goes on, but by now, you probably get the picture: implementing complete applet support is not a three-minute hack.

That said, it is still the case that some simple applets can be run from a stand-alone application with a minimum of extra coding. You can't call `getImage()`, `getParameter()`, or other routines that require the implementation of `AppletContext()`, but you can draw text and simple graphics (lines, polygons, ovals, etc.) to the applet's screen.

Example: AppletFrame

To find out if your applet can be easily adapted to run in a stand-alone application, simply "frame" your applet. An easy way to do this is to first create a subclass of Frame as shown in AppletFrame.java. Next, create a Java class that extends your applet, adding a main() method to make the class suitable to run as an application. Your main() method should be similar to MyMain.java.

If you are attempting to run the application and it results in a NullPointerException, then you're going to have to do some more coding if you want the applet to work as a stand-alone application.

AppletFrame.java

```
import java.awt.Event;

public class AppletFrame extends java.awt.Frame {
    public AppletFrame() {
        this("Applet Frame");
    }

    public AppletFrame(String title) {
        super(title);
    }

    public boolean handleEvent(Event e) {
        if (e.id == Event.WINDOW_DESTROY)
            System.exit(0);
        return false;
    }
}
```

MyMain.java

```
public class MyMain extends MyAppletClass {

    public static void main(String argv[]) {

        // create a frame for the applet
        AppletFrame f = new AppletFrame("MyAppletTitle");

        // instantiate the applet
        MyMain app = new MyMain();

        // start up the applet
        app.init();
        app.start();

        // add the applet to the frame
        f.add(app);

        // pack all the components on the frame
        f.pack();

        // resize the frame to at least the size of the applet
        f.resize(app.size().width, app.size().height);

        // show your applet
        f.show();
    }

}
```

N O T E

You should subsitute the class name of your applet and an appropriate title for *MyAppletClass* and *MyAppletTitle* in the preceding code.

Understanding the Code

What's a Frame?

A `Frame` is a subclass of class `java.awt.Window`. Thus, when you create a `Frame`, you have in fact created a kind of `Window`. `Frame` adds to `Window` the capability of having a menu bar, a window title, some cursor utilities, and resizability.

Our `AppletFrame` class is simply a subclass of `Frame` that knows how to destroy itself when passed a `WINDOW_DESTROY` event. Any time you create a `Frame`, you should make sure you instantiate a subclass of `Frame` that responds to `WINDOW_DESTROY`; otherwise, when the user tries to close the window, it will remain on the screen and continue to use local system resources. If you want closing the window to exit your application—as in this case—you should handle `WINDOW_DESTROY` by calling `System.exit(0)`; otherwise you should handle `WINDOW_DESTROY` by first calling the `Frame`'s inherited `hide()` method to make it invisible and then calling its `dispose()` method to free up any local window system resources allocated to it.

NOTE

Recall that you never have to worry about freeing up the memory for Java objects that you create; the Java garbage collector handles this for you. However, in this case, Java is communicating with your local window system so that top-level windows created from Java programs will have the look and feel of your local system. As a result, the resources allocated to that window by the local system are outside the realm of the garbage collector, and you need to call `dispose()` to tell the local system to destroy the window.

```
// create a frame for the applet
AppletFrame f = new AppletFrame("MyAppletTitle");

// instantiate the applet
MyMain app = new MyMain();
```

There are two objects created in `MyMain.main()`. The first is an `AppletFrame`, our home-grown subclass of `Frame` that knows how to destroy itself. The second is an instantiation of the applet itself. Why do we need to do this? Remember that `main()` is a static method, but the methods `init()`, `start()`, `stop()`, and `destroy()`, which we need to call to make the applet run, are instance methods. The instance methods access instance variables, which will only be created if an object of the class is instantiated. As a `static` method, `main()` is shared among *all* instantiations of the class; it cannot simply call `init()`, it must call `someSpecificInstance.init()` (see Chapter 8). Thus, we must instantiate the applet so that we can call its instance methods:

```
// start up the applet
app.init();
app.start();
```

We start the applet running by first calling its `init()` method and then its `start()` method. The applet is no longer being controlled by a browser; it's now our job to direct the applet's life cycle.

```
// add the applet to the frame
f.add(app);
```

The class `java.applet.Applet`, as you recall, is a subclass of both `java.awt.Component` and `java.awt.Container`. (When we say *subclass*, we do not necessarily mean "immediate subclass." If A is subclassed from B, which is subclassed from C, which in turn is subclassed from D, then it is also true that A is a subclass of D, even though A's declaration only says `extends` B.) A `Frame` is also subclassed from these two classes. A `Container` is a `Component` that can contain other `Components`. In this case, we would like the `Frame` to contain the `Applet`, so we call the `Frame`'s `add()` method to add the `Applet` to the `Frame`.

```
// pack all the components on the frame
f.pack();

// resize the frame to at least the size of the applet
f.resize(app.size().width, app.size().height);

// show your applet
f.show();
```

Next, we call `f.pack()`, which is necessary if you have more than one component to pack into the `Frame`. We resize the `Frame` using the height and width obtained by a calls to `app.size()`. Finally, we call `f.show()` to make our `Frame` visible on the screen.

Example: "Hello Internet" Applet as an Application

Having demonstrated the basic technique for framing an applet, let's use our `AppletFrame` class on a real applet. We'll use the most basic applet we can—the `HelloInternet` applet from Chapter 4. The applet is so simple that, rather than subclassing it, we'll just rewrite it, creating a single class `HelloInAFrame`, which functions as an applet or a stand-alone application. `HelloInAFrame` relies on our `AppletFrame` class. In order for the compiler and interpreter to load `AppletFrame` when it is referenced, you need to do any *one* of the following:

- Make sure the compiled file `AppletFrame.class` is in the same directory as `HelloInAFrame.java` during compilation and in the same directory as `HelloInAFrame.class` at run time.

- Add a package statement to `AppletFrame.java` and recompile it, storing it in an appropriately named directory that is accessible in your CLASSPATH. If you do this, you will want to add an `import` statement to the beginning of `HelloInAFrame.java`, importing the class *yourNewPackage*.`AppletFrame`.

- Put the class declaration for AppletFrame in the same compilation unit (i.e., source file) as that for HelloInAFrame, but remove the public keyword from AppletFrame's declaration.

HelloInAFrame.java

```
import java.awt.Frame;
import java.applet.Applet;
import java.awt.Graphics;

public class HelloInAFrame extends Applet {
    public void init() {
        resize(300, 300);
    }

    public void paint(Graphics g) {
        g.drawString("Hello Internet", 100, 100);
    }

    public static void main(String argv[]) {
        HelloInAFrame app = new HelloInAFrame();

        AppletFrame f = new AppletFrame("Here's the Title");

        app.init();

        // add the applet to the frame
        f.add(app);

        // resize the frame to at least the size of the applet
        f.resize(app.size().width, app.size().height);

        // show your applet
        f.show();
    }

}
```

Understanding the Code

Note that there are a few ways in which `HelloInAFrame.java` differs from the generic code presented in `MyMain.java`. For one, we don't call `start()` on the applet object, because this applet does not have a `start()` method (other than the default `start()` method, which we know does nothing).

We also skip the step of calling `pack()` on the `Frame`. It's only necessary to call `pack()` when you have more than one component in the `Frame`.

Basic Client-Server Concepts

We're about to move on to create a networked client-server application. If you've ever done any network programming with sockets in C or C++, you'll find network programming in Java to be much simpler; if you haven't, Java makes it easy enough that you shouldn't have any trouble.

What's a Socket?

A *socket* is an abstraction that is useful for handling networked input and output (I/O). Network I/O with sockets is very similar to file I/O. In fact, it's useful to think of a socket as a file, to which both a client and a server have access.

What Does Client-Server Mean?

Client-server is a communication architecture where one entity, the *client*, requests a *service* (a return of some information or the execution of some program) from another entity, the *server*, which performs the requested service. In client-server programming, the client and the server are two separate programs, typically communicating with one another across a network.

The server program sits idle, typically running a loop in which it "listens" to a port waiting to receive a request for service. Servers do not initiate communication; they wait for a client to issue a request, at which point it performs the requested service and typically returns some information to the client.

The client program, on the other hand, does not sit idle and wait for requests; instead, it initiates communication by sending a request to the server. Because it is the client's job to initiate communication, the client must know the port number and network address of the server; otherwise it cannot issue a request.

What's a Port?

It's quite likely that more than one kind of client or server will be running on the same machine. In order to distinguish messages intended for one program from those intended for another, every message is tagged with a *port number*. A program only receives incoming messages if they are tagged with a port number to which that program is bound. No more than one program may use a given port number.

In the TCP/IP protocol stack (the set of protocols used for communication on the Internet) there are a fixed number of ports that can be used for communication. Port numbers 0 through 1024 are reserved for common ("well-known") services such as telnet (port 23) and HTTP (port 80). Port numbers 1024 through 65535 are available for any program to use (although you must make sure there is not already another program using that port on your machine).

What's a Protocol?

Ports, sockets, and the client-server model provide a foundation on which communication between programs can be built. But now that the programs can talk to each other, what do they say?

How does the client get the server to understand a request? This is where application-level protocols come in. A *protocol* is a set of specific rules for communication. The protocol establishes who may initiate communication, what types of messages may be sent, what their content may be, and how each party is supposed to respond to that content. If data is sent that violates the protocol, it ceases to be meaningful, because it can no longer be interpreted. A protocol may also specify what either party does if it receives information that violates the protocol. Creating a client-server application involves either following a well-known protocol (such as HTTP, FTP, or telnet) or creating a new specialized protocol to which both the client and the server must be programmed to adhere.

HTTP and the Client-Server Model

HTTP, the Hyper-Text Transfer Protocol, which forms the basis for the World Wide Web, is a perfect example of the client-server model. A Web server program makes itself available on a host machine, typically on port 80. It runs as a *daemon*, a background program, listening for any client to make an HTTP request on that port. If there is no request, it sits idle.

Your Web browser is a client program. In order for you to retrieve a Web page from a host, you must tell your Web browser—via a URL—the network address of the machine on which the server is running. (If you don't specify a port, it assumes the server is running on port 80, the well-known port for HTTP traffic.) The URL contains additional information—typically a relative path name—that is used to form the specific request. Your Web browser sends that request to the server at its network address and its port.

If all goes well, the request reaches the host machine in the form of message tagged with the server's port number. The message also contains the network address and port number of your client program so that the server can reply. The server program, seeing that a request has come in on its port, "wakes up" and processes the request, sending the requested Web page to your client program, at your browser's network address and port.

HTTP is a connectionless protocol, in that once the server sends the requested information, the connection closes and the server goes back either to an idle state or to process requests from other clients.

NOTE

Even if you use a port number higher than 1024, you can't be certain that another program hasn't already chosen that port. If you want to open up a socket—as we will do in our next example—and you need to know what port to open it on, you can either send mail to everyone who has access to your Web server, asking them if they have any programs using that port or you can simply use trial and error. If you start up a server program and it hears something it doesn't understand—something that violates its protocol—it may be listening on a port that is already reserved for use by another program.

Client-Server Example: Java Counter

This example demonstrates how to create a basic client-server application in Java, using the `Socket` object provided in the package `java.net`. In order to use this example, you need to have access to a site on which an HTTP server (Web server) is running. If you have a place you can put Web pages for others to access, then you can use this program.

The following client-server program keeps track of how many people use a Java-enabled browser to visit your page. A drawback of this program is that it can only keep track of Java-enabled traffic—the client is a Java applet; only a Java-enabled browser can execute it.

However, an advantage of the program is that you can run this program even if you cannot run CGI programs. In order to run CGI programs, your system administrator must have specified one or more directories in which CGI programs may reside. If your system administrator has not granted you access, then you can't run CGI programs.

Another advantage is that if the client reloads your Web page, the counter will not be incremented. Remember that, at least in Netscape, reloading a page does not cause applets on the page to be reloaded. Therefore, your counter won't "double count" if a visitor goes back and forth between your page and other pages.

Consistent with the client-server model, you need two programs to implement the Java Counter: a client program and a server program. The client is a Java applet; the server, a Java stand-alone application.

Let's start by examining the server program.

The Server: `CounterServer.java`

```java
import java.io.RandomAccessFile;
import java.io.PrintStream;
import java.io.IOException;
import java.net.ServerSocket;
import java.net.Socket;

// This is the server program
public class CounterServer {
    Socket clientSock;

    // file to store the current count
    String counterFileName;

    // port number
    int ourPort;

    public static void main(String argv[]) {
        try {
            // Get arguments: a file name, and a port number
```

```java
            String givenName = argv[0];
            int givenPort = Integer.parseInt(argv[1]);

            // Instantiate the CounterServer
            CounterServer cs =
                new CounterServer(givenName, givenPort);

            // You're a server, so act like one
            cs.takeRequests();

        } catch (ArrayIndexOutOfBoundsException e) {
            // Not enough arguments
            System.out.println("Usage: java CounterServer" +
                                       "counterFile portNumber");
        } catch (NumberFormatException e) {
            // Port number is not an integer
            System.out.println(argv[1] +
                                   "is not a valid port number.");
        } catch (java.io.IOException e) {
            // Something went wrong with the server
            e.printStackTrace();
        }
    }

    // Construct a new CounterServer
    //   using the given filename, and the given port
    public CounterServer(String givenName, int givenPort) {
        counterFileName = givenName;
        this.ourPort = givenPort;
    }

    // create socket and wait for request
    private void takeRequests() throws IOException {
        // create a ServerSocket, bound to the ourPort
        ServerSocket serverSock = new ServerSocket(ourPort);

        // start listening
```

```java
        while (true) {
            // block here until a request is received
            clientSock = serverSock.accept();

            // increment the counter in the counter file
            updateCounter();

        }
    }

    // This method reads the count from the file,
    //   increments it, and overwrites it with the new value.
    private synchronized void updateCounter() throws
IOException {
        PrintStream ps;
        int counter;

        // Open a file for random access,
        //   allowing us to read and write
        RandomAccessFile counterFile =
                new RandomAccessFile(counterFileName, "rw");

        if (counterFile.length() == 0) {
            // File does not exist; this is the first hit.

            // Write the String "1" to the file
            counterFile.writeBytes("1");

        } else {
            // read file to a String
            String line = counterFile.readLine();

            try {
                // increment the counter
                counter = 1 + Integer.parseInt(line);

                // Rewind the pointer to the beginning of the file.
                counterFile.seek(0);
```

```
                    // Overwrite the previous value with the new one.
        counterFile.writeBytes(String.valueOf(counter));

                    // Chain the socket's OutputStream
                    //   to a PrintStream so that data can
                    //   be "printed" to the socket
                    ps = new
PrintStream(clientSock.getOutputStream());

                    // "Print" counter to the socket
                    // (so the client can receive it)
                    ps.println(counter);

            } catch (NumberFormatException e) {

                    // Data in the counter file is not an integer string.
                    System.out.println("Invalid integer string in " +

counterFileName);
                    System.exit(-1);
            } finally {
                    // no matter what, close the socket
                    try {
                        clientSock.close();
                    } catch (IOException alreadyClosed) {
                        // who cares?
                    }
                }
            }
        }
    }
}
```

}Understanding the Code

The server works by storing a counter in a file. Actually, what it stores in the file is a representation of an integer as a string of characters (decimal digits), where each character is one byte in the file.

The reason we use a character representation of the decimal digits, rather than simply a binary representation of an int is that it's better to have a human-readable file. This way, a person can read what's in the file without having to write a program to read it.

When the server gets a request from the client, it reads the data in the file, increments the counter, stores the new value back in the file, and transmits the value to the client. Then it goes back to listening for requests.

There are four methods in the class:

- `main()` takes parameters from the command line indicating the name to use for the file and the port number to listen on. Next, it instantiates an object of class `CounterServer()` and tells it to `takeRequests()`.

- `CounterServer()` is the constructor for our class.

- `takeRequests()` simply waits for a request, calls `updateCounter()` when it gets one, and then loops back around to wait for the next request.

- `updateCounter()` actually performs the service for which this server was created: reading in the data from the file, updating the counter, and sending the information back to the client.

main()

Our program takes two arguments from the command line (and complains if it doesn't get them): the name of a file to store the counter in and a port number to listen for connections on.

Notice the use of exception handling in `main()`. Rather than place each method that could cause an exception within its own `try/catch` block, we use a single `try/catch` block and catch all the individual exceptions at the end. This makes the code more readable, as we can focus on what is intended rather than what might go wrong at each juncture. This is in fact the purpose for which exceptions were designed.

CounterServer()

We use a constructor to instantiate an object of class CounterServer. Recall that we need to do this so that we can access CounterServer's instance variables and call its instance methods.

takeRequests()

This is a classic server method. The server program must first create an object of class java.net.ServerSocket, binding it to a specified port. Then it blocks waiting for a connection. Notice that although this method contains an infinite loop, it does not present a problem in the sense that Chapter 9's SimpleTickerTapeBad did. It doesn't monopolize the processor, because of the nature of the method ServerSocket.accept(). When we say that this method *blocks* until it receives a connection, we mean that it goes to sleep until it is woken up by a message from a client. This relinquishes the CPU to other processes. Thus, rather than looping frantically, takeRequests() iterates only once per request.

When presented with a request, ServerSocket.accept() instantiates and returns a new client socket (class Socket), which is used for further communication with client. Thus, the classic form for the accept loop of a server is:

```
ServerSocket servSock;
Socket clientSock;

servSock = new ServerSocket(port);
while (true) {
    clientSock = servSock.accept();
    // Got a client; now perform the service
}
```

NOTE

Notice the two kinds of sockets in use here. The `ServerSocket` is only used to accept connections; it does not have an associated `InputStream` or `OutputStream`, because there is not yet a connection in place. It is only after a connection is requested by the client that a full-fledged `Socket` object is constructed, through which the real communication will take place.

updateCounter()

```
private synchronized void updateCounter() throws IOException {
```

We have declared `updateCounter()` as a `synchronized` method, because it could cause inconsistencies if more than one client request can update the counter at the same time. It is wise to use `synchronized` methods or `synchronized` blocks when reading from or writing to a file. It is `private` for similar reasons. We don't want anybody else messing with this file.

```
RandomAccessFile counterFile =
    new RandomAccessFile(counterFileName, "rw");
```

We use a `RandomAccessFile` object to handle the file I/O because we want the ability to read and write to the same file. We could have used a `DataInputStream` to read the file and a `PrintStream` to write to the file, but this would have been more burdensome than necessary. It's easier to use a single stream object.

```
// read file to a String
String line = counterFile.readLine();

try {
    // increment the counter
    counter = 1 + Integer.parseInt(line);
```

Reading a `String` from a `RandomAccessFile` is trivial with `readLine()`. We simply convert the `String` to an integer and increment it.

```
// Rewind the pointer to the beginning of the file.
counterFile.seek(0);

// Overwrite the previous value with the new one.
counterFile.writeBytes(String.valueOf(counter));
```

Having incremented the counter, we rewind the file pointer to the beginning of the file so that we can overwrite the previous value. Notice that because the value is always increasing, we can be sure the number of digits will not decrease, and thus we know we are always overwriting the entire contents of the file; no artifacts will be left from previous writes.

```
// Chain the socket's OutputStream
//   to a PrintStream so that data can
//   be "printed" to the socket
ps = new PrintStream(clientSock.getOutputStream());

// "Print" counter to the socket
// (so the client can receive it)
ps.println(counter);
```

Here's where the network output comes in; if you don't look carefully you could miss it. We create a new `PrintStream` object, and we pass the client socket's `OutputStream` in to the `PrintStream` constructor.

Recall that it is useful to think of a socket as a file to which both the client and server have access. As such, the client `Socket` has an `OutputStream` to which we can write, thereby sending data to the client. An object of class `PrintStream` is a stream to which we can easily write text. By chaining a `PrintStream` to the `Socket`'s output stream, we facilitate the "printing" of text to the client `Socket`. Constructing a

`PrintStream` from a socket's `OutputStream` makes sending data over the network as simple as printing to the console. Next, when we create the client program, we'll see what this looks like to the client.

N O T E

Note the `finally` block in `updateCounter()`. Regardless of what happens, you want to make sure we close the socket. If the operation to close the socket fails, it's because the socket is already closed, in which case you can just catch the error without doing anything special.

WARNING

In Windows 95/NT, sockets do not close properly. This is an acknowledged bug.

The Client: `CounterClient.java`

```
import java.applet.Applet;
import java.net.Socket;
import java.io.DataInputStream;
import java.io.IOException;

public class CounterClient extends Applet {
    int counter;

    public void init() {
        try {

            // get DNS name of the host
            String host = getCodeBase().getHost();

            // the port is specified in a <param> tag
            int port = Integer.parseInt(getParameter("port"));

            // Open a socket and bind to the port the
            //    server is listening on.
            Socket s = new Socket(host, port);
```

```
    // Get input from socket and chain it
    //   to a data input stream
    DataInputStream inStream =
        new DataInputStream(s.getInputStream());

    String line = inStream.readLine();
    counter = Integer.parseInt(line);

} catch (IOException e) {
    showStatus("Can't read from Socket");
    e.printStackTrace();
} finally {
    // close the socket.
    try {
        s.close();
    } catch (IOException alreadyClosed) {
        // so what?
    }
}
}

public void paint(java.awt.Graphics g) {
    // print the counter
    g.drawString(Integer.toString(counter), 5,
size().height);
}
}
```

Understanding the Code

The client program is quite simple. It gets the DNS name of the host and uses that—along with the server's port number, passed in as a parameter from the HTML file—to create a Socket with which to communicate with the server. The creation of the socket prompts the server to perform the service; our client receives the server's output and prints it to the applet window. After that, we close the socket.

```
// get DNS name of the host
String host = getCodeBase().getHost();

// the port is specified in a <param> tag
int port = Integer.parseInt(getParameter("port"));

// Open a socket and bind to the port the
//   server is listening on.
Socket s = new Socket(host, port);
```

The client program is an applet. For security reasons that we will discuss in more detail in Chapter 12, it can only open a socket to the host from which the applet was loaded. Recall that an applet need not necessarily reside on the same host as the HTML file that references it. The call to `getCodeBase().getHost()` gives us the name of the host from which the applet's **.class** file was loaded. Note that because we open a socket to this host to make our connection, the server application must reside on the same host as that from which the applet's `.class` file was loaded.

```
// Get input from socket and chain it
//   to a data input stream
DataInputStream inStream =
 new DataInputStream(s.getInputStream());

String line = inStream.readLine();
counter = Integer.parseInt(line);
```

N O T E

The distinction between `getCodeBase()` and `getDocumentBase()` is an important one and bears repetition. `getCodeBase()` returns a URL object identifying the location from which the executable `.class` file was loaded, whereas the URL object returned by `getDocumentBase()` indicates the location from which the HTML file is loaded. If these two URLs are on the same host, then calling either URL's `getHost()` method will yield the same results. If, on the other hand, they are on different hosts, then a call such as:

```
Socket s = new Socket (getDocumentBase().getHost(),
somePort);
```
will not succeed. This is why we use `getCodeBase().getHost()` instead.

We chain the input from the socket to a `DataInputStream` so that we can use the method `readLine()`, the counterpart of `println()`. After chaining the input in this way, reading a `String` from the network becomes as simple as reading from the console.

```
} catch (IOException e) {
    showStatus("Can't read from Socket");
    e.printStackTrace();
} finally {
    // close the socket.
    try {
        s.close();
    } catch (IOException alreadyClosed) {
        // so what?
    }
}
```

As in the server program, we need to handle `IOException`, and we need to close the socket without complaining if it's already closed.

Client Applet, Server Application

The model that we have used here—where the server is a stand-alone application and the client is an applet—is a very commonly used model. The server, as a stand-alone application, has some freedom that an applet does not have. It can access local files on the server side, connect to other hosts on the network, and load native libraries. Most meaningful services will require this type of freedom. Even our simple Java Counter example needed to read and write local files in order to function. An applet could not do this.

A server typically provides "back-end" functionality, such as searching databases and facilitating communication between different clients, and therefore does not need the GUI functionality that applets provide. In fact, a GUI unduly increases the burden of the server.

The client, on the other hand, is typically a front-end program and needs to provide a comfortable interface for the user; this generally means a GUI, and that's what applets are built for.

For a more advanced example of a client-server pair implemented in this way, take a look at the source code for Paul Burchard's Chat Touring, supplied on the CD-ROM accompanying this book.

CGI Script

A discussion on the `comp.lang.java` newsgroup a while back centered on the possibility of using Java to write CGI programs. This is certainly possible. CGI only specifies an interface by which a program may interact with an HTTP server; it does not force you to use one language rather than another. Perl is the most popular language for CGI scripting, because of its rich set of string-manipulation functions that make it easy to develop CGI applications quickly and efficiently. Still, there are plenty of programmers programming CGI in other languages, such as C, Visual Basic, and various shell-scripting languages. For the most part, all CGI programs need to be able to do is read the standard input, manipulate text, and write to the standard output.

One obstacle to writing CGI programs in Java is the fact that Java cannot read environment variables; such variables are system-dependent, and Java aims to be platform-independent. There are ways around this obstacle, however, such as invoking the Java program from a one-line script that passes environment variables in via the command line to the `java` interpreter.

Our Java Counter example can be implemented as a CGI program (with much less coding). About all you need to do is take out the networking code from the server program and use the standard output instead. You wouldn't need to have it run as a daemon, waiting for connections; you wouldn't even need a client program. Of course, you would need access to the CGI-bin directory in order to place our program there so that the Web server may invoke it.

Summary

As a full-featured object-oriented language, Java can do much more than add animation and interactive GUIs to Web pages. Above and beyond applets, you can write virtually any type of program in Java that you can in any other language, but it is likely that the most compelling reason to program in Java will be its built-in support for networking.

This chapter introduced the basic concepts of the client-server model: clients, servers, sockets, ports, and protocols. We first created a server program, a stand-alone Java application taking advantage of both networked I/O, and file I/O as well. We then implemented a client applet to initiate a connection to that server and receive a response.

We have only scratched the surface of what is possible with Java. In fact, the language itself is so new that many of the applications for which it will be used simply have not been devised yet. With the basic techniques acquired from this book and your own creativity and initiative, perhaps you will be one of those to devise new applications for the language, shaping the future not only of Java, but of the Internet as a whole.

Part Four
Other Issues

CHAPTER 12

Security

Security—A Language Issue?

If you look in any book on C, C++, Pascal, or Ada, you will not find discussions of security. Security is not traditionally a language issue. Books on operating systems discuss security; books on networking discuss security. Why is it that with the introduction of Java, security has suddenly become a language issue?

The reasons are fairly straightforward. Java has, with good reason, been touted as the language of the Internet. One of the most powerful and innovative features of Java is the ability to download executable code from a server and run that code directly on the client. This reduces traffic on the network, because once the code is downloaded, interactivity can be handled directly on the client's machine without clogging the network. This important feature, however, shifts the burden of security from the server to the client.

In the past, the only thing exchanged transparently over the Web was data: text, images, audio, messages between client and server applications, etc., but not executable instructions and logic for the receiving machine to execute on its arrival. Of course, you could download programs and then run them on your machine, but only if you made two very important conscious decisions:

- You intentionally initiated the download of that executable code.

- After the code was downloaded, you actively invoked the new program.

Programs written in traditional languages like C or C++ are installed on your machine only with your permission and executed when you tell them to run. A user must make a conscious decision to run such a program, and wise users do not run a given program if they don't know where the program came from or how it will behave.

Java programs, on the other hand, can load from the network *transparently* when you go to a Web page and then run *themselves*. You have no way of knowing when you click on a hyperlink whether the destination page will contain an applet. Furthermore, it is quite possible for you to go to a Web page that contains an applet with no visible user interface. The program could be running on your machine, and you would never know it! It would clearly be disastrous if such a program could overwrite your hard drive, insert virus code into your executable applications, or read your password file and transmit it via the Internet to a hostile program running on another machine. There are any number of dangerous scenarios one can devise that make the unprotected distribution of executable code a highly dangerous enterprise.

Fortunately, the designers of Java realized that users would not want to take the risk that potentially dangerous programs could automatically run themselves without authorization. What user in their right mind would use a product that exposed them to such unacceptable security risks? This is why security features are built into the Java language.

Generally speaking, there are two levels at which security occurs in Java. First, there is the language level. If the programmer attempts to do certain things, the compiler will flag them as an error, and no executable code will be generated. Also at the language level, there are certain constructs (such as pointers) that are entirely absent from the Java language, preventing a programmer from intentionally or unintentionally compromising system security.

The second level is the run-time level. Depending on decisions made at the user's machine, either via default settings of the browser or Java application or via settings specifically overridden by the user, applets or applications can be disabled from performing certain suspicious activities, such as writing to files or initiating network connections.

As you read the following discussion of security, you will notice that we point out many ways in which C and C++ are "deficient" in terms of security features. We do not in any way mean to imply that C and C++ are "unsafe" languages. It is important to realize that for these languages, security is not so much an issue as it is in Java, for the reasons we have described. This chapter points out many ways in which C or C++ programs, if run unwittingly by a user, could conceivably compromise the security of the user's system. The knowledge that this could happen is probably not new to you. Surely you have heard of programs that contain viruses, worms, or Trojan Horses.

Educated users only run those programs they trust. The security features built into Java are intended to provide the user with some measure of assurance that many kinds of suspicious programs cannot be generated in the first place, and that programs that should not be trusted will not be allowed to access sensitive data or perform suspicious operations. Some of these features can be configured by the user or by a stand-alone Java application, and the default configuration provides protection against many—but not necessarily all—kinds of risks. Any user wishing to use a Java-enabled browser should make themselves aware of the extent of protection that is provided as a default, and any user who wishes to experiment with configuring the security features should make sure he or she understands the nature of the settings being changed.

Security at the Language Level

Protection from Programmer Error

Java's security features are aimed at preventing a broad range of potential security hazards, including programmer error. Languages such as C or C++ are extremely powerful in that the programmer is given a great deal of freedom in the manipulation of data types and in dealing directly with memory at a low level. Basically, the compiler trusts the programmer to know what he or she is doing, even when something seems a little out of the ordinary, like accessing the 101st element of an array that was declared to have 100 elements. This type of power can be an advantage, because it allows sophisticated programmers to use all sorts of tricks that may supercharge the performance of a program. Quite obviously, however, this kind of power can also be a drawback, because it is possible for the programmer to make careless errors that have extreme consequences, often without a warning from the compiler. In short, if you want to shoot yourself in the foot, the compiler will let you.

Java, on the other hand, has features built into it that, as we shall see, effectively prevent several common types of programmer errors from ever making it into compiled code.

WARNING

If you are a C or C++ programmer and you are accustomed to using all the tricks of the language, such as pointer arithmetic and arbitrary type-casting, you will need to adapt and learn alternatives in order to program in Java; these tricks will not work.

No Pointers

In C and C++, the programmer may declare pointers to data items. A *pointer* is essentially a physical address in memory where an item is stored. Additionally, C and C++ allow something called *pointer arithmetic*, which allows one to add or subtract a number to or from a pointer, thereby making that pointer point to an address somewhere else in memory. It is a very common error for programmers to carelessly misuse pointer arithmetic and to end up reading or writing the wrong data.

Additionally, with or without pointer arithmetic, the data to which a pointer points may accidentally be deleted, and a new item may be stored in that location. The language itself has no means of alerting the programmer that such a thing has happened, and the programmer may use that pointer to read or write data he thought was still there, which has in fact vanished. This can result in the reading of spurious data or, worse, the overwriting of some crucial piece of data with an erroneous value.

Java removes the possibility of such common errors by eliminating pointers entirely at the user programming level.

Java programs access blocks of memory using logical pointers, known as *references* or *handles*. For example, in

```
Button       btn = new Button ("OK");
```

btn is a handle to a `Button` object. The only way for a Java programmer to refer to the block of memory where `btn` lives is by the name of a valid handle for an object of that type. There is no way for a Java programmer to refer to the physical memory address in which that object lives or to assign that handle to point to anything other than another `Button` object. There is no such construct in Java as pointer arithmetic, by which the programmer could refer to the memory location at, say, 64 bytes higher than that held by `btn`. Only the Java run-time code, to which the programmer does not have access, can refer to the physical memory location for `btn`.

NOTE

In fact, Java's built-in automatic memory manager/garbage collector, which will be discussed soon, may move `btn`'s physical location in memory in a way that is completely transparent to the programmer. This sort of memory management demands that programmers not rely on the physical addresses of objects. Java takes this idea to its logical conclusion, entirely removing the construct of a physical address from the programmer's vocabulary.

Compile-Time Checking

The Java compiler also does extensive compile-time checking so that careless mistakes may be corrected before execution. For example, the compiler will not allow a programmer to access a primitive-type variable before it has been initialized. (In C or C++, you could simply access the variable, even if there might be a garbage value in it.)

Automatic Memory Management/Garbage Collection

Another common problem in C and C++ is that of memory leaks. A *memory leak* occurs when a programmer allocates memory for a given object and then deletes the reference to that memory without explicitly informing the memory manager that he no longer wants it to reserve the space it allocated for this object. Thus, the system still considers this space reserved and looks elsewhere when the application needs to allocate memory for new objects. If a memory leak occurs in a commonly used portion of the program, it can cause the program to gradually run out of available memory while it is running. The program is said to be *leaking* free memory. This is clearly not a desirable state of affairs.

In traditional programming languages, it is up to the programmer to ensure that the program takes care of managing dynamically allocated memory. Sloppy, careless, or inexperienced programmers may write programs that allocate memory inefficiently, asking for large blocks early in the program simply to avoid having to test for available space or improperly estimating the amount of memory actually needed in the specific circumstances. Another common error is to accidentally free up the wrong block of memory, allowing it to be overwritten with new data.

To the rescue comes the Java garbage collector. In Java, you cannot explicitly free objects. If an object you have declared goes out of scope or if memory you allocated can no longer be accessed by any part of your program, the garbage collector takes care of it for you, de-allocating the space and allowing that space to be re-allocated for new objects.

The Java garbage collector runs as a separate thread, with a low-priority value. When the processor becomes idle, the garbage collector is activated. Although the specific implementation of the garbage collector may be different on various platforms, most implementations use a *mark and sweep* mechanism, whereby the garbage collector *marks* each currently active object in the system and follows references within that object to other objects, marking these in turn. Once it has marked all objects that can possibly be referenced by the program, it knows that all the remaining space is memory that the program could not possibly access again while it is running. It then *sweeps* away this memory, freeing it to be allocated later. After freeing up unused space, the garbage collector *compacts* the remaining objects (i.e., moves them so that they are adjacent), thus removing small gaps between them and collecting this free space into larger blocks where new objects can be allocated. This cycle produces a highly efficient use of memory, with barely noticeable performance side-effects, thus allowing the programmer to allocate memory for objects as needed without having to be concerned with the complexities and pitfalls of memory management.

Regardless of how the garbage collector is implemented on various platforms, it always takes care of memory management for you.

Protection from Malicious Code

There is a popular image in the media of computer programmers as devious, criminally minded sociopaths whose sole source of satisfaction in life is stealing people's credit card numbers and erasing their hard drives, wreaking all sorts of havoc in their path. This image is perpetuated in part through movies like *Jurassic Park*, in which a self-serving rogue programmer, as part of a corporate espionage plot, brings down a security system that is the only thing standing between the gnashing jaws of a horde of cloned carnosaurs on one side of an electric fence and several nice, respectable people on the other. In the news, cases of computer crime arouse almost the same kind of morbid fascination as high-profile murders do.

The truth is that the vast and overwhelming majority of programmers are law-abiding, honest, and principled people who dutifully turn their eyes away when other people are entering their passwords, would never dream of stealing a credit card number, and grow slightly faint at the thought of *anyone's* hard drive being erased. Nonetheless, it cannot be denied that there are a few who make life difficult for the rest of us, and in the real world, we cannot afford to ignore security issues.

Fortunately, there are aspects of the Java language that make it much more difficult for programmers to access or manipulate data that should not be available to them or to perform operations that could compromise the security of the user.

Stringent Type-Checking

As an object-oriented language, Java allows objects to be declared with `private` data members. These members may not be accessed by other classes. Languages like C++ provide similar data-hiding mechanisms, but in the case of C++, there is a crucial difference: C++ allows pointers of any type to be cast to pointers of any other type. When you *cast* an object from one type to another, you essentially tell the compiler, "I know this is an object of type A, but between you and me, let's treat it as if it were an object of type B, just for now." (Fortunately for the programmer, the syntax for casting is much more concise than this.) The compiler complies dutifully, regardless of any differences between these two data types, including the rules regarding access to their constituent members. Thus, there are ways for a malicious programmer to use type-casting to evade the data-hiding features built into the C++ language.

For example, let's imagine a hypothetical scenario. Suppose there is a class `Password` and an object of this class contains a user name and password, as well as a `private` method to access the password data. However, a programmer who knows how the `Password` object was declared could declare a data type—called, for example, `OpenPassword`—with the same layout, but whose members were `public`. By casting the `Password` object to an object of type `OpenPassword`, a C++ programmer could then access—and even alter—the so-called `private` members of the `Password` object.

In Java, however, there are strict typing rules. You can only cast objects to objects from which they are inherited, never to an unrelated object or even an object of a sibling class. As a result, the data-hiding features remain intact, even in the very narrow set of circumstances where casting is allowed. The language allows no way to circumvent the data-hiding features of the language, and any code that attempts to do this would simply not compile.

The example just given is, again, hypothetical. It is *not* meant to imply that it's foolhardy to run programs written in C++ because they might contain some such code. Remember, you should only run programs that come from a person or company that you *trust*. You make a judgment that the program is safe, and then you run it. As we have already pointed out, however, Java programs are downloaded to your machine and may simply run themselves when you navigate to their URL. It is wise that Java enforces stricter rules with regard to data hiding. Remember, the Java run-time code itself has access to information about your system, some of which may be sensitive, such as the location of your home directory or other sensitive files. To a running Java program, this information appears to be stored in the `private` fields of Java objects. It would not be appropriate for outside Java applets to be able to use casting in order to access the `private` members of these objects.

Late Binding

Late binding means that objects are not loaded or assigned a memory location until they are needed. If an object has members that are themselves objects, then the member objects themselves are not loaded until *they* are needed, and so on. As a result, the physical layout in memory of a given class is very run-time-dependent and may vary from one instance of the class to another. This makes it impossible for a Java program to predict the physical memory layout of a class on the client machine.

Bounds Checking

In C or C++, as in Java, you can declare an array of objects and then access those objects using an index relative to the beginning of the array. In Java, however, it is a compile-time error to attempt to access an object beyond the boundaries you set for the array when you instantiated it. That is, if you have an array of 100 objects, it is an error to ask for the 101st object in that array. C and C++, on the other hand, allow the programmer to make such a reference, and they will simply return whatever is in that memory location as if it were an object of that type. This conceivably allows the programmer to access memory to which they would not normally have access.

The Java compiler checks array references at compile time to the extent that such bounds checking is possible. In cases where it cannot be predicted at compile time, out-of-bounds array references will generate run-time errors that halt the program's execution. In either case, any attempt to access privileged information via out-of-bounds array references will be thwarted.

Security at the Run-Time Level

To understand the system safeguards that protect your system during run time, consider Figure 12.1.

Figure 12.1 illustrates the various security components of the Java *run-time* code. The run-time code can be thought of as the entity that orchestrates, controls, and monitors the execution of Java code and acts as a liaison to, and stand-in for, the client machine when Java programs request information about or services from their environment. The run-time code is responsible for coordinating the modules that perform, among other things, memory allocation, garbage collection, and thread management, as well as security.

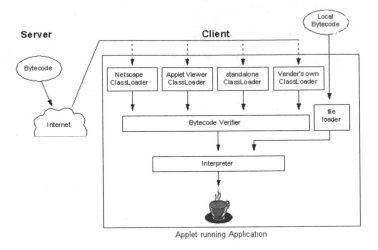

Figure 12.1 Loading and verifying a bytecode file.

Class Loaders

When you use your Web browser to visit a page with an applet, your browser will first download the applet's **.class** file from the applet *host* (server) and then pass that file to a `class loader`. A *class loader* is a Java object that is smart enough to determine whether a class is downloaded from the network or if it originated on the local file system. The class loader separates out the class files, based on their origin: files from different hosts are separated from one another, and files from the local file system are separated from those that came from the network.

Stand-alone programs (but not applets themselves) can implement their own class loaders, simply by subclassing the `abstract` class `ClassLoader`, provided in the Java API. The `ClassLoader`, as implemented by that program, decides the policy by which classes will be loaded into the system. The `appletviewer`, the Netscape Navigator 2.0 browser, and the HotJava browser have their own `ClassLoader` implementations. We will discuss some of the differences later, but there are certain basic mechanisms that these implementations share.

Bytecode Verification

After the classes have been separated by origin, the bytecodes comprising the classes that originated from the network are met with a series of checks from the *bytecode verifier*, which makes sure that the bytecodes do not violate any of the language-level security rules, some of which we have described here.

If the compiler checks these things anyway, why do we need to check them again? The answer is that we don't want to take the risk that a poorly written compiler will have missed some check it should have made or, worse, that someone has improperly modified the compiler or written his or her own compiler that allows invalid or dangerous bytecode to be generated. Furthermore, there is no guarantee that any data sent over the Internet will not be intercepted and modified in transit. For all these reasons, it is only *after* the bytecode verifier has validated the code that it is passed to the interpreter, which executes the code.

Note that, by default, this verification process is bypassed for classes loaded from the local file system (using the `file://` protocol). These classes are considered to be trusted. As such, they are handled by a file loader, which imposes only minimal checking before dispatching them directly to the interpreter, resulting in better performance for code that originates from the local file system.

For more information about the bytecode verifier, you may wish to look at:

`http://java.sun.com/sfaq/verifier.html`

System Properties

A *system property* is a variable that contains some information about the environment in which an applet or application is running. In general, system properties consist of a *key* (essentially the name of that property) and a *value*. You can see the values for all your system properties using the following Java code, included on the CD-ROM in two versions, as both an applet and a stand-alone application. Following is the application version:

```
import java.util.Properties;
import java.util.StringTokenizer;
public class PrintProperties {
    public static void main(String args[]) {
            Properties p = System.getProperties();
            String propString = p.toString();
            StringTokenizer st = new StringTokenizer(

propString, ",{}", false);

            while (st.hasMoreTokens()) {
                    System.out.println(st.nextToken());
            }
    }
}
```

Some system properties are perfectly appropriate—and may, in some cases, be necessary—for any applet or application to have access to; for example, the property `java.version`. Others, however, may represent a security risk if accessed by an outside applet, for example, `user.name` or `user.dir`. You may not wish for an applet to transmit your user name and home directory path back to the host machine from which the applet was downloaded.

As a result, certain properties are, by default, hidden from outside applets. As with most issues of applet security, the specifics are highly dependent on the policy of the program loading the applets. Table 12.1 shows which system properties can be read by applets loaded by Netscape, the `appletviewer`, and Java stand-alone applications.

Table 12.1 System Properties—Modified from http://java.sun.com/sfaq

Key	Meaning	Default Access				
		NN	NL	AN	AL	JS
java.version	Java version number	Y	Y	Y	Y	Y
java.vendor	Java vendor-specific string	Y	Y	Y	Y	Y
java.vendor.url	Java vendor URL	Y	Y	Y	Y	Y
java.class.version	Java class version number	Y	Y	Y	Y	Y
os.name	Operating system name	Y	Y	Y	Y	Y
os.arch	Operating system architecture	Y	Y	Y	Y	Y
file.separator	File separator (e.g., / or \)	Y	Y	Y	Y	Y
path.separator	Path separator (e.g., : or ;)	Y	Y	Y	Y	Y
line.separator	Line separator	Y	Y	Y	Y	Y
java.home	Java installation directory	N	N	N	Y	Y
java.class.path	Java classpath	N	N	N	Y	Y
user.name	User account name	N	N	N	Y	Y
user.home	User home directory	N	N	N	Y	Y
user.dir	User's current working directory	N	N	N	Y	Y

NN = Netscape Navigator 2.0, loading applets over the Net

NL = Netscape Navigator 2.0, loading applets from the Local file system

AN = `appletviewer`, loading applets over the Net

AL = `appletviewer`, loading applets from the Local file system

JS = Java stand-alone applications

Application Security

Java is a general-purpose programming language. Although Java has specific features that make it ideal for Internet applications, these are by no means the only applications for which Java can be used. When you run a Java stand-alone application, you do so as you would an application written in any other language. Thus, there are virtually no security restrictions imposed by default on a Java application other than those that are intrinsic to the language itself (such as bounds checking and type restrictions). A Java application may, by default, read and write files, make calls to `native` methods, and open connections with arbitrary hosts on the network; in short, a Java application can do anything any other program can do.

This is not to say that security features are not available to the designer of the application. Applications that load classes from the network (such as Java-enabled Web browsers), will most likely want to implement their own security policies. The API provides a class called `java.lang.SecurityManager`, which may be overridden in order to define an application's own policy with regard to security issues. An application may have only one `SecurityManager`, loaded at the start of its execution. Additionally, the application can define its own class loaders, which define specific policies based on the origin of loaded classes.

The bottom line is that the security of Java stand-alone applications is highly application-dependent, and application designers have complete flexibility with respect to how they wish to implement security features. A good indication of what kind of options are available is provided by an investigation of the security policies governing Java applets, as implemented in currently available applications that support them.

Table 12.2 Security rules imposed by different Java applications—Modified from http://java.sun.com/sfaq

	stricter ——————> less strict				
	NN	NL	AN	AL	JS
Read file (`acl.read=null` or not specified)	N	N	N	Y	Y
Read file (`acl.read=`*readPath*)	N	N	Y	Y	Y
Write file (`acl.write=null` or not specified)	N	N	N	Y	Y
Write file (`acl.write=`*writePath*)	N	N	Y	Y	Y
Get file info(`acl.read=null` or not specified; `acl.write=null` or not specified)	N	N	N	Y	Y
Get file info(`acl.read=`*readPath*; `acl.write=`*writePath*)	N	N	Y	Y	Y
Delete file, using `File.delete()`	N	N	N	N	Y
Delete file, using `Runtime.exec()`	N	N	N	Y	Y
Read the `user.name` property	N	Y	N	Y	Y
Load library	N	Y	N	Y	Y
`exit(-1)`	N	N	N	Y	Y
Create a pop-up window without a warning	N	Y	N	Y	Y

NN = Netscape Navigator 2.0, loading applets over the Net

NL = Netscape Navigator 2.0, loading applets from the Local file system

AN = `appletviewer`, loading applets over the Net

AL = `appletviewer`, loading applets from the Local file system

JS = Java stand-alone applications

Applet Security

Applets from anywhere in the world can be downloaded and executed on your machine through your Web browser. Although the Java run-time code can check the validity of bytecode and make sure that a downloaded class is indeed what it claims it is, the fact that applets may run themselves automatically when you navigate to their URLs demands that a browser (or the `appletviewer`) place further restrictions on applets with regard to what activities they may and may not engage in. The idea is that applets—particularly those loaded from the Net—must be treated as untrusted, and therefore need to be run in a trusted environment, that is, an environment that isolates them from any sensitive information or activities on the client machine.

At the time of this writing, there are only two programs that can run Java 1.0 applets: Netscape Navigator 2.0 and the `appletviewer` that comes with the JDK. Each imposes its own rules with regard to applet privileges. By the time you read this, however (or shortly afterwards), it is very likely that Sun will have released a version of the HotJava browser that will run Java 1.0 applets. It is also quite possible that other parties will have released Java-enabled browsers or other programs that can load and run applets. This has an impact on the way we frame any discussion of applet security.

A program that loads and runs Java applets may be a Java stand-alone application, such as the HotJava browser, or, like Navigator, it may be a program written in another language, which contains an embedded Java interpreter. Either way, this program itself will have no restrictions on it per se. The applet-security features of that program, whether or not it is written in Java, will be dependent on the way in which it implements the `SecurityManager`. Thus, any of our discussions about what privileges applets may or may not have are merely features of a specific program and do not necessarily apply to all programs that run Java applets. Table 12.2 summarizes the security rules imposed on applets by Netscape Navigator 2.0, the JDK's `appletviewer`, and Java stand-alone applications.

Despite the application-specific nature of applet security, the following discussion of the individual security features of

Navigator and the `appletviewer` can serve to give you an idea of the various ways in which a program may restrict applets in order to protect the client system (and other systems on the network). An investigation of these features should give you an idea of what questions a security-conscious user needs to ask before running an application that can load and run applets.

appletviewer

The security model implemented by the JDK's `appletviewer` is based on a distinction between applets loaded from the local file system (*local applets*) and those loaded from the network (*outside applets*). Applets loaded from the local file system are, by default, considered trusted. The logic behind this is that an applet on your file system, just like any other program on your file system, is there because *you* put it there, and if you choose to run it, you make that choice knowingly. Therefore, the restrictions on such applets can be loose, as it is up to you to decide whether you trust them.

Applets loaded over the network are, on the other hand, considered untrusted. Because they come from the outside and execute on your machine, they need to undergo more rigorous scrutiny, and they must obey tighter restrictions than applets loaded from the local file system.

The `appletviewer` uses separate class loaders for classes loaded from the network and those loaded from the local file system. Those loaded from the network pass through the applet class loader, and those loaded from the file system pass through the file loader. The file loader passes its classes directly to the interpreter, while the local classes must first go through the bytecode verifier and must conform to several additional restrictions.

Restrictions on Outside Applets

Unless you choose to override the default settings (as we will discuss shortly), outside applets:

- **cannot read from, write to, or delete files on the client's local file system, including floppy disks, hard disks, and other media**. The reasons for these restrictions are fairly obvious. Reading files represents a security risk because what can be read can also be sent back to the server (host) from which the applet was downloaded. Writing files represents a risk because of the danger that an applet could overwrite the user's data or damage files crucial to the operation of the system. It would be inappropriate for a browser to operate on the assumption that the local system has its file permissions set adequately. Thus, the browser assumes that this is not the case, so that the user does not have to worry about it.

- **can only initiate a network connection (i.e., open a socket) to the host it was downloaded from**. Imagine that a malicious programmer has stolen some credit card numbers (or figured out the access codes to a security system in a park full of carnivorous prehistoric reptiles). He has a plan that involves transmitting information over the Internet, but he does not wish for the communication to be traced to his machine. He writes an enticing applet, perhaps featuring some lurid animation. That applet, once running on your machine, initiates the connection that will allow him to wreak the havoc he has dreamed up. When the transaction is discovered and its source is traced, the only information about it is that it was running on your machine on an obscure port number. As you await your trial without bail, visions of Duke, the Java mascot, haunt your nightmares, while the true perpetrator sucks down piña coladas somewhere in the tropics. Fortunately, this scenario cannot occur because applets cannot initiate connections to an arbitrary host on the network.

WARNING

On February 18, 1996, two graduate students from Princeton University announced that they had discovered a security leak with respect to this aspect of Java. For important information, see the sidebar "How Bulletproof are Java's Security Features?"

- **cannot execute any program on a client machine (i.e., a Java applet cannot start a Java stand-alone application)**. It would clearly be inappropriate for an applet to invoke, for example, the program you use to format your hard disk.

- **cannot load libraries from the client machine or define `native` method calls**. Remember that `native` methods do not go through any of the security checks that Java code does; they are written in languages like C, which were not designed for distributed execution; they do not have to pass through a class loader or a bytecode verifier, and they have direct access to the client machine, rather than running on the Java virtual machine.

Unlike outside applets, local applets run by the `appletviewer` can read and write files, execute system commands, exit the virtual machine, load libraries, and call `native` methods. In short, they can do all the things that outside applets are restricted from, with the exception of deleting files.

Customizing the `appletviewer`'s Security Settings

If you want to, you can configure the `appletviewer` in such a way as to relax some of the default restrictions on outside applets. You do this by means of the **properties** file. The **properties** file is located in a subdirectory called **.hotjava** under the Java home directory.

To enable outside applets to read specific files or directories, include the following line in your **properties** file, substituting for *readPath1*, etc., full path names for the files or directories to which you want to allow access:

```
acl.read=readPath1:readPath2:...
```

To enable applets to write to specific files or directories, include the following line:

```
acl.write=writePath1:writePath2...
```

WARNING

When you enable applets to read or write a directory using `acl.read` or `acl.write`, you automatically enable reading or writing to *all* subdirectories of that directory! It is safer to allow reading or writing only to specific files.

You can also elect to hide a system property that is accessible by default (see Table 12.2 for the default settings). To hide a system property that is visible by default—for example, `os.name`—include the following line in your **properties** file:

```
os.name=null
```

To show a system property that is hidden by default—such as `user.dir`—include the following:

```
user.dir=true
```

N O T E

Netscape does not read the **properties** file. Thus, under Netscape Navigator 2.0, applets can only read those properties that are visible to them by default. Other than replacing the Netscape Navigator SecurityManager with one of your own implementation, there is no way to make a hidden property visible to applets run under Netscape, nor is there any way to hide those properties that are visible by default.

WARNING

Changing the default security settings may introduce severe security holes. Do *not* do this if you aren't 100% certain of what you're doing! For example, if you include `acl.write=~` in your **properties** file under UNIX (or `acl.write=\` on Windows), you are opening up your home directory (and all its files and subdirectories) to be written in by any applet you run, essentially making all your files free territory for anyone who writes applets. You may think that your home directory is protected by the local file permissions under UNIX, but as far as your local system is concerned, it is *you* doing the writing, because the process executing the applet is being run under your user ID. If this doesn't scare you, it should. If you absolutely *must* allow applets to read or write files, set the `acl.read` or `acl.write` property to a specific directory that holds the files the applet needs to read or write, or better yet, to the specific files themselves. This is still not risk-free, but it is somewhat less risky than exposing your entire home directory.

How Bulletproof are Java's Security Features?

On February 18, 1996, Drew Dean and Dan Wallach, two graduate students at Princeton University, announced that they had discovered a serious flaw in the implementation of one of Java's security features. They found the flaw to be present in both the `appletviewer` and the Netscape 2.0 browser.

Outside applets are not, by default, supposed to be able to open network connections from the client machine to any machine other than the host from which the applet was loaded. However, the Princeton students discovered that the Java security system on the client machine used the domain name (e.g., `applethost.somenet.org`) rather than the actual IP address (e.g., 10.10.10.2) in order to make the determination as to whether or not to honor a request for connection.

Because it is fairly easy for a malicious user with an understanding of network infrastructure to set up a spurious domain-name server (DNS), it is possible for such a DNS to fool the client machine into making a connection with an arbitrary machine, thinking it was only connecting back to the host. Such a scenario could, in certain circumstances, enable an applet to use a client machine inside a firewall to connect to other machines inside the firewall, thus bypassing any security provided by the firewall.

The applet itself would not necessarily have to contain the code that directs the attack; rather, it could send information back and forth to the original host, enabling that host machine to conduct sophisticated direction of the attack. Additionally, the attacker could conceivably take advantage of the illicit connection it has established in order to become a kind of "Web virus," by appending <APPLET> tags to any HTML pages it finds on the victim's machine, thus effectively implanting itself in those pages.

A more detailed discussion of these students' ongoing work with regard to Java security can be found at:

`http://www.cs.princeton.edu/~ddean/java/`

Sun responded to the announcement on February 22, 1996, acknowledging the existence of the flaw and promising a fix within a matter of days. By the time you read this, the issue should be ancient history.

Nonetheless, the story illustrates two important concepts about security in general. First, no security system can be guaranteed to be totally secure. If the right attacker tries hard enough to evade the security rules, it is possible through ingenuity and determination for that attacker to find a weak point and exploit it. Second, there are plenty of people who are just as determined to find these security bugs for less pernicious purposes. These people direct their intelligence and hard work to discovering security flaws in order to make them public and beat the malicious few to the punch. People who do this gain a great deal of publicity in the industry, go on to get very lucrative job offers, and have their names printed in books like this one. They find these rewards much more attractive than the satisfaction of doing damage or the prospect of going to jail.

Netscape Navigator 2.0

Netscape Navigator imposes more severe restrictions on applets than does the `appletviewer`, making virtually no distinction between local applets and those loaded over the network. That is, under Netscape's security policy, *all* applets, whether loaded from the network or from the local file system, are loaded by Navigator's applet class loader, not the file loader. As a result, they all must follow the default rules outlined earlier, and they all go through the bytecode verifier. Navigator also restricts local applets to the same system property rules imposed by default on outside applets.

Also unlike the `appletviewer`, Navigator does not have a **properties** file, nor does it read the `appletviewer`'s. Thus, there is no way to alter the default security settings for Java applets under Navigator. The only thing you can do in Navigator to customize your Java security settings is to disable Java entirely by selecting the **Security Settings...** item in the Options menu.

Summary

How Risky are Java Applications?

A Java application is no riskier than any application written in any other language. In terms of robustness and protection from inadvertent programmer error, it may, in fact, be somewhat safer. However, no language can entirely guarantee that the programmer has not written the application with malicious intent in mind.

Have you ever asked yourself, "How much risk am I taking when I run my word processor?" After all, what guarantee do you have that your word processor will behave honestly? Ultimately, it depends on trust and common sense. You make a judgment with any application as to whether you trust the person or company who wrote that application.

NOTE

Even a word processor can be a risky application. Microsoft Word 6.0, for example, provides a powerful macro language, which turned out to be so powerful that someone wrote a virus, called *Concept*, using that language. The virus was capable of infecting both Windows and Macintosh documents created in Word. Microsoft itself even distributed the virus inadvertently on a CD-ROM.

If you run the application, it's because you are reasonably sure that it will do what it says it does and that it will not attempt to harm your system in any way. It is no different with a Java application. Unlike a Java applet, which is typically loaded from the network and thus lives only in the memory of your machine, a Java application must be loaded and run from your file system. You must treat a Java application with exactly the same caution with which you would treat any other application.

How Risky are Java Applets?

The answer to this question is dependent on two things: the security features enabled by the application running the applet and the ability of the Java interpreter used by that application to ensure that it is bug-free.

Any application that runs Java applets should specifically make users aware of what default restrictions it imposes on applets and to what extent it allows users to modify those defaults. We have included in this chapter an analysis of the security features of two specific programs: Netscape Navigator 2.0 and the `appletviewer` included with JDK 1.0. The default features of these programs provide fairly strong assurances that applets cannot do damaging things to your system—provided, of course, that there are no bugs in the way in which these features are implemented.

Like all software, however, there is no guarantee that these programs are completely bug-free. The designers are sensitive to the fact that security issues are an important concern, and it can only be in their best interests to make sure there are no bugs in their security features. However, should such weaknesses be discovered—as has already happened (see the sidebar "How Bulletproof are Java's Security Features?")—one can only hope that they are discovered first by those without malicious intent and that the designers of programs that run Java applets will move quickly to implement any necessary fixes. Surely they are aware that it is in their own benefit to do so. If companies can be counted on to do anything, they can certainly be counted on to do those things that they know are in their best interests.

JAVA
PROGRAMMING
BASICS

CHAPTER 13

The Future of Java

Within a few years, Java will become the most important object-oriented programming language, eclipsing Smalltalk and C++. This will be due to the convergence of several factors.

Java will participate in the success of the World Wide Web. The Web was the necessary ingredient that turned the technical, hard-to-use Internet into a mass medium. There are now millions of people accessing the Web—eight million in the United States who have direct Internet access, according to one fairly conservative count, plus several million more who have access via online services such as Prodigy and CompuServe. The Web now takes its place alongside the telephone, radio, and television as an instrument of mass communications, to which people will turn for information and entertainment. Java, as the only full-featured language customized for the Web, will be carried along by the Web's success.

Java will permit the full flowering of the Web as a multimedia instrument. Today, the Web is largely a static, passive environment with little interactivity; it is a place where people go to read documents and view graphics. Listening to sound or viewing animation typically requires the launching of a program external to your browser and not tightly integrated with it. Interactive presentations, where a user fills out an HTML form and gets a customized HTML page as a result, are slow and rudimentary, implemented with CGI scripts. The Web, when it is not restricting you to reading text, typically only allows you to carry out one task at a time on an interactive Web page, due to the limitations of the environment.

Java has already changed all that. Its flexibility, reusability, and the unique way in which it implements distributed computing will allow programmers and content providers to exploit the full power of the Web as a graphical user interface to other applications, a server for video and sound, and a way of delivering dynamic, constantly updated information such as stock market prices. Java is the "glue" that will allow serious, complex business and entertainment applications on the Web.

We are in the early stages of a technological convergence that may either result in the computer, telephone, and television merging into a single appliance or in the computer taking on aspects of the other two. CU-SeeMe, first a shareware and now a commercial product from White Pine, allows for inexpensive videoconferencing via the Net. Comdex TV uses the Net to broadcast special trade show events (check out http://www.comdextv.com). Internet Phone permits the user to make free international phone calls by digitizing voice and sending it via modem. These products are fascinating examples of how the Internet is already being used to deliver video and sound. Although they are primitive and suffer from bandwidth problems, delays, and slow refresh rates, they symbolize the immense potential of the Internet as a multimedia server.

In any such environment, an inexpensive standard programming language is needed to fuel and support the innovative uses of the technology. In the world of the early personal computer, that language was Basic; Basic allowed users and programmers to create a wide variety of utilities and applications that contributed greatly to the success of the machine and the DOS and Windows operating systems. The parallel to today's Internet developments is exact; the Web browser represents a platform-independent operating system, and Java is today's equivalent of the Basic language, which allows flexible and innovative uses of the technology.

Java and the Information Superhighway Paradigm

Two competing paradigms exist for the information superhighway. Although one of them seems to be triumphing, Java has a role to play in either one.

The winning paradigm appears to be the Internet itself, a huge, somewhat chaotic network of computers of all sizes, a "pluralistic world of small communicators" exchanging data, text files, graphics, voice, and video with one another. Java can play a wide variety of roles in this environment, including traffic cop, security guard, chauffeur, administrative assistant, and quality controller.

The second paradigm, which today appears to be fading in importance, is the "set-top box" view of the world, in which many users will be connected to the superhighway via a somewhat intelligent television set, allowing limited interactivity, retail ordering, and the purchase of services such as video on demand. In one of its earlier permutations (as we saw in Chapter 1), Java was to be used to create the operating system for the set-top box that would give the TV set its intelligence. While Internet usership grows geometrically and Netscape and Sun see their stock prices soar because of their Net-related products, development of the set-top box approach has not fared well. "Baby Bells" such as Bell Atlantic, cable giants like TCI, and entertainment conglomerates like Time Warner have been scratching their heads about how to proceed, announcing and canceling media mergers and video on demand projects. However, if this paradigm comes back to life—and there is no reason why it cannot coexist with the more vital Internet paradigm—Java is well-positioned to be the standard language for set-top box development, acting as the electronic "traffic cop" for the video server and the "chauffeur" for retail ordering data.

Recent announcements of stripped-down Internet computers costing $300 to $500 are an attempt to revitalize the set-top box concept using the Internet as a delivery medium. These computers may incorporate Java-compliant Web browsers in ROM. A television remote will take the place of a mouse, and an infrared keyboard will be optional. Sun has announced three microprocessors with Java embedded for use in these machines and other appliances such as printers, cellular phones, and game machines.

Java and the Client-Server Paradigm

Not many years ago, data was stored in huge DB2 databases on mainframes and accessed via dumb terminals on the desktop. These character-based terminals had little or no local memory and contributed no processing; they served merely as vehicles to display the data.

Simultaneously with the PC revolution, we saw the client-server revolution, in which the desktop machine became smarter and application processing started to be partitioned between the server—now often a minicomputer or workstation rather than a mainframe—and the desktop. X terminals handled much of the display processing, providing the user with a graphical user interface and mouse control of the application. The use of increasingly powerful PCs and workstations as desktop "clients" allowed the application processing to be partitioned and allocated between the server and the client, leading to sophisticated new developments in client-server analysis and design methodologies. Complex discussions began to take place about the proper way to set up client-server systems, involving questions such as whether business rules should be placed on the client or server and whether the "fat" client is preferable to the "thin".

Business rules constitute the sum of the "metadata" in a database application and include statements like "invoices more than 90 days overdue should be flagged for the collections department" and "collections should be notified when overdue invoices are paid." Somewhere along the line, a sophisticated application will carry out the work necessary to enforce these rules or remind the user to do so. In the meantime, the application will police the enforcement of simpler data-integrity rules, such as "a project number consists of four digits," by refusing the entry of inconsistent information. The debate about where to place business rules involves considerations of convenience, flexibility, and bandwidth. Because business rules are frequently updated—a decision might be made, for example, to send overdue invoices to collections after 60 days—it may be more convenient to have them reside on the server, where a single update allows them to be changed for all users. If business rules reside on the client, practical problems arise in ensuring that when a change is needed, it is made everywhere; otherwise client machines will get out of synch with one another and with updated versions of the server-side application. However, if business rules can vary—for example, user A can only enter data for projects in the 4000 series, while user B can enter data for any project—placing the rules on the client makes sense. Placing the business rules on the client may also offer other bandwidth benefits, taking some of the pressure off the server and limiting network traffic to the raw data. In addition to the business rules, other elements of the application's work, such as CPU-intensive calculations, may be partitioned between client and server. A client machine that handles display processing and relatively little else is known as a *thin* client; a *fat* client handles a significant share of the application processing.

Another variation on the client-server theme is the *three-tier architecture*, where significant processing may be placed on a third machine between the client and the server. One common, not very complex implementation found in many companies is the X terminal connected to an intermediate application server, while the database server resides in the background. In larger systems, an online transaction processing (OLTP) server may serve as watchdog, ensuring that transactions initiated on the client are not committed to the database until completed (for example, not writing a debit to the database until a corresponding credit has been entered on the client and is ready to be written).

Java brings new possibilities to the client-server paradigm. Rather than debating where to place the business rules, for example, designers can now implement solutions where the rules, embodied in applets, reside on the server but run on the client when needed. This allows the convenience of storing the business rules in a central repository, while avoiding the bandwidth problems that result from having the processing done on the server, tying up the network. Business rules and associated watchdogs, such as the feature that prevents user A from entering data on projects outside the 4000 series, can now travel across the network to the machine where they are needed, allowing the thin client to fatten itself up when appropriate!

Similarly, Java offers new possibilities for the three-tier architecture; as a full-featured programming language, it can be used to create OLTP-style watchdogs residing in places other than the client or database server, or even traveling around the network to where they are needed.

Java and the Application Builder Paradigm

Without Java, the Web browser is the universal data-viewer, allowing users to look at certain standardized sources—primarily HTML documents—from any client platform. With Java, the browser rivals application-building environments such as PowerBuilder, by functioning as the *universal client* for client-server applications, saving developers and customers a great deal of expense.

In the past, when developing a client-server application, developers had to worry about both ends of the equation. Once they completed design of the application, which involved deciding on partitioning and resolving the question of the thin or fat client, they had to create both sides of the application from scratch. Existing applications such as spreadsheets offered very limited possibilities for customized client-side solutions. Although it is technically possible to use an Excel spreadsheet via an ODBC connection as a client-side "viewer" for your SQL data, the resulting application may be frustrating to users who prefer databases to spreadsheets or who need to massage the data in ways not supported by a spreadsheet. Therefore, it was almost always necessary to create the client-side application from the ground up, using either a programming language such as C or an application builder such as PowerBuilder.

Although Java can still be used, like any other programming language, to develop such soup-to-nuts applications, it can also easily be used in conjunction with the browser to create a quick, versatile client. Unlike a spreadsheet or database application, which makes assumptions about the way in which the user wants to use the data, the browser only makes assumptions about the way the user wants to *view* the data. These assumptions—involving objects such as buttons, scrollbars, and fields for the entry of data—are exactly the same as those presented by X toolkits, Visual Basic, and PowerBuilder. More than any of these, however, the browser presents the developer with a ready-made operating environment, saving a lot of work. A Java developer choosing to use the browser as a "universal client" only needs to make sure that the browser is fully Java-compliant and that the application complies with any appropriate application programming interfaces (APIs). This saves a lot of development time and contributes significant economies by allowing one application—the browser—to be used as the client for any number of client-server applications.

Several companies have already released or announced products that facilitate Java application development. Symantec Corporation announced a visual development environment called Cafe, which it described as "a standalone Java development tool" including "graphical tools that dramatically speed up the development of Java applets and applications." The product features a native Java compiler that Symantec claims will allow "builds of Java programs several times faster than Sun's Java Development Kit compiler." In addition, the product will include Cafe Studio, a tool allowing the visual design of forms and menus by dragging and dropping the appropriate objects from a toolbar. Rogue Wave announced a similar product, JFactory, which "enables developers to quickly create applications by dragging and dropping typical controls such as buttons, list boxes, and menus."

Java and Distributed Computing

Java has the potential to rival Lotus Notes in the creation of operating environments for distributed applications. Notes is frequently used by large corporations for the replication and sharing of text files and databases. For example, prior to the Web and Java, a company wishing to create a distributed knowledge base for its customer service representatives around the country would probably have regarded Lotus Notes as the most appropriate development platform. Although Notes has dropped its client-side prices to about the cost of a browser, it still costs thousands of dollars for the Notes server; moreover, although it has been ported to many platforms, Notes is not universally available on all hardware.

IBM, which now owns Lotus, hopes that Notes and Java will complement each other rather than compete for distributed applications. The company announced on its Web site that it has licensed Java so that it may make Notes Java-compliant.

Because it is inexpensive, flexible, and platform-independent, companies are increasingly turning to the Web as a platform for so-called *intranet* applications running on a company's internal network. The Web, assisted by Java, is an appropriate environment for the types of applications for which Notes is commonly used. For example, a customer service application might involve all representatives being equipped with a browser. Whenever a representative needed to enter a new customer problem report or query existing data, the browser would call the appropriate applet from an internal Web server. New customer problem reports would be entered into a Java data entry screen feeding a common repository of files on the Web server or on a third machine. A query screen, also implemented in Java, would permit a customer service representative to search the repository for problems using certain keywords, converting the query results into HTML and displaying them within the browser. A "mailto" function would allow the service rep to notify other employees of actions taken; the rep would be able to update an existing problem file and store it back to the server, and so forth.

Companies are attracted to the Web and Java for these applications because the development tools and client-side application—the browser—are much less expensive than Notes and because, in many cases, they already have all the necessary infrastructure (the Web server and browser) installed and in use for other purposes.

Java and Databases

Java represents the latest exciting opportunity to open up the corporate database and make it available to the masses. Older technology on the mainframe and on the PC made little distinction between the *data* and the *application*; the latter was a set of forms and reports built in a rudimentary language included, almost as an afterthought, with the database product. One sensed back then that the real interest of database developers was in tables and queries rather than friendly ways of getting the information in and out of the database.

Over the years, a wide variety of tools, such as JAM and PowerBuilder, and standards, such as ODBC, OLE, and CORBA, have promoted the concept that the database itself is a specialized repository of data to be used by other applications. The SQL database on the large corporate server can now be called on by your spreadsheet, desktop database, or PowerBuilder, Visual Basic, C++, or Smalltalk application.

Java will be of great assistance in adding the Web browser to the list of applications that can use the corporate database. Of course, vendors have not waited for Java to connect databases to the Web. Federal Express was an early innovator, allowing customers to check the status of their packages via an innovative World Wide Web front end. Just as it will in the client-server world in general, Java will provide the transport mechanism to allow corporate users to feel comfortable distributing SQL data via the Web.

By itself, HTML is not very well suited to serving as a front end to the database. Its forms capability is still very rudimentary. Compare HTML to a highly detailed desktop development tool like Microsoft Access: in the latter, you can generate a form from a table or paint fields on a form, "telling" the form what database table to feed and what type of data each field should expect. An Access form, like a PowerBuilder form, is capable of "knowing" the business rules pertaining to data: a field on the form may know, for example, that it expects four characters of alphanumeric information and should reject anything else or that it is to accept data only if another field has been filled in with a certain value.

In its present incarnation, HTML offers few such capabilities. It cannot be customized, using native HTML capabilities, to give you an error message if wrong data is entered, nor can it be told to which database table it pertains. Current workarounds frequently place a CGI script "behind" the HTML form; the script reads the form and submits the data to the database. If you have entered wrong data into the form, you will not find out until the information has made the round trip to the corporate database and back, typically accompanied by an obscure SQL error message. Using current technology to replicate the marvelous functionality of an Access form, you would have to bypass HTML altogether and write the form in a programming language. In the near future, all such projects will be done with Java, and toolkits of standard Java functions—akin to Visual Basic OCXes—are already becoming available to streamline this task. A form implemented as a Java applet could contain the native intelligence, for example, to tell you that you cannot enter a five-digit project number or cannot mark an invoice ready for collections if it is less than 90 days overdue.

Of course, users don't only want to put information into the database, but to retrieve it as well. By placing HTML tags into report templates and outputting them to disk instead of to the printer, it is already possible to customize standard reports to create HTML files that can be passively viewed on the Web. Java again adds the possibility of much more customization and interactivity; Java can pass a user-customized SQL query to the corporate database, capture the results, arrange them in a format pleasing to the eye, and present them to the user via the Web browser.

Java database applications may consist of applets, used within the browser, or of stand-alone applications used instead of the browser. Using the applet approach enables the developer to create a sort of intelligent object—a package of data and associated functionality with which the user can manipulate and understand the data. For example, a car dealership's Web site might allow a user to request information about a particular type of car. The applet delivered to the user's browser would contain data on that car, along with functions that would allow the user to compare pricing packages with different options, calculate lease options, and the like.

Similarly, Java could be used to create the front end to a software analysis database containing requirements documents and diagrams pertaining to an application under development. A developer might check out a package consisting of the description and diagrams pertaining to a particular module. A flag would be set on the server preventing anyone else from working on— or at least writing to—the same module. At the same time, an applet delivered to the developer's browser would allow him to examine and modify the associated text and diagrams. Clicking the **Enter** button would result in the entire package being submitted to the server as modified, and the flag on the server would be reset, allowing the module to be edited by other developers.

Sun is developing a SQL interface for Java, known as JDBC. According to Sun, JDBC "defines Java classes to represent database connections, SQL statements, result sets, database metadata, etc. It allows a Java programmer to issue SQL statements and process the results." Daryl Collins, a computer systems manager in Australia, has released a shareware product called MsqlJava, a class library allowing Java applets or applications to communicate with MiniSQL databases (`http://mama.minmet.uq.oz.au/msqljava/`).

Java and the Object-Oriented Paradigm

Java brings the advantages of object orientation into the new universe of the World Wide Web. From the perspective of a software development manager, the well-known advantages of the object-oriented (OO) paradigm include:

- **A more rational approach to analysis.** Using the old procedural approach, an analyst reviewing a business function would write down a list of processes and then correlate them with particular "entities," often inaccurately. In OO, the analyst begins with a list of possible classes and then assigns functions to them, leading to a more robust result.

- **Reuse and related economies.** In the old, disfavored world of spaghetti code, programmers frequently reinvented the wheel rather than reusing code. Attempts at reuse were frequently clumsy: routines might be cut and pasted, but if they were later modified in one application, they might remain unmodified elsewhere. Evolving business rules might have to be changed in dozens of different places in the code. Object-oriented programming allows the programmer to create a class containing some common functionality, and then to create classes inheriting from it that contain additional data and functions. Class libraries and associated "browsers" would allow developers to search for similar work done by colleagues or predecessors, looking to see if a particular class exists before creating one. If no larch class was found, the programmer might examine the birch and elm classes, to see which is most similar and might therefore be added to create a new larch class.

- **Collaborative model of systems function.** Object-oriented systems are constructed according to a collaborative model in which classes collaborate to do work and communicate by exchanging messages with one another. A popular analysis approach called *CRC* involves the identification of classes, responsibilities, and collaborators. For example, a timesheet object might collaborate with an invoice object by sending it hourly billing data to produce a bill for the client.

Java applies all these benefits in the context of the exciting new world of the Internet. Just as the availability of Visual Basic fueled an entire industry creating OCXes to carry out common business functions, an immense trade is already beginning in Java classes which will aid in the creation of user interfaces, database access, workflow, and every other imaginable use of Java. Within a few years, the concept of "intelligent agents"—until now talked about more than implemented—may find its realization through Java; we may see autonomous intelligent applets flying around the network searching out information and performing other tasks for their "owners."

(See Chapter 1 for a more complete discussion of Java and the object-oriented paradigm.)

Real-Time Java

Java will be used to distribute real-time data via the Web. Java applets will carry continuously updated data, such as stock prices, to your screen. Existing vendors of stock, commodities, and other constantly changing information are already beginning to consider the Web as an alternative way of delivering data to their customers. Vendors who refuse to consider the Web as a platform will be eclipsed by those who eagerly adapt to it. The PC or X terminal with a Web browser—in many cases, already owned by the client—will provide a low-cost alternative to the proprietary terminal or PC software sold by the data vendor.

Entertaining Java

Companies are already spending hundreds of thousands of dollars creating customized Web sites to market their products and services to the public. In order to differentiate themselves from the myriad other Web sites and to capture the attention of potential customers, companies will seek the color and movement available in television advertising, coupled with the interactivity made possible by the computer. Java will become the premiere platform for the creation and delivery of colorful, animated product marketing via the Web. While in many ways its most trivial capability, Java's ability to deliver animation in the midst of an otherwise static Web page, has already served to arouse enormous public interest in the language.

Macromedia's Shockwave product (`http://www.macro-media.com`) delivers multimedia presentations to your Java-enabled Netscape browser.

Who will Use Java?

In a word, everybody.

Software vendors will first turn to Java to create Web-based versions or extensions of existing products. The more adventurous will create products specially for the Web. Eventually, the Web will be regarded as another operating environment, like Windows or UNIX.

Hardware vendors will write device drivers, data transporters and interpreters, which will provide the intelligence of the new "converged" appliance, the telephone-television-computer. As Nicholas Negroponte of MIT observed in *Being Digital*, this futuristic appliance may receive an undifferentiated stream of bits via cable, satellite, broadcast, or fiber optic; an interpreter—a set-top box or plug-in card—will determine which bits represent text, television, email, and voice communications. Java is an excellent candidate for the systems that will run the converged appliance.

Banks and brokerages will use Java to automate workflow, distribute real-time data to brokers, and provide account information to customers.

Publishers will use Java in connection with new multimedia applications as a convenient alternative way of delivering data inexpensively to their clients.

Insurance companies will use Java in applications that help their salespeople quote premiums for new policies. It will replace or extend existing character-based applications that allow a salesperson to dial in from a client's house, fill out an online questionnaire and obtain an immediate price quote.

Airlines will use Java to allow travelers to check schedules and the availability of seats, and to purchase tickets online.

Online services will use Java to spice up their existing forums and resources. Shareware may be "wrapped" in a Java applet that will assist in downloading and help the user install and customize the program. Taking advantage of Java's built-in security, these "wrappers" might also serve a second purpose— to reassure users that the software they are downloading does not contain viruses or other malicious features dangerous to the user's environment.

Overnight delivery companies will use Java to help you track your package.

Newspapers will use Java to help create and deliver customized versions of the daily paper via the Web. You will download an applet that asks you what types of articles you wish to see. The newspaper's server will deliver a daily applet to you that will allow you to view the information you want; by clicking on links you will request the server to send you more details on stories that interest you. Your electronic daily paper will include everything the newsprint version does and more—audio, video, and animation.

Energy companies will use Java for underground resource visualization in making drilling decisions.

Engineering companies will use it for CAD/CAM.

Everyone doing software development will use it for CASE.

Every product company will use it for a distributed customer service database.

The Department of Defense will rely on Java for a system that will permit the President to launch global thermonuclear warfare from any Web browser anywhere in the United States, using a 40-bit key (just kidding).

Caveats

As you can tell, we are big fans of Java. However, we would be dishonest if we didn't also express a couple of concerns.

As we go to press, Java is not yet a finished product. Users are still reporting bugs to Sun, many of them trivial, some of significant concern. Java security (see Chapter 12) is not yet thoroughly tested, and holes are still being found. For example, Sun recently discovered that it was possible to write an applet that would read and forward a user's email without his or her knowledge.

Given the amount of time, energy, and money that companies and individuals are pouring into Java development, we are confident that Java will emerge as a robust, mature product on which businesses and individual users can rely.

(See Chapter 2 for more information on the origins and history of Java.)

Catch the Java Wave

By buying this book, you've declared your interest in being a pioneer. Getting in on the ground floor of a new programming language is exciting enough; imagine being the first developer on your block to learn C++, Smalltalk, or Visual Basic. Ten times more exciting than that is being one of the first to learn the language that will unlock the full potential of the World Wide Web as a new mass communications medium. We hope you find Java as rewarding as we do—and that this book helps light your way.

Java Tools

Tools Included with the Java Development Kit (Version 1.0)

When the Java Development Kit is unpacked, creating the `java` directory, the tools discussed in this chapter are placed in `java/bin`. For convenience, it is recommended that you set your path variable to include this directory; this saves you from having to type the entire path each time you run one of these commands. Our discussions of these tools assume that you have already added the directory in which the tools are stored to your path.

Sun provides online manual pages for all of these tools at:

`http://java.sun.com/JDK-1.0/tools/`

Sun's pages are more comprehensive than this appendix in describing all of the options available for each tool. What we are attempting to do is to distill the most important aspects of these tools and focus our attention on those aspects in detail, describing them in a way that makes it easy to understand how to use them. As you become more of an expert in Java programming, you will want to refer to Sun's online manual pages for more technical details concerning each command and its available options.

Some of the tools are supplied in two versions, one of which has a _g appended to the end; for (e.g., `java_g`, `javac_g`.) These versions are not substantially different from the normal versions; they were built using special debugging options. For advanced debugging, you may find these versions useful; however, for normal use, and even normal debugging, you will not need to explicitly use these versions; when you do, they are often invoked automatically—for example, `java`, when invoked with the `-debug` option, automatically runs `java_g`. For the most part, we will leave the _g versions out of our discussion.

`appletviewer`

The `appletviewer` allows you to view applets without using a Web browser. This is useful for viewing applets while they are under development. It requires less RAM than a full-fledged Web browser, but more importantly, you can run the `appletviewer` with a `-debug` option, so that it runs under the Java debugger, `jdb`, allowing you to use the console to control the execution of your applet.

Here is the syntax for an invocation of the `appletviewer`:

```
% appletviewer [-debug] appletURL
```

The URL specified in `appletURL` must be the URL of an HTML file containing tags specifying at least one applet. As a shortcut, if you are invoking the `appletviewer` from within the same directory of the HTML file, you can simply specify the name of the HTML file; this is because it serves as a relative URL. Following are some examples. In UNIX:

```
% appletviewer MyAnimator.html
% appletviewer file:///users/boris/tetrahedron.html
% appletviewer http://java.sun.com/
```

In Windows:

```
C:\> appletviewer MyAnimator.html
C:\> appletviewer file:///C:/my_dir/fascinating.html
C:\> appletviewer http://java.sun.com/
```

The `appletviewer` will not display any of the text, links, or other HTML elements in the HTML file; it only displays applets.

As an alternative to running the `appletviewer` with the `appletviewer` command, you can use the Java interpreter, `java`, on the `Appletviewer` class, as follows:

```
% java [javaOptions] sun.applet.Appletviewer URL
```

This is useful for taking advantage of options specific to `java` (discussed soon), such as `-mx` and `-ms`, which allow you to set the heap size, and `-verbosegc`, which prints informational messages tracking the behavior of the garbage collector.

java

When you compile a stand-alone Java application, you can run it using the Java interpreter, which is invoked by the command `java`. This command executes Java bytecodes stored in `.class` files output from the compiler. (*Note*: In order to use the `-t` option to generate an instruction trace, you must use `java_g`. It is only for advanced debugging purposes that you would use this option.) Note that you don't typically use the `java` command to run a Java applet; you use the `java` command to run stand-alone Java applications. To view Java applets, you typically use either a Java-enabled Web browser or the `appletviewer`. (Note that there is an exception to this, described in the section on the `appletviewer`.)

The syntax for an invocation of `java` is as follows:

```
% java [options] className [arguments]
```

`className` is the name of a Java class, stored in a file named `className.class`. (The `.class` extension is added automatically by the compiler when the class is compiled. The `.class` extension is not part of className.) It is necessary for the class `className` to have a method called `main()`, declared with access specifiers `public static` and return type `void`, taking as an argument an array of `String` objects:

```
class myApplication {
    public static void main(String args[]) { ... }
    ...
}
```

The interpreter will execute `main()`, passing as arguments anything appearing on the command line after `className`. (The passing of arguments to stand-alone applications is discussed in Chapter 11.) If `main()` initiates one or more threads, then the interpreter will exit after the last thread has completed. Otherwise, the interpreter will simply exit when `main()` has completed.

To run `myApplication`, you would simply type:

```
% java myApplication
```

There are quite an assortment of options to `java`, which can be specified on the command line. The `-debug` option allows the interpreter to be attached to the Java debugger, `jdb`, during execution. When you run `java` with the `-debug` option, you are presented with a password, which you'll need to enter later when you execute the jdb command to run the debugger.

Other commonly used options include -checksource (-cs will work, too), which automatically recompiles any classes whose source files have changed since they were last compiled; and -t, which generates a trace of each instruction executed (only available with java_g).

NOTE

-checksource and -cs only work on UNIX systems.

There are three options for verification: -verify, -verifyremote, and -noverify. *Verification* is a process by which the Java interpreter, while it is running, can check bytecodes to ensure that they do not violate the rules of the language (such as stack overflow or underflow and illegal data conversions). This prevents even hand-assembled Java bytecodes from doing things that would normally be disallowed by the Java compiler. Verification increases security, but it also slows down the loading of classes, and so comes the desire for flexibility: to increase security by turning on verification or to optimize performance by turning off verification under certain (or all) conditions. Specifying -verify (or -v) turns on verification for all code, whether it originates on the local machine or from a remote machine on the network; conversely, specifying -noverify turns off verification for all code, local or remote. If you do not specify a verification option, then the default setting, -verifyremote, will be in place. -verifyremote, whether specified explicitly or by default, enforces verification on classes loaded from a remote host but not on classes loaded locally. This produces a speed optimization for local code, but ensures that remote code is checked for validity.

N O T E

Classes compiled with the -o (optimization) option to javac will *not* pass verification, because they inline private variables. For this reason, it is inappropriate to use the -o option to compile applets for use on Web pages.

Several additional options are available, such as -D, -verbosegc, -noasyncgc, -ss, -oss, -ms, -mx, and -classpath. For a discussion of the -classpath option, see the sidebar "About the CLASSPATH Variable and -classpath Options." The others are discussed in more detail in Sun's online manual pages.

javac

The Java compiler is invoked with the command javac (or javac_g, which generates debugging symbols and includes them in the compiled bytecodes). The syntax for an invocation of the Java compiler is:

```
% javac [options] sourceFile.java [moreSourceFiles.java ...]
```

javac takes one or more source files (whose filenames end in the .java extension) and creates Java bytecodes, which it stores in one or more .class files. Each class in the source files is put into its own output file, whose filename consists of the name of the class, followed by the .class extension.

The .class files are stored in the same directory as the .java source files, unless an alternative destination directory is specified with the -d option. This option allows the user to specify a different root directory for the class hierarchy of output .class files. For example:

```
% javac -d /my_dir MyApplication.java
```

would cause the output file, MyApplication.class, to be stored in the directory /my_dir. A more complicated scenario would involve packages:

```
% javac -d /my_dir MyPackage/Module1.java MyApplication.java
```

This call would cause the file `Module1.class` to be stored in the directory `/my_dir/MyPackage/` and the file `MyApplication-.class` to be stored in `/my_dir`.

After you have finished testing and debugging a class, you may wish to recompile it using the -o option (that's a capital O, not a zero), which instructs the compiler to produce code optimized for speed. The amount of speedup is dependent on the specific application, and using this option may increase the size of the bytecode file. So if you are concerned about the size of your classes (particularly if download time is an issue), you may wish to test the -o option to see if the performance enhancement is significant enough to merit the increased code size.

While you're still debugging your classes, you should compile them with the -g option. This causes the compiler to generate debugging tables, allowing the debugger to give you clearer messages about the values of local variables and information about what line of code it is executing at a given time. You should make sure not to use the -o (optimization) option while debugging; optimization reorganizes the instructions generated from your code, removing the direct relationship between a given line of source code and the instructions that it compiles to. You rely on this relationship when you communicate with the debugger.

NOTE

Classes compiled with the -o (optimization) option to `javac` will *not* pass verification, because they inline `private` variables. For this reason, it is inappropriate to use the -o option to compile applets for use on Web pages.

Additional options for `javac` commands include: -verbose, which causes the compiler to print a message each time it loads a class or compiles a source file; -nowarn, which turns off

compiler warnings (use this one at your own risk); and
-classpath. For more information on the -classpath option,
see the sidebar "About the CLASSPATH Variable and -classpath
Options."

javadoc

javadoc makes it possible to automatically generate HTML
documentation, complete with hypertext links, from the source
code files (i.e., .java files) for a class or a package of classes.
This is made possible by a special type of comment used in the
Java language, called the *doc comment*. These comments start
with /** and end with */. In between, the programmer places
marked-up text (HTML) for inclusion in automatically generated
documentation. Doc comments are typically placed immediately
before the declaration for a class, interface, method, or variable.
The syntax for a call to javadoc is as follows:

```
% javadoc [options] packageName | className.java [moreNames
...]
```

javah

In order for C/C++ "native methods" to access the instance
variables of Java objects passed to them as parameters, it is
necessary to create header files (.h files) containing declarations
of the objects as C structs. The javah command creates these
header files, as well as *stub files*, C source code files (.c files)
that provide C definitions connecting the C structs with their
Java counterparts. Working with native methods is not
discussed in detail in this book.

In general, you run javah twice; once to create header files
and again with the -stubs option to create stub files. By
default, one output file is generated for each class specified,
and all output files are stored in the current working directory.
If, however, the -d option is used, output files will be stored in
the directory specified on the command line after the -d. Also

useful is the -o option, which you use to specify a filename into which all the output files are to be concatenated. This option is convenient because you will likely want all the headers and stubs for a particular group of classes to be stored in a single header file and a single stub file.

Additional options include: -td, which allows the user to override the default temp directory (/tmp on UNIX, %TEMP% or %TMP% on Windows 95 and Windows NT) in which javah stores temporary files it creates while it runs; -verbose, which enables detailed reporting of the status of output files as they are created; and -classpath, which is described in the sidebar later in this appendix.

javap

javap is a disassembler for Java classes. Depending on the options with which it is invoked, javap can list various types of information about a Java class. The syntax is as follows:

```
% javap [options] className
```

The option you will probably find most interesting is the -c option, which prints out a representation of the bytecodes comprising the specified class—essentially assembly language for the Java virtual machine. For example, the command

```
% javap -c HelloApplet
```

will cause a listing of the bytecodes for our HelloApplet class from Chapter 4, as follows:

```
Compiled from HelloApplet.java
public class HelloApplet extends java.applet.Applet {
    public void paint(java.awt.Graphics);
    public HelloApplet();
```

```
Method void paint(java.awt.Graphics)
   0 aload_1
   1 ldc #1 <String "Hello, Internet!">
   3 bipush 50
   5 bipush 25
   7 invokevirtual #6 <Method
java.awt.Graphics.drawString(Ljava/lang/String;II)
V>
  10 return

Method HelloApplet()
   0 aload_0
   1 invokenonvirtual #5 <Method java.applet.Applet.<init>()V>
   4 return


}
```

Note that the argument to javap is the name of a class, *not* the filename of a .class file. If invoked with no options, javap prints out the public fields and methods of the class passed to it. Other options include -p, which prints out private and protected methods as well as public ones; -h, which prints out a C header file, suitable for linking to this class from a native method; and -v, which results in a more verbose form of output. Additionally, as with many of the other tools, there is a -classpath option, discussed in the sidebar, "About the CLASSPATH Variable and -classpath Options."

jdb

The Java debugger is invoked by the command jdb. If you invoke jdb with the name of a class as an argument, jdb will load that class and pause before executing its first instruction. If you have already started a Java stand-alone application using the interpreter's -debug option and have taken note of the password as it started up (see our discussion of java), you can invoke the debugger to attach it to the already-running Java interpreter.

The debugger puts you in a command-driven environment from which you can control and examine your program's execution. The syntax for invoking `jdb` is as follows for ordinary invocations:

```
% jdb [interpreterOptions] [className]
```

For attaching `jdb` to an application while it is running, the syntax is as follows:

```
% jdb [-host hostname] [-password password]
```

Notice that when you start up a Java program with the interpreter, you specify the interpreter options just as you would for `java`, but you substitute `jdb` for `java` on the command line. There are only two options that are specific to the `jdb` command itself, and they are only used when attaching the debugger to a running interpreter. You can attach `jdb` to an interpreter running on a remote host using the `-host` option. It is this feature that raises the necessity of a password to avoid the security risk of `jdb` being used to seize unauthorized control of Java interpreters running on the network. In order to attach `jdb` to a running interpreter, either locally or on a remote host, you need to have been present when the interpreter was invoked with the `-debug` option and to have noted the password presented at the start of execution. Here are some examples of calls to `jdb`:

```
% jdb -verify -checksource myApp
% jdb -host thelonious.nyu.edu -password id92u
```

Table A.1 shows some of the debugger commands you will find yourself using most frequently.

Table A.1 Debugger commands used frequently.

Debugger Command	Function
help (or **?**)	Print to the console a list of all available commands, with a brief description of their syntax and function.
stop at className:lineNumber	Insert a break point immediately before the specified line number in the source code.
stop in className.methodName	Insert a break point immediately before the first instruction of the specified method.
run	Start executing.
step	Execute the current line.
cont	Continue execution from the breakpoint at which execution is currently suspended.
clear className:lineNumber	Clear the specified breakpoints.
clear	When the **clear** command is used without arguments, it causes a printout to the console of all currently set breakpoints and their line numbers.
list	Print to the console a list of the source code currently being executed, with an arrow indicating the point where execution is currently suspended. In order for this very useful command to work, you need to have compiled your source code using the -g option to `javac`.
print identifier	Print to the console a human-readable representation of the value currently stored in the object, variable, or field named by the identifier.
locals	Print to the console a list of local variables and the values stored in them.
!!	Repeat the last command.
exit (or **quit**)	Quit the debugger.

About the CLASSPATH **Variable and** -classpath **Options**

When you run the appletviewer or javac (or just about any of the other JDK tools), these programs need to load some Java classes from your local file system. Sometimes these are the classes that came with the JDK, such as the AWT classes or other classes in the API. Sometimes, they may be special packages of classes on your local machine that you have written and compiled yourself.

The Java tools need you to specify a starting point or a list of starting points, where they may begin to look for classes that they need. This is the purpose of the CLASSPATH variable.

The CLASSPATH variable is an environment variable, consisting of a list of directories, separated by semicolons under Windows 95 and Windows NT or by colons under UNIX. This list of directories specifies, in order, the locations in which the Java tools should look when they need to load additional classes. Once a class with a matching name is found, the interpreter loads it and stops looking. Thus, a class located in an earlier directory in the CLASSPATH can "mask" a class with the same name, located in a directory listed later in the CLASSPATH.

If the class is still not found after searching all the directories in the CLASSPATH and a remote connection is in place (such as to an applet host), then an attempt is made to load the class from the remote host. Thus, if the class is located locally, it does not need to be loaded from the remote host.

One aspect of the CLASSPATH that is sometimes confusing to newcomers is that the interpreter does some manipulation of the CLASSPATH behind the scenes. When the interpreter starts up, it automatically appends the location of the standard Java API classes to the end of your CLASSPATH. As a result, you shouldn't need to do anything to the CLASSPATH in order for the interpreter to find the classes are bundled with the JDK. Thus, even if you manually set the CLASSPATH environment variable, the interpreter should still know where to look when it needs to load these classes.

How should you set your CLASSPATH? For most purposes, there are only two items you might need to put in your CLASSPATH. It's a good idea to put "." ("dot") as the first location in your CLASSPATH. This way, the first place the interpreter will look is in whatever directory it is invoked from. This way, if you're working on a new project, you can test it out from the project's home directory, and the interpreter will know to look there first for any classes it needs to load. Additionally, there are certain conditions under which the JDK tools fail to add the appropriate location to the end of the CLASSPATH as described earlier. For this reason, it's a good idea to add the path to the classes.zip file to the end of your CLASSPATH. In Windows 95 and Windows NT, the following command should set your CLASSPATH appropriately:

```
C:\> set CLASSPATH=.;C:\java\lib\classes.zip
```

In UNIX, you would use the following command:

```
% setenv CLASSPATH .:~/java/lib/classes.zip
```

These commands assume that the Java home directory is located on the root level of your hard disk under Windows or in your home directory under UNIX. If this is not the case, you will need to alter the paths accordingly. (*Note:* If any of the directories in your CLASSPATH have spaces in their names, which is allowed in Windows 95, you will need to surround the CLASSPATH with double quotes.)

WARNING

Do *not* unzip the `classes.zip` file!

If you want to set your CLASSPATH as above, once and for all, without having to reset it when you restart the computer, then place the above statement into your AUTOEXEC.BAT file (in Windows 95 and Windows NT) or your `.cshrc` file (in UNIX, under the C-shell). After that, you should never have to think about your CLASSPATH variable again.

For those times when you may wish to override the CLASSPATH variable, many of the tools included with the JDK have a `-classpath` option, which allows you to temporarily override the value of the CLASSPATH variable. For example, under UNIX:

```
% java -classpath /k/acme_corp/classes;.;~/classes
MyProgram
```

will cause the interpreter to look in the directory `/k/acme_corp/classes` before looking in the current directory or the user's own `classes` directory. Note that if you use the `-classpath` option to override the default or environment CLASSPATH variable, then the home directory of the JDK is *not* automatically appended to the path you specify. Thus, using the `-classpath` option gives you total control over the CLASSPATH variable for those instances in which you need such control.

JAVA PROGRAMMING BASICS

Applet Class Quick Reference

This appendix should help you understand how the class `java.applet.Applet` fits into the Java class hierarchy. When you create a class that `extends java.applet.Applet`, your class inherits functionality from five successive generations of classes, outlined here:

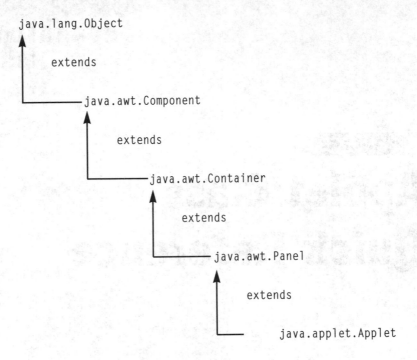

Table B.1 provides a list of some of the most commonly used methods from each of these classes. A class that `extends` `java.applet.Applet` inherits *all* methods and variables from *all* of these classes. Knowing from which class each method is inherited should make it easier to find the API documentation for that method.

Some of the methods (e.g., `resize()`) are defined in more than one class in the hierarchy. In such cases, the subclass *overrides* the method from superclass; it is the *overriding* method (the one in the subclass) that is inherited by `java.applet.Applet`.

Table B.1 Commonly used methods in classes.

java.lang.ObjectM	extends

Constructor

public Object( )

Methods

public final Class getClass( )

public int hashCode( )

public boolean equals(Object obj)

protected Object clone( ) throws CloneNotSupportedException

public String toString( )

public final void notify( )

public final void notifyAll( )

public final void wait(long timeout) throws InterruptedException

public final void wait( ) throws InterruptedException

protected void finalize( ) throws Throwable

---

java.awt.Component

Constructor

invoke Object()

Methods

public Dimension size( )

public Color getForeground( )

public synchronized void setForeground(Color c)

public Color getBackground( )

public synchronized void setBackground(Color c)

public Font getFont( )

public synchronized void setFont(Font f)

public void resize(int width, int height)

public void resize(Dimension d)

public Dimension preferredSize( )

public Dimension minimumSize( )

---

public Graphics getGraphics()

public boolean handleEvent(Event evt)

public boolean mouseDown(Event evt, int x, int y)

public boolean mouseDrag(Event evt, int x, int y)

public boolean mouseUp(Event evt, int x, int y)

public boolean mouseMove(Event evt, int x, int y)

public boolean mouseEnter(Event evt, int x, int y)

public boolean mouseExit(Event evt, int x, int y)

public boolean keyDown(Event evt, int key)

public boolean keyUp(Event evt, int key)

public boolean action(Event evt, Object what)

public void addNotify( )

public synchronized void removeNotify( )

public String toString( )

public Insets insets( )

extends

java.awt.container

Constructor

invoke Object( )

Methods

public int countComponents( )

public synchronized Component getComponent(int n)

public synchronized Component[ ] getComponents( )

public Insets insets( )

public Component add(Component comp)

public synchronized Component add(Component comp, int pos)

public synchronized Component add(String name, Component comp)

public synchronized void remove(Component comp)

public synchronized void removeAll( )

public LayoutManager getLayout( )

public void setLayout (LayoutManager mgr)

public synchronized void layout( )

public synchronized void validate( )

public synchronized Dimension preferredSize( )

public synchronized Dimension minimumSize( )

public void paintComponents (Graphics g)

public void printComponents (Graphics g)

public void deliverEvent (Event e)

public Component locate (int x, int y)

public synchronized void addNotify()

public synchronized void removeNotify( )

protected String paramString( )

public synchronized void removeNotify( )

protected String paramString( )

public void list(PrintStream out, int indent)

extends

java.awt.Panel

Constructor

public Panel( )

Methods

public synchronized void addNotify( )

continued

extends

---

java.applet.Applet

Constructor

public Applet( )

Methods

public final void setStub(AppletStub stub)

public boolean isActive( )

public URL getDocumentBase( )

public URL getCodeBase( )

public String getParameter(String name)

public AppletContext getAppletContext( )

public void resize(int width, int height)

public void resize(Dimension d)

public void showStatus(String msg)

public Image getImage(URL url)

public Image getImage(URL url, String name)

public AudioClip getAudioClip(URL url)

public AudioClip getAudioClip(URL url, String name)

public String getAppletInfo ( )

public String [ ] [ ] getParameterInfo ( )

public void play (URL url)

public void play (URL url, String name)

public void init( )

public void start( )

public void stop()

public void destroy()

JAVA
PROGRAMMING
BASICS

JavaScript: Introduction to JavaScript

JavaScript is a scripting language introduced by Netscape in December 1995. The very first thing to say about JavaScript is that, while its syntax may be "Java-like," the language is not, in fact, Java. It was originally called "LiveScript"—a term that persists in its headers and elsewhere—but, in a stroke of marketing genius, in late 1994 Netscape worked out a deal with Sun to pre-pend the "Java" name. LiveScript, which up to that time had seemed a bit dowdy, was suddenly associated with something hot and sexy, and JavaScript was born.

That said, what is JavaScript? Basically, a JavaScript is just that, a *script*—source code maintained and transmitted in plain ASCII text format—that is interpreted by browsers such as Netscape Navigator, starting with Netscape Navigator version 2.0. These scripts are contained, for the most part, in the header portion of HTML pages. JavaScripts are, as of this writing, always public and viewable. There are few secrets among JavaScript programmers.

The JavaScript interpreter is built into the browser. The interpreter looks at the JavaScript source in the HTML document and, when appropriate, executes it. In this, what the browser is doing is not much different from interpreting HTML codes, except that HTML codes are basically designed to control text and graphics, whereas JavaScript manipulates the kinds of data structures that programmers are familiar with: strings, database records, and so on. A JavaScript program generally outputs or inserts text into the HTML page: an HTML page can be considered the standard output for JavaScript. This HTML text is, of course, then interpreted by the browser for presentation to the user. One immediate consequence of this is that a JavaScript can change the appearance of an entire HTML page, whereas Java applets are normally limited to appearing in a rectangle pre-determined by the browser. JavaScript interpretation happens before HTML interpretation; Java happens after.

Because the results of a JavaScript are usually visible, JavaScript is generally a step up the complexity ladder for authors previously writing HTML, whereas Java is often an additional language for those who know C or C++. JavaScript allows a great deal of "sloppiness" that makes it easier for nonprogrammers to learn and use. Its sloppiness can be somewhat maddening for trained programmers. In particular, the variables in a JavaScript need not be declared as to type: they are, as in Perl, simply used, and the interpreter "guesses" their type from context. This makes errors in JavaScript syntax difficult to make, but semantic errors—the script compiling but not doing what is intended—are much more of a danger in JavaScript than in Java or C++.

In addition, in contrast to Java, JavaScript is intimately connected with the event-processing (mouse clicks and keypresses, etc.) of the browser. It is a fair statement to say that JavaScript was designed primarily to simplify dealing with forms in HTML pages. As a side benefit, however, it has allowed preprocessing of HTML text in some innovative ways. Netscape introduced a menu system on its home page in early 1996 that shows where a user has been and where they can go next, which makes intense use of JavaScript.

Off the Server

JavaScript is generally used to customize a section of an HTML page that requires interaction with a server. JavaScript's main attraction, and its reason for being, is to shift as much work as possible from servers to the user's local PC. The architecture of the Web and the design of HTML, unfortunately, date in many ways from the "big server, dumb terminal" days, in which it was assumed a server would and should control everything. HTML was designed to be a relatively non-dynamic view-only language. A user views a page, clicks on a link, and is served up another page. Interactive HTML pages can be made, but to date this involves cumbersome exchanges between browser and server. These exchanges are typically managed by the server through a CGI script. A simple animation on a page, for example, is often done by running a script on the server that causes the server to do what is know as a *server push*, in which it keeps shoving frames of the animation down to the browser over the Internet.

This sort of thing may work and add life to otherwise dull Web pages, but it is ultimately rather silly and wasteful of bandwidth. The computer on which the browser is running can probably run Doom—that is, it can probably run highly interactive animation in local mode. These days it may well be as powerful as—or more powerful than—the server. The basic point is that as the Internet expands, servers need to do less, and browser or user computers need to do more. In the future, server push animation will seem like using two tin cans and a piece of string in place of a telephone.

Another factor in the shift toward local browser-machine control is that interactive CGI scripts can quickly become cumbersome, difficult to write, more difficult to debug, and organizationally involved. Developing a complex CGI script requires access to both the server and client sides of a system. That often means interacting not only with a server, but with an organization's MIS department, which controls access to the server. An HTML author who is comfortable working on a PC or Macintosh may find him- or herself coping with the ins and outs of the UNIX file system or needing to pester others who know those ins and outs.

A JavaScript, in contrast to a CGI script, can usually be written and debugged by an individual armed with only a browser and a text editor. This can often be done in *local mode*, that is, without being connected to the Internet at all. The browser acts much like a development tool, such as a C or C++ compiler, and the script author works on the script until it's done or ready for live testing.

The Look and Feel of JavaScript

As mentioned earlier, JavaScript code is interpreted, not compiled. A script is stored as text and downloaded as part of the HTML file being viewed. To prevent confusing browsers that don't support JavaScript, it's a general practice to bracket the JavaScript with HTML comments of the form `<!-- ... -->`. The Netscape browser will look for JavaScript code inside HTML comments.

JavaScript is marked off by the hard-to-miss markers `<SCRIPT LANGUAGE ="LiveScript">` and `</SCRIPT>`. JavaScript can be located in several places in an HTML document, or it can be imported from another by a link. However, the usual place for a JavaScript is in the document's `<HEAD>` (as opposed to its `<BODY>`). This use is not unlike the "Prolog" in PostScript, unit defines in Pascal, or library headers in C. Smaller snippets of JavaScript that invoke the functions defined in the head follow in the document's HTML text bracketed with `SCRIPT` tags.

JavaScript looks a lot like simplified C, C++, and Java. A variable is indicated by a word name and is case-sensitive. Variable names can use the underscore (_), but no other nonalphanumeric character, and they may not begin with an underscore or number. The operators are identical to those in C or Java; the few that are not are relatively intuitive. A plus sign, for example, can be used for string concatenation (`"my " +` `"name" = "my name"`).The four basic data types are the *object* (a generic data thing with named things attached), the number (floating-point or decimal), the *string* (a set of text characters), and the *Boolean* (true or false values). Unlike C or C++, there are no pointers or address variables in JavaScript: all references are by name.

JavaScript's syntactic similarity to C and Java can be deceiving. In fact, it is very useful to think of a JavaScript "program" as not being a program at all in the usual sense, but rather as a series of operations on an associative database in which each object in the database has various named "things" (properties and methods) attached. The number of things that can be attached to an object is not limited or predefined; one tends to just pile on additional properties and methods. You can "compose" your objects as you go, adding properties when you like, as if in C++ you could add new methods in a **.cpp** file without needing to edit the **.hpp** file.

This can get confusing or ambiguous, however, so taking or maintaining a series of "snapshots" of the state of the JavaScript object database is the best way to debug JavaScripts that don't seem to be doing what they should. These snapshots often use circles for objects with named lines going out to the attached properties and methods. Here is a very useful JavaScript function for dumping the list of properties of an object:

```
// general function to write a list of properties of an object
function write_all_props(obj, obj_name) {
    for (i in obj)  {
    var result = obj_name + "." + i + " = " + obj[i] + "\n";
    document.write(result);
    }
}
```

JavaScript "Hello World"

A little program that prints "Hello World" is the traditional first effort in programming. If you were reading this in a browser, this JavaScript would now output "Hello World":

```
<SCRIPT LANGUAGE = "JavaScript">
document.write("Hello World!")
</SCRIPT>".
```

Note that this "program" is one line of script. The only odd thing about this line is the term, `document.write`. JavaScript is object-oriented: a document is a class of object, and "write" is one of its methods. Objects have properties as well as methods. One should generally think of *properties* and *methods* as adjectives and verbs, respectively.

While it may help to think of them as "functions" or "subroutine calls," the politically correct term for JavaScript routines is *methods*. If you know C++, the analogies are: a JavaScript *object* is a C++ "class"; a JavaScript *method* is a class function (e.g., `className::Function(x,y)`); and a JavaScript *property* is a public variable belonging to the class.

Properties are relatively intuitive, methods slightly less so. A displayed object might have one or—let's say—two color properties, with values like "red" and "green". Call these properties `color1` and `color2`. For such an object, `blend` might be a method. So a method is an action or operation that makes sense, given the properties of the object. The keyword `this` is, as in C++, a kind of magic word that translates to "the current object I'm in."

Using JavaScript in the Real World

While it is possible to define custom objects in JavaScript and use the language for general programming, in everyday use the JavaScript programmer is most likely going to write scripts that attach to standard HTML page objects. These scripts will get run by the browser when certain events occur. For example, a particular JavaScript function might be run when the user clicks on a button in a form. So the process of JavaScript programming becomes one of writing a script (or function), deciding what to attach it to, and attaching it to that thing.

There are a number of standard objects predefined in JavaScript. `document`, used in the preceding example, is one of them. Writing to a document is an operation that makes sense; `write` is a method of the document class. So the "Hello World" program simply uses this document's `write` method to output the string `Hello World!`.

The properties of objects are accessed like structure fields in C: to get the title of the current document, use `document.title`. These lines print more properties of a document:

```
document.write("<p><b>document.title:</b> " + document.title)
document.write("<p><b>document.location: </b> " +
document.location)
document.write("<p><b>document.Forms.length:</b> " +
document.forms.length)
document.write("<p><b>document.links.length:</b> " +
document.links.length)
```

JavaScript predefines many useful objects, including forms, form elements, HTML links, and anchors. The following is a reasonably complete list of all the built-in objects (or classes) defined in Netscape Navigator:

anchor	the HTML anchor tag object
applet	a Java applet object
button	an HTML input tag of type `button`
checkbox	an HTML input tag of type `checkbox`
Date	an object that contains a variety of methods to print, calculate, and interchange dates
document	the object describing an HTML page
form	the controlling object for an entire HTML form
history	an object of the current browser's history list
link	an HTML link object
location	an object describing a URL
Math	an object that contains mathematical constants, trigonometric functions
password	an HTML input tag of type `password`
radioButton	an HTML input tag of type `radio`
reset	an HTML input tag of type `reset`
selection	a text selection within the HTML textArea or input type `text` tags
string	the string data type with a variety of methods for printing and manipulating strings
submit	the HTML input tag of type `submit`
text	the HTML input tag of type `text`
textArea	the HTML textArea tag (Note that the selection object is separate from the textArea object itself.)
window	the object describing the current browser or document window

Events

Most of the functions of JavaScript are invoked within an HTML form or document with the help of the browser's event handlers. Each form type has a set of events that it responds to such as selecting a check box or *defocusing* or (blurring the focus) of a text field. A reasonably complete list of event handlers is:

onBlur   when a text, selection, or textArea field loses focus

onChange   when a selection, text, or textArea field is modified or loses focus

onClick   when a button, check box, link, or radio object is clicked or selected

onFocus   when a selection, text, or textArea field is focused

onLoad   when a window or a frame is loaded

onMouseOver   when the mouse is moved over a hyperlink

onSelect   when text in a text or textArea field is selected

onSubmit   when a form is submitted

onUnload   when a window or frameset is closed or a new page is displayed

An event handler is attached to a button by adding a parameter to a given tag, for example,

```
<INPUT TYPE="button" VALUE="Total Amount"
ONCLICK="doTotalAmount(this)">
```

Creating Your Own Objects

While you may not need to create your own objects, it helps to understand JavaScript's internals to create one and give it properties. JavaScript, to repeat, is a sort of small-scale database manager.

Creating a new object has two steps. First, write a function whose name is the name you want to use for this general class of thing. (This is something like a `constructor`, if you know C++; your function can take parameters used to set the initial values for the properties of the object.) Then, to make an individual object of this class, use the built-in function `new`.

Let's try it. The following JavaScript first sets up a way to create things called `usState`. I might want to have a bunch of state objects around for reference. Let's say I want to make an object to hold some information about Texas. I'll name this particular object `myHomeState`. To create `myHomeState`, I make a call that essentially tells JavaScript that "`myHomeState` is a new U.S. state":

```
<p><center><tt>var myHomeState = new usState</tt>.</center>
```

As parameters, I pass the name `Texas` and some other information.

The constructor function as written does one nice thing for me. It slugs, with a simple string, a `type` field that lets me remember what this object was supposed to be when I made it. If I start creating lots of objects, I may not want to compare apples with oranges or try to look up the Zip codes when I'm dealing with former Yugoslav republics.

Here's the code so far:

```
<pre>// This function definition is similar to a C++
constructor...
function usState(name, cap, pop) {
   this.type = "usState"
   this.name = name
   this.capital = cap
   this.pop = pop
}


/* This statement creates a new object */
var myHomeState = new usState("Texas", "Armadillo", 50000)
/* At this point, Texas has a total of 4 properties ... */
</pre>
```

Let's see if it worked by listing the properties of myHomeState. We'll do this with a useful little function in the header of this page called write_all_props.

```
<SCRIPT LANGUAGE = "LiveScript">
document.write("<PRE>")
write_all_props(myHomeState,"Texas")
document.write("</PRE>")
</SCRIPT>
```

But let's say that we later decide there are other important things to remember about Texas and that we got mixed up when we set the name of the state capital (at least we knew it started with an *A*). We can fix that and add two more properties to our object, with these JavaScript statements:

```
<pre>myHomeState.stateBird = "Roadrunner"
myHomeState.officialDrink = "Dr. Pepper"
myHomeState.capital = "Austin"
</pre>
<SCRIPT LANGUAGE = "LiveScript">
myHomeState.stateBird = "Roadrunner"
myHomeState.officialDrink = "Dr. Pepper"
myHomeState.capital = "Austin"
</SCRIPT>
```

Let's see what myHomeState looks like:

```
<SCRIPT LANGUAGE = "LiveScript">
document.write("<PRE>")
write_all_props(myHomeState,"Texas")
document.write("</PRE>")
</SCRIPT>
```

Summary

Where Java is potentially revolutionary and its goal of platform-independence is something like the Holy Grail of computing, JavaScript was far more pragmatic in its origins and was designed to solve some very real problems involved in communicating with browsers. JavaScript is perhaps closer to languages such as MacroMedia's Lingo or Apple Computer's AppleScript than Java. Still, JavaScript is a much-needed intermediary with the browser. In addition, the interface between Java applets and JavaScript will evolve: it may well turn out that Java applets will communicate with browsers in JavaScript.

JAVA
PROGRAMMING
BASICS

Java HotLinks

This appendix contains a selection of URLs useful to Java programmers. Many, but not all, of these URLs also appear in the chapters of this book.

Java Basics Home Page

http://www.pencom.com/javabasics/

Sun's Java Pages

Java Home Page

http://java.sun.com/

Documentation for JDK Version 1.0

http://java.sun.com/JDK-1.0/index.html

Java Frequently Asked Questions (FAQ) Index

`http://java.sun.com/faqIndex.html`

Java-Related Commercial and Shareware Products

Netscape Communications Corporation (Netscape Navigator 2.0)

`http://home.netscape.com/`

Natural Intelligence, Inc. (Roaster IDE)

`http://www.roaster.com/`

Symantec (Café, Caffeine IDEs)

`http://cafe.symantec.com/index.html`

Borland (Debugger for Java)

`http://www.borland.com/Product/java/debugger/bugform.html`

Rogue Wave (JFactory Visual Interface Builder)

`http://www.roguewave.com/rwpav/products/jfactory/jfactory.htm`

ModelWorks (JPad Java Text Editor)

`http://www.csn.net/express/`

Quintessential Objects, Inc. (Diva IDE)

http://www.qoi.com

Ports of Java to Alternate Platforms

Linux

http://www.blackdown.org/java-linux.html

IBM's Centre for Java Technology

http://ncc.hursley.ibm.com/javainfo/index.html

The Unofficial OS/2 Java Home Page

http://www.3cat.com/java_os2/javaos2.html

Java Resource Sites

Gamelan

http://www.gamelan.com/

JARS (Java Applet Rating Service)

http://www.jars.com/

The Java Developer

http://www.digitalfocus.com/digitalfocus/faq/

Club Java

`http://www.io.org/~mentor/jnIndex.html`

Online Publication

JavaWorld

`http://www.javaworld.com/`

Newsgroups

comp.lang.java

`news:comp.lang.java`

Digital Espresso
(Extracts from comp.lang.java)

`http://www.io.org/~mentor/jnIndex.html`

Applets

PC Scoreboard

`http://www.cnet.com/Content/Reviews/Compare/Pc100/`

Financial Portfolio Demo

`http://java.sun.com/applets/applets/StockDemo/index.html`

CyberAgent

http://www.mks.com/tools/java/dale/agent/CyberAgent.html

Chat Touring

http://www.cs.princeton.edu/~burchard/www/interactive/chat/

The NPAC Visible Human Viewer

http://www.npac.syr.edu/projects/vishuman/VisibleHuman.html

Utilities

WinZip Compression/Decompression Utility for Windows

http://www.winzip.com/winzip/winzip_x.htm

StuffIt Expander Decompression Utility for Macintosh

ftp://mirrors.aol.com/pub/info-mac/cmp/stuffit-
-expander-352.hqx

PFE (Programmer's File Editor) for PC

http://www.lancs.ac.uk/people/cpaap/pfe/

Alpha Text Editor for Macintosh

http://www.cs.umd.edu/~keleher/alpha.html

Miscellaneous Links

World Wide Web Tutorials

`http://www.stars.com/Vlib/Misc/Tutorials.html`

Emacs Java Modes

`ftp://java.sun.com/pub/java/contrib/emacs/`
`http://www.io.org/~mentor1/java-mode.txt`

JAVA
PROGRAMMING
BASICS

CD-ROM Contents

The CD-ROM is divided into three portions: one for UNIX, one for Windows, and one for Macintosh. Each portion contains the latest version of the JDK for its respective platform, along with all of the source code examples from this book and a directory full of additional examples collected from the Internet.

The Macintosh portion also contains version 6.1.2 of Alpha, a shareware text editor for the Macintosh, which includes a Java syntax-coloring mode and many other cool features useful to anyone programming the Mac in any language. Note that Alpha is included with the permission of the author, Pete Keleher, but he is not directly making any money from the sale of this book. The purchase price for this book does *not* include the shareware fee for Alpha; if you decide to use Alpha for more than 30 days, you should pay the registration fee to the author. Information on how to register is included on the CD with the Alpha package. Also included for Mac users is a limited demo version of Natural Intelligence's *Roaster* IDE for Java.

The Windows portion contains version 0.06.002 of Alan Phillips' freeware PFE (Programmer's File Editor) for Windows 95 and Windows NT. This editor includes such useful features as template definitions and the ability to execute command lines from the menu bar. Also included on the Windows partition is the freeware Kalimantan IDE. (Note that Kalimantan is free only for noncommercial use; see the included license for details.)

The UNIX portion of the CD-ROM also contains Kalimantan.

For any additional information about CD-ROM contents, look on the disc itself for the appropriate **README** file for your platform.

Index

ROASTER™ LICENSE
IMPORTANT: READ CAREFULLY BEFORE INSTALLING THE ROASTER SOFTWARE!
NATURAL INTELLIGENCE LICENSES THE ENCLOSED ROASTER SOFTWARE TO YOU ONLY UPON THE CONDITION THAT YOU ACCEPT ALL OF THE TERMS CONTAINED IN THIS LICENSE AGREEMENT. INSTALLING THE SOFTWARE CONSTITUTES YOUR ACCEPTANCE OF THESE TERMS. IF YOU DO NOT AGREE WITH THIS LICENSE, DO NOT INSTALL THE SOFTWARE.

License
The Roaster software which accompanies this license, including the program(s) and electronic documentation (referred to collectively throughout this agreement as the "Software") is the property of Natural Intelligence, Inc. or its licensors and is protected by United States copyright law and international copyright conventions. Natural Intelligence and its licensors retain all intellectual property rights including but not limited to patent, trademark, copyright, and trade secret rights in the Software. You agree that the Software is confidential and is a trade secret of and is owned by Natural Intelligence, Inc. You agree to do nothing inconsistent with such ownership. While Natural Intelligence and its licensors continue to own the Software, you will have certain rights to use the Software after your acceptance of this license. Except as may be modified by a license addendum which accompanies this license or an upgrade to the Software, your rights and obligations with respect to the use of this Software are as follows:

You may
(1) use one copy of the Software on a single computer at any one time. This means that you can use the Software at home, at work, or on another computer provided that only you, the licensee, use the program and that you use only one copy at a time. You must purchase a license for each additional user. Site licenses and multi-user licenses are available. Please contact Natural Intelligence for further details.
(2) make one copy of the software for archival purposes, or copy the software onto the hard disk of your computer and retain the original for archival purposes. All copies of the Software must contain all copyright and restrictive legends appearing in the original copy of the Software in their entirety and must not be omitted, obscured or otherwise misrepresented.
(3) use the Software over a network, provided that you have a licensed copy of the Software for each user that can access the Software over that network and that each user is only using the Software from one computer at a time in accordance with (1) above; and
(4) after written notice to Natural Intelligence, transfer the Software on a permanent basis to another person or entity, provided that you retain no copies of the Software and the transferee agrees to the terms of this agreement. All of your rights to use the Software will revert back to Natural Intelligence upon the termination of this license.

Because the Software is a Natural Intelligence development environment product, you have a royalty-free right to include object code derived from the libraries in programs that you develop using the Software and you also have the right to use, distribute, and license such programs without payment of any further license fees, so long as a copyright notice sufficient to protect your copyright in the program is included in the graphic display of your programs and on the labels affixed to the media on which your program is distributed. (Example: "Copyright © 1996 [Licensee's Name]. All rights reserved.")

 You may not
(1) copy the electronic documentation that accompanies the Software except as provided above;
(2) sublicense, rent or lease the Software in whole or in part;
(3) reverse engineer, decompile, disassemble, modify, translate, make any attempt to discover the source code of the Software, or create derivative works from the Software; or
(4) use a previous version or copy of the Software after you have received a disk replacement set or an upgraded version as a replacement of the prior version unless specifically authorized to do so in an addendum to this agreement. The upgraded version constitutes a single product with the Software that you upgraded. You cannot allow or make both versions available for use by two different people at the same time, nor can the versions be transferred separately.

Limited Warranty
MIS Press warrants that the physical media on which the Software is distributed will be free from defects in materials and workmanship for a period of 90 days from the date of delivery of the Software to you. MIS Press and Natural Intelligence's entire liability and your sole remedy will be a replacement of the defective media. To obtain a replacement you must return the entire package, including receipt, to the authorized dealer from whom it was purchased, or to MIS Press, within the 90 day warranty period.

Natural Intelligence does not warrant that the Software will meet your requirements or that operation of the Software will be uninterrupted or that the Software will be error-free, or that the defects in the Software will be corrected. You expressly acknowledge and agree that use of the Software is at your sole risk. The Software is provided "AS IS" without warranty of any kind. Natural Intelligence does not warrant or make any representations regarding the use or the results of the use of the Software, including the documentation, in terms of their correctness, accuracy, reliability, or otherwise.

THE ABOVE WARRANTIES ARE EXCLUSIVE AND IN LIEU OF ALL OTHER WARRANTIES, WHETHER EXPRESS OR IMPLIED, INCLUDING THE IMPLIED WARRANTIES OF MERCHANTABILITY, FITNESS FOR A PARTICULAR PURPOSE AND NON-INFRINGEMENT. THIS WARRANTY GIVES YOU SPECIFIC LEGAL RIGHTS. YOU MAY HAVE OTHER RIGHTS, WHICH VARY FROM STATE TO STATE.

Disclaimer of Liability
IN NO EVENT WILL NATURAL INTELLIGENCE BE LIABLE TO YOU FOR ANY SPECIAL, CONSEQUENTIAL, INDIRECT OR SIMILAR DAMAGES, INCLUDING ANY LOST PROFITS OR LOST DATA ARISING OUT OF THE USE OR INABILITY TO USE THE SOFTWARE, EVEN IF NATURAL INTELLIGENCE HAS BEEN ADVISED OF THE POSSIBILITY OF SUCH DAMAGES. SOME STATES DO NOT ALLOW THE LIMITATION OR EXCLUSION OF LIABILITY FOR INCIDENTAL OR CONSEQUENTIAL DAMAGES SO THE ABOVE LIMITATION MAY NOT APPLY TO YOU. IN NO CASE SHALL NATURAL INTELLIGENCE'S LIABILITY EXCEED THE PURCHASE PRICE OF THE SOFTWARE. The disclaimers and limitations set forth above will apply regardless of whether you accept the Software.

US Government Restricted Rights
RESTRICTED RIGHTS LEGEND. Use, duplication, or disclosure by the Government is subject to restrictions as set forth in subparagraph (c) (1) (ii) of the Rights in Technical Data and Computer Software clause at DFARS 252.227-7013 or subparagraphs (c) (1) and (2) of the Commercial Computer Software-Restricted Rights clause at 48 CFR 52.227-19, as applicable.

General
This agreement will be governed by the laws of the Commonwealth of Massachusetts. This agreement may only be modified by a license addendum which accompanies this license or an upgrade to the Software, or by a written document which has been signed by both you and an officer of Natural Intelligence. This license automatically terminates if the licensee violates any of the requirements of this license. You agree to abide by the rules, regulations, and restrictions for export established by the United States Government.